Palgrave Studies in European Union Politics

Edited by: **Michelle Egan**, American University USA, **Neill Nugent**, Manchester Metropolitan University, UK, **William Paterson**, University of Birmingham, UK.

Editorial Board: **Christopher Hill**, Cambridge, UK, **Simon Hix**, London School of Economics, UK, **Mark Pollack**, Temple University, USA, **Kalypso Nicolaïdis**, Oxford UK, **Morten Egeberg**, University of Oslo, Norway, **Amy Verdun**, University of Victoria, Canada, **Claudio M. Radaelli**, University of Exeter, UK, **Frank Schimmelfennig**, Swiss Federal Institute of Technology, Switzerland.

Following on the sustained success of the acclaimed *European Union Series,* which essentially publishes research-based textbooks, *Palgrave Studies in European Union Politics* publishes cutting edge research-driven monographs.

The remit of the series is broadly defined, both in terms of subject and academic discipline. All topics of significance concerning the nature and operation of the European Union potentially fall within the scope of the series. The series is multidisciplinary to reflect the growing importance of the EU as a political, economic and social phenomenon. We will welcome submissions from the areas of political studies, international relations, political economy, public and social policy, economics, law and sociology.

Submissions should be sent to Amy Lankester-Owen, Politics Publisher, 'a.lankester-owen@palgrave.com'.

Titles include:

Ian Bache and Andrew Jordan (editors)
THE EUROPEANIZATION OF BRITISH POLITICS

Richard Balme and Brian Bridges (editors)
EUROPE–ASIA RELATIONS
Building Multilateralisms

Derek Beach and Colette Mazzucelli (editors)
LEADERSHIP IN THE BIG BANGS OF EUROPEAN INTEGRATION

Milena Büchs
NEW GOVERNANCE IN EUROPEAN SOCIAL POLICY
The Open Method of Coordination

Dario Castiglione, Justus Schönlau, Chris Longman, Emanuela Lombardo, Nieves Pérez-Solórzano Borragán and Mirim Aziz
CONSTITUTIONAL POLITICS IN THE EUROPEAN UNION
The Convention Moment and Its Aftermath

Morten Egeberg (editor)
MULTILEVEL UNION ADMINISTRATION
The Transformation of Executive Politics in Europe

Kevin Featherstone and Dimitris Papadimitriou
THE LIMITS OF EUROPEANIZATION
Reform Capacity and Policy Conflict in Greece

Palgrave Studies in European Union Politics
Series Standing Order ISBN 978-1-4039-9511-7 (hardback) and
ISBN 978-1-4039-9512-4 (paperback)

You can receive future titles in this series as they are published by placing a standing order. Please contact your bookseller or, in case of difficulty, write to us at the address below with your name and address, the title of the series and one of the ISBNs quoted above.

Customer Services Department, Macmillan Distribution Ltd, Houndmills, Basingstoke, Hampshire RG21 6XS, England

The Limits of Europeanization

Reform Capacity and Policy Conflict in Greece

Kevin Featherstone
Professor of Contemporary Greek Studies, London School of Economics, UK

Dimitris Papadimitriou
Senior Lecturer in European Politics, The University of Manchester, UK

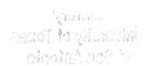

First published 2008 by
PALGRAVE MACMILLAN

Palgrave Macmillan in the UK is an imprint of Macmillan Publishers Limited, registered in England, company number 785998, of Houndmills, Basingstoke, Hampshire RG21 6XS.

Palgrave Macmillan in the US is a division of St Martin's Press LLC, 175 Fifth Avenue, New York, NY 10010.

Palgrave Macmillan is the global academic imprint of the above companies and has companies and representatives throughout the world.

Palgrave® and Macmillan® are registered trademarks in the United States, the United Kingdom, Europe and other countries.

ISBN-13: 978-0-230-00706-2   hardback
ISBN-10: 0-230-00706-6   hardback

This book is printed on paper suitable for recycling and made from fully managed and sustained forest sources. Logging, pulping and manufacturing processes are expected to conform to the environmental regulations of the country of origin.

A catalogue record for this book is available from the British Library.

Library of Congress Cataloging-in-Publication Data

Featherstone, Kevin.
   The limits of Europeanization : reform capacity and policy conflict
   in Greece / Kevin Featherstone and Dimitris Papadimitriou.
      p. cm. — (Palgrave studies in European Union politics)
   Includes bibliographical references and index.
   ISBN 0-230-00706-6 (alk. paper)
   1. Greece—Economic policy—1974– 2. European Union—Greece. I.
   Papadimitriou, Dimitris, 1972– II. Title.

   HC295.F415 2008
   330.9495—dc22   2008016312

10   9   8   7   6   5   4   3   2   1
17   16   15   14   13   12   11   10   09   08

Printed and bound in Great Britain by
CPI Antony Rowe, Chippenham and Eastbourne

For the new philhellenes: Nina, Chris, and Emily

&

For Zouzou and Konstantinos, an Athenian single-parent family in 2008

Contents

Tables

Preface

This book represents something of an intellectual odyssey for both of us: a quest to understand better the impact of European Union membership on Greece set against the constraints and continuities of the domestic society. We have also wanted to place our consideration of Greece in a framework that allows for international parallels to be drawn, rather than to settle for the comfortable arguments of Greek exceptionalism. This has led us to see Greece as a case study of 'Europeanization', charting the depth and extent of domestic change and appreciating its limits. This should make the national focus of much wider interest, addressing issues of the capability and reach of EU-level initiatives. Further, our focus was on the new agenda of structural economic and social reform – testing the limits of EU competences and the ability of the domestic system to respond to indirect and 'soft' policy instruments.

While there is much attention paid to 'Europeanization' in Greece, the study of public policy remains in its infancy. Similarly, though there have been studies of the labour system, there have been few attempts to consider the political economy of the system in the round. Such a task is relevant to understanding continuities of interest and the strategic interactions between the key players. Again, detailed empirical investigation entailing large numbers of interviews with the key actors remains all too rare in the study of Greek politics. This book attempts to address these shortcomings. It makes no grand claim to fill all the gaps; rather, it seeks to identify the key systemic characteristics alongside three detailed empirical case studies, so that one may inform the other.

The research for the case studies has been spread over a number of years. Some of our findings have been published as journal articles.[1] The present studies greatly extend these in time period, breadth, and depth. They are also placed in a more extended conceptual frame.

A work of this kind requires the help and support of a number of individuals and institutions. We wish to record our gratitude to all those who granted us personal interviews and conversations (listed in the appendix); their time and insight were essential to our task. We have respected their right to anonymity in the text. We have also been helped by academic advice from a range of colleagues, too numerous to list. But special mention must be made of Vassilis Monastiriotis, George Pagoulatos, David Soskice, Dimitris Sotiropoulos, and Platon Tinios for their comments and advice at different stages. In addition, various anonymous reviewers for our different publications have provided useful stimuli. Our documentary searches and editorial work were greatly eased by the professionalism of Eleni Xiarchogiannopoulou at the LSE. Our colleagues and students have been a regular source of stimulus. We are also grateful to the Hellenic Studies Programme at Princeton University for affording generous time and resources to Dimitris Papadimitriou for completing parts of this book during the fall of 2006. Above all, we are grateful to the Hellenic Observatory at the LSE for providing us with a conducive working environment and logistical support which nourished our collaboration and made this book possible.

Finally, we wish to close by thanking our respective wives and families for their tolerance and support. Our busy schedules imposed on them, and we are grateful for the space we had to complete this work.

Kevin Featherstone

Dimitris Papadimitriou

Abbreviations

ADEDY	Higher Command of Unions for Public Sector Employees (ΑΔΕΔΥ: Ανώτατη Διοίκηση Ενώσεων Δημοσίων Υπαλλήλων)
ALC	Athens Labour Centre (ΕΚΑ: Εργατικό Κέντρο Αθήνας)
ASEP	Higher Council for the Selection of Personnel (ΑΣΕΠ: Ανώτατο Συμβούλιο Επιλογής Προσωπικού)
BA	British Airways
BEPG	Broad Economic Policy Guidelines
DAKE	Democratic Independent Workers' Movement (ΔΑΚΕ: Δημοκρατική Ανεξάρτητη Κίνηση Εργαζομένων)
DEI	Public Enterprise of Electricity (ΔΕΗ: Δημόσια Επιχείρηση Ηλεκτρισμού)
DEKO	Public Utilities (ΔΕΚΟ: Δημόσιες Επιχειρήσεις Κοινής Ωφέλειας)
DIKKI	Democratic and Social Movement (ΔΗΚΚΙ: Δημοκρατικό Κοινωνικό Κίνημα)
ECJ	European Court of Justice
ECU	European Currency Unit
EDP	Excessive Deficit Procedure
EEC	European Economic Community
EES	European Employment Strategy
EIRO	European Industrial Relations Observatory
EISF	Union of Flying Attendants (ΕΙΣΦ: Ένωση Ιπταμένων Συνοδών και Φροντιστών)
EMU	Economic Monetary Union
ESEE	National Confederation of Greek Commerce (ΕΣΕΕ: Εθνική Συνομοσπονδία Ελληνικού Εμπορίου)
ESSE	National General Collective Agreement (ΕΣΣΕ: Εθνική Συλλογική Σύμβαση Εργασίας)

ETAM	Single Social Security Fund for the Salaried (ETAM: Ενιαίο Ταμείο Ασφάλισης Μισθωτών)
ETEAM	Single Auxiliary Social Security Fund for the Salaried (ETEAM: Ενιαίο Ταμείο Επικουρικής Ασφάλισης Μισθωτών)
EU	European Union
EXPA	Union of Civil Aviation Pilots (ΕΧΠΑ: Ένωση Χειριστών Πολιτικής Αεροπορίας)
GSEE	General Confederation of Greek Workers (ΓΣΕΕ: Γενική Συνομοσπονδία Εργατών Ελλάδος)
GSEVEE	General Confederation of Professionals, Medium and Small Businesses and Traders (ΓΣΕΒΕΕ: Γενική Συνομοσπονδία Επαγγελματιών Βιοτεχνών Εμπόρων Ελλάδος)
IKA	Social Security Foundation (ΙΚΑ: Ίδρυμα Κοινωνικών Ασφαλίσεων)
IMF	International Monetary Fund
INE	Institute of Labour (ΙΝΕ: Ινστιτούτο Εργασίας)
KKE	Communist Party of Greece (ΚΚΕ: Κουμουνιστικό Κόμμα Ελλάδας)
LAOS	Popular Orthodox Rally (ΛΑ.Ο.Σ: Λαϊκός Ορθόδοξος Συναγερμός)
NAP	National Action Plan
NAT	Seamen Pension Fund (ΝΑΤ: Ναυτικό Απομαχικό Ταμείο)
ND	New Democracy (ΝΔ: Νέα Δημοκρατία)
NSSG	National Statistical Service of Greece (ΕΣΥΑ: Εθνική Στατιστική Υπηρεσία Ελλάδος)
OA	Olympic Airlines (ΟΑ: Ολυμπιακή Αεροπορία)
OAEE	Social Security Organisation for the Self Employed (ΟΑΕΕ: Οργανισμός Ασφάλισης Ελεύθερων Επαγγελματιών)
OECD	Organization for Economic Cooperation and Development

OGA	Agricultural Social Security Fund (ΟΓΑ: Οργανισμός Γεωργικών Ασφαλίσεων)
OIYE	Greek Federation of Private Sector Employees (ΟΙΥΕ: Ομοσπονδία Ιδιωτικών Υπάλληλων Ελλάδας)
OKE	Economic and Social Committee (ΟΚΕ: Οικονομική και Κοινωνική Επιτροπή)
OMC	Open Method of Coordination
OMED	Organization for Mediation and Arbitration (ΟΜΕΔ: Οργανισμός Μεσολάβησης και Διαιτησίας)
OSPA	Federation of Civil Aviation Unions (ΟΣΠΑ: Ομοσπονδία Σωματείων Πολιτικής Αεροπορίας)
OTE	Greek Telecommunications Organization (ΟΤΕ: Οργανισμός Τηλεπικοινωνιών Ελλάδας)
OTOE	Greek Federation of Banking Unions (ΟΤΟΕ: Ομοσπονδία Τραπεζοϋπαλληλικών Οργανώσεων Ελλάδας)
PASKE	Fighting Union Movement of Greek Employees (ΠΑΣΚΕ: Πανελλήνια Αγωνιστική Συνδικαλιστική Κίνηση Εργαζομένων)
PASOK	Pan-Hellenic Socialist Movement (ΠΑΣΟΚ: Πανελλήνιο Σοσιαλιστικό Κίνημα)
PAYG	Pay as you go
PPP	Purchasing Power Parities
R & D	Research and Development
SELPE	Greek Federation of Retail Enterprises (ΣΕΛΠΕ: Σύνδεσμος Επιχειρήσεων Λιανικής Πώλησης Ελλάδος)
SEV	League of Greek Industries (ΣΕΒ: Σύνδεσμος Ελληνικών Βιομηχανιών)
SYN (Synaspismos)	Coalition of the Left, Movements and Ecology (ΣΥΝ: Συνασπισμός της Αριστεράς, των Κινημάτων και της Οικολογίας)
SYRIZA	Coalition of the Radical Left (Συνασπισμός της Ριζοσπαστικής Αριστεράς)

TAE	Technical Aviation Undertakings (ΤΑΕ: Τεχνικαί Αεροπορικαί Εκμεταλεύσεις)
TEVE	Greek Social Security Fund for Craftsmen and Small Traders (ΤΕΒΕ: Ταμείο Επαγγελματιών και Βιοτεχνών Ελλάδας)
TEP	Territorial Employment Pact
YPA	Civil Aviation Authority (ΥΠΑ: Υπηρεσία Πολιτικής Αεροπορίας)

1
Introduction

1.1 The focus of the book

The European Union (EU) plays an increasingly important part in the political and economic life of its member states. Indeed, this fact has been recognized by the new attention given to processes of 'Europeanization'. Somewhat akin to 'globalization', Europeanization represents a seemingly pervasive but variable intrusion of an external dimension into domestic systems. The dividing line between the EU and domestic politics is thus blurred. The relevance of the EU to the policies and public debates witnessed at the domestic level is evident, for example, from the attention given to the single European currency, the euro; the authority exercised by the EU Commission on mergers and acquisitions and against state aids; the development funding provided to poorer regions of the EU; the relevance of the EU to sensitivities on asylum and migration issues; and the contrast between reported policy splits and the aspiration to a 'Common Foreign and Security Policy'.

'Europeanization' testifies to the capabilities of the EU. It is not only a matter of how the EU impacts on domestic systems – setting laws, creating obligations – but also of how national governments seek to shape the agenda of the EU as a whole, inserting their interests and preferences into common policies and understandings. In other words, the relationship between a member state and the EU is two way: ideas and pressures flow in both directions, shaping the politics and economics of each other. Indeed, the relationship takes on further interest; the EU is more than the sum of its parts, given that its institutions and processes mediate and shape agendas and outcomes in a distinctive manner. National actors participate in a structured environment and in one that affects their strategies and ideas. These complex features define the EU system of governance.

But what is the *reach* of the EU's system of governance? How *effective* is it in steering and shaping the major policies found across its member states? What are the *limits* to Europeanization? Why do EU stimuli sometimes lead to domestic *change*, but at other times have little effect? These questions are at the heart of this book.

It can be tempting to identify the impact of 'Europeanization' in a wide variety of areas and settings. To some, the limits of Europeanization may seem boundless. New drinking habits, a change of identity in football, the historic movement of ethnic groups, and a shift in ideology – each of these topics has been explained by prime reference to the term (Featherstone and Radaelli, 2003). Yet none has any significant, direct connection with the politics of the EU. The meaning of 'Europe' here is much wider and non-institutional. Where the direct connection with the EU is stronger – as with compliance with an EU legal obligation, such as a 'directive' – the type of impact at the domestic level is more readily discernible. Though even here the process of explaining, let alone predicting, domestic change as a result of the EU obligation is far from straightforward (e.g. Haverland, 2003). More challenging still are the areas where the power of the EU to act is less clear. A government announcing the privatization of a state-owned enterprise or the adoption of a new welfare policy, or a government urging the need to make employment patterns more open and flexible – each of these moves may be ascribed politically to the EU, but the reality is of varying competences and instruments available to the EU to act. In the social sciences, explanation depends on identifying a cause and effect relationship. Claims of 'Europeanization' need to meet these same tests; they cannot to settle for presumed impacts.

This book explores the impact of the EU across areas where the power of the EU to act varies. It is set in the general context of the EU's plan of 'structural reform' enunciated in its 'Lisbon programme' of 2000. At a meeting of the 'European Council' – of heads of government/state – in Lisbon that year, the EU set itself a new mission for the period up to 2010. It declared:

> The Union has today set itself *a new strategic goal* for the next decade: *to become the most competitive and dynamic knowledge-based economy in the world capable of sustainable economic growth with more and better jobs and greater social cohesion* [emphasis in original].
>
> (European Council, 2000a: 2)

The Lisbon Programme elaborated a set of priorities, mixing economic liberalization, sound finances, and social solidarity. The key themes were a European area for research and innovation, a more friendly environment for small business, efficient and integrated financial markets, education and training for the knowledge society, a fully operational internal market, the sustainability of public finances, an active employment policy, modernizing social protection, and promoting social inclusion. A set of ambitious targets was set to underscore the programme. Subsequent progress was disappointing, however. By 2005, while economic growth in the EU was sluggish at 1.6%, in the USA growth was more than double at 3.6%. Whereas at Lisbon bold employment targets had been set, unemployment in France and Germany remained at around 10%. In response to these problems, the European Council updated the programme in 2005 (European Council, 2005).

The Lisbon Programme recognized that the goals being set were ones where the EU had only limited competences. The European Council did not seek to extend the powers of the EU institutions to fill the gaps. Instead, it placed them in the context of a system of policy coordination, embracing the national governments and the Commission. The Lisbon Council declared that

> Implementing this strategy will be achieved by improving the existing processes, introducing a ***new open method of coordination*** at all levels, coupled with a stronger guiding and coordinating role for the European Council to ensure more coherent strategic direction and effective monitoring of progress. A meeting of the European Council to be held every Spring will define the relevant mandates and ensure that they are followed up[1] [emphasis in original].
>
> (European Council, 2000a: 2)

The 'Open Method of Coordination' (OMC) process tackled the programmatic objectives on the basis of a benchmarking of national progress and a system of mutual learning, sharing good practice, etc. The OMC involves a wider range of bureaucratic and technocratic actors – national government and Commission officials along with some civil society actors such as the social partners (unions and employers), NGOs, and local and regional authorities – but it has been criticized for its lack of transparency and low public profile.

In any event, the strategy behind the Lisbon Programme had a vulnerable character: to its critics, it involved soft policies and soft processes. The rhetoric was ambitious and general, but the substance lacked authority to oversee its implementation across the EU. There were many objectives, but little that was binding. The politics of EU-level exhortation replaced the legal constraint of treaty commitments or legislative directives. To its supporters, the Lisbon Programme and the OMC were the best attempts to bring the EU closer to the needs and aspirations of Europe's citizens, tackling core issues of growth, jobs, IT, social protection, and adaptation to a new global economy. Rather than involving yet another institutional reform, it focussed in a pragmatic manner on policy learning in key areas.

By focussing in the main on the Lisbon Programme of structural economic reform and its concomitant OMC, this book defines a severe test for assessing the domestic relevance of 'Europeanization'. As an area of soft instruments to support non-enforceable policy goals, the stimulus to domestic reform is weaker than where the EU acts on the basis of treaty competences and legislative directives. Actors at the national level could not benefit from the kind of external empowerment that marked the binding convergence criteria that governed entry into the 'euro' single currency (Featherstone, 2004). If Lisbon could be shown to be central to a domestic reform process, then 'Europeanization' is indeed a credible hypothesis here.

At the same time, the cases covered in the book combine 'soft' instruments with some aspects of 'hard law'. The book comprises three empirical case studies: pension reform, labour market reform, and the privatization of a national airline. The first two were affected by the 'hard' constraint of Greece seeking to meet the Economic and Monetary Union (EMU) entry criteria. In addition, both were linked to the Lisbon Programme of adapting the social model and creating a more competitive economy and its 'soft' instruments of implementation. Privatization cuts across several agendas and involves both 'hard' and 'soft' EU interventions. The liberalization of the single European market and the anti-state aid strictures of the EU's competition policy created new and severe regulatory constraints on state monopolies. At the same time, the policy signals emanating from the Commission urged governments to pursue liberalization to the full, shedding inefficient state enterprises to the private sector. There was an implicit link to the Lisbon stress on competitiveness.

The combination of these three sectoral case studies thus provides a varied range on which to assess the reach of the EU's broad agenda on reform. The case studies have been chosen to reflect a variety of EU instruments across policy sectors – many sectors incorporate different types of instruments – and because they each relate to so-called supply-side reforms. As a part of an agenda of economic and social 'modernization', they serve to test the reform capacity of a member state such as Greece in such areas, when the latter is challenged by EU stimuli of varying types. The analytical framework of 'Europeanization' will be explored in Chapter 2.

1.2 Why this case?

This book has selected a member state for study that represents a 'critical case' for the Europeanization hypothesis in this context: Greece. A critical case is one where it can be asserted that if the hypothesis is not valid for this case, then it is unlikely to apply to other cases (Flyvbjerg, 2006; Eckstein, 1975). Greece can be regarded as a 'least likely' case in relation to structural reform: the prevailing domestic conditions contrast markedly with the Lisbon Programme; it has a tradition of 'statism' in the economy; and its pension system has been distorted by entrenched domestic interests. Indeed, historically, successive Greek governments have struggled to achieve significant reform in the key areas of structural reform. If the following case studies show significant domestic impacts as a result of the EU stimuli, then this would validate that the EU has 'teeth' when it acts in these areas. Either way, the Greek case will provide important causal insights, whether it tends to confirm or falsify the 'Europeanization' hypothesis (Brady and Collier, 2004: 283).

The choice of policy sectors can be revealing in the Greek case. Over the last decade or more, Greece has enjoyed greater success than most of her EU partners with respect to macroeconomic growth. Yet progress on 'supply-side' economic reforms and on the 'modernization' of social provision has proved difficult. The three case studies analysed here – of pensions, labour market reform, and privatization – will clarify the politics of the relevant processes, indicating the mix of power and interests to determine policy outcomes in these sectors. They will reflect, at one level, the politics of *who gains* from the macroeconomic success, in defending their interests, though this is more a result of inertia than collective choice.

More generally, Greece is an EU member state that has had a reputation for being the 'black sheep' – standing aside from common declarations on foreign policy, failing to meet agreed targets, and misusing EU funds. Further, it has had one of the poorest records in implementing and upholding EU legislation.[2] Table 1.1 shows the infringement proceedings undertaken against the 15 longer-term members of the EU (EU 15) from 1980 to 2005. Over this period, Greece has consistently been

Table 1.1 The number of established infringements – classified by the stage of proceedings and the member state

	Letters of formal notice						Reasoned opinions						Referrals to Court					
	'80	'85	'90	'95	'00	'05	'80	'85	'90	'95	'00	'05	'80	'85	'90	'95	'00	'05
BE	34	68	67	80	92	68	10	37	29	19	34	33	8	23	13	6	5	7
DA	15	27	35	42	54	37	2	4	5	1	7	6	1	2	3	0	0	2
DE	14	29	61	92	92	63	3	17	20	25	40	27	1	9	5	10	11	12
EL	*	69	121	113	115	104	—	30	39	26	35	70	—	10	10	12	23	18
ES	—	—	114	81	93	73	—	—	15	15	32	35	—	—	3	6	8	6
FR	34	93	76	97	110	77	10	36	17	17	43	48	4	14	6	6	27	12
IE	25	33	52	67	91	54	5	10	17	3	27	28	1	9	3	6	17	9
IT	39	70	110	114	118	136	19	61	58	36	50	93	11	31	24	17	24	34
LU	26	37	43	71	78	75	5	16	14	9	40	49	2	6	4	3	16	18
NL	21	48	61	59	64	57	7	11	20	4	16	20	—	4	2	0	12	9
AT	—	—	—	4	85	59	—	—	—	0	33	22	—	—	—	0	8	9
PT	—	—	176	115	120	85	—	—	11	22	46	65	—	—	2	4	10	6
SE	—	—	—	0	72	48	—	—	—	0	13	18	—	—	—	0	3	6
FI	—	—	—	0	63	59	—	—	—	0	14	21	—	—	—	0	4	10
UK	19	29	44	77	70	60	7	11	6	15	30	22	—	5	2	2	4	7
EU 15	227	203	960	974	1317	1055	68	233	251	192	460	561	28	113	77	72	172	165

Sources: (1) European Commission (2006b), Document de Travail des Services de la Commission. Annex au 23eme Rapport Annuel de la Commission Sur le Controle De'l Application Du Droit Communitaire (2005), COM (2006) 416 Final, SEC (2006) 1005, Brussels 27 July 2006; (2) European Commission (2005a), 22eme Rapport Annuel Sur le Controle De'l Application Du Droit Communitaire (2004). Document de Travail des Services de la Commission Annexes Statistiques Annexe au COM (2005) 570. SEC (2005) 1447. Brussels 23 December 2005; (3) European Commission (1999a), XVIth Report on Monitoring the Application of Community Law, COM (1999) 301 Final, 9 July 1999; (4) Commission of the European Communities (1986), Third Annual Report to the European Parliament on Commission Monitoring of the Application of Community Law – 1985, Official Journal of European Communities, C 220, 1 September 1986; (5) Commission of the European Communities (1992), Ninth Annual Report on Commission Monitoring of the Application of Community Law – 1991, Official Journal of European Communities, COM (92) 136 Final, 12 May 1992.

*Greece joined the EC in 1981; by 1983 it had 26 letters of formal notice, 4 reasoned opinions, and 2 references to the Court of Justice.

among the worst two or three offenders in not implementing or following EU laws. Table 1.2 shows the relative delays in transposing the internal market legislation of the EU by member states. Here, the Greek record has fluctuated significantly: in 1997 it scored relatively well, but in 2000 it was the worst performer by far, then improvement in 2003 was followed by Greece being one of the three worst performers in 2006. More relevant here have been the evident problems experienced by Greece in implementing the Lisbon Programme. By June 2005, Greece ranked twenty-fourth in the EU 25 in the transposition of the Lisbon Programme directives, with just 66.7% transposed. Table 1.3 represents the full data of the EU Commission's report of 2004. It indicated that Greece had the second-lowest score on labour productivity and the employment rate in the EU 15, the lowest investment in Research and Development (as percentage of GDP); the second highest at-risk-of-poverty rate and long-term unemployment. In December 2006, the EU Commission reported that Greece 'is making limited progress in the implementation of its National Reform Programme' (European Commission, 2006a: 44). Specifically, 'Regarding governance, better coordination and stronger ownership among administrative levels is needed' (European Commission, 2006a: 44). While it noted good progress in the consolidation of public finances and other areas, it listed the high-priority areas for reform as the pension system, public administration, employment participation, unemployment and undeclared work, employment protection and labour mobility, and the quality of education and training (European Commission, 2006a: 45). The list touched on the foci of the case studies presented here, confirming Greece as a critical case and posing the question of what has happened to the reform attempts. Across the various sets of indicators, the Greek record suggests a major problem in state administration and reform capacity.

On the other hand, the long-term trend of public opinion in Greece has displayed one of the highest levels of support for further European integration. Table 1.4 shows the exceptional levels of public support in Greece for the EU. Accession and early membership of the EU were controversial domestically, but in 1990, 1995, 2000, and 2005 the Greek public were consistently among the top two or three in Europe in their belief that membership had 'benefited' their country. Similarly, Table 1.5 shows that in the same years Greek voters were among the highest in Europe believing that EU membership had been a 'good thing'. Again, Table 1.6 indicates that Greek support for the single currency was well above the EU average in 1990, 1995, and 2000. The introduction of

Table 1.2   Transposition deficit of internal market legislation (per cent)

Country	1997	2000	2003	2006
AT	10.1	3.6	3.4	1.4
DE	8.5	3.6	3.0	1.8
BE	8.5	3.1	1.8	2.0
IT	7.6	3.4	3.9	3.8
GR	7.5	7.3	3.3	3.8
FR	7.4	5.2	3.3	1.9
LU	6.5	4.6	3.2	3.8
SK	6.2	1.5	1.0	1.4
PT	5.9	6	3.7	3.7
IRL	5.4	4	3.5	2.0
ES	4.7	1.5	1.2	1.7
UK	4.6	3	1.5	1.3
FIN	4.3	1.4	1.0	1.5
NL	3.5	3	2.0	1.5
DK	3.2	2	0.6	0.5

Sources: (1) European Commission (2006c), Internal Market Scoreboard No. 15, July; (2) European Commission (2003a), Internal Market Scoreboard No. 12, May; (3) European Commission (2000a), Single Market Scoreboard No. 6, May; (4) European Commission (1997), Single Market Scoreboard No. 1, November.

the 'euro', however, led to a significant public backlash. In 2005, only 46% of Greeks were recorded as being in favour of the currency, well below that recorded elsewhere.

In the same period, there was some evidence of a new, though limited, 'euroscepticism' in Greece. Archbishop Christodoulos of Athens – a new and populist figure on the domestic scene, who was to provoke strong reactions from supporters and opponents alike – had launched a strident campaign suggesting that 'Europe' was encroaching on Greek 'identity'.[3] In 2000, his opposition to a revision of the Greek identity card – where it was proposed to remove a question about religious identity and it had been claimed that this was required by the EU[4] – produced a petition of over three million signatures. A new 'eurosceptic' party also emerged (LAOS: Popular Orthodox Rally/ΛΑ.Ο.Σ: Λαϊκός Ορθόδοξος Συναγερμός), with its leader George Karatzaferis winning a seat in the European Parliament in June 2004. The latter remained fringe, with both the major parties being overwhelmingly pro-EU. Indeed, this was evident in the trouble-free ratification of the EU Constitution by the Greek Parliament on 19 April 2005, which produced a majority of 268 to 17 votes.

But what this evidence suggests is a differentiated profile of Greek membership of the EU. Thus, general patterns appear in the limits to

Europeanization in Greece. The state administration is weak in implementing and upholding EU commitments. Within government and between government and other domestic actors there is a political struggle over the adaptation to EU policies, especially where there are distributional issues involved. More widely, there is a cultural resistance concerning national identity, traditions, and habits. To some extent this is a matter of cultural pride in the Greek 'way' and is based on distinct social values of heritage, reciprocity, and loyalty. Resistance involves both sectional interests and cultural choice. Yet, at the same time, the major parties and the majority of the public are strong and consistent supporters of the development of the EU. It is a profile of contradictions: in crude terms, the Greek system welcomes 'Europe' for its political and resource advantages while sustaining barriers to its legal, economic, and cultural adaptation. The profile contrasts self-confidence about Greece's place in Europe with a sense of vulnerability on matters of policy substance and a defensiveness about the Greek way of 'doing things'.

It is this differentiated profile that makes Greece such an interesting focus for this study. There is clear evidence of political will to engage with the EU. Yet the record suggests significant problems of administrative and reform capacity when doing so. If the EU's structural reform agenda (notably, the Lisbon Programme) have a significant effect on Greece, then this would be a strong endorsement of their domestic reach, penetrating a system that has shown resistance. Beyond this, the policy case studies question the governability and membership of a national system that seemingly struggles to deliver. More generally, they have significant implications for the EU's sense of purpose in managing economic reform.

1.3 The domestic political context

The historical period discussed in this book mainly covers the period from 1996 to late 2007. The period began with the premiership of Costas Simitis between 1996 and 2004. The election of Simitis as leader of PASOK (Pan-Hellenic Socialist Movement / ΠΑΣΟΚ: Πανελλήνιο Σοσιαλιστικό Κίνημα) and his appointment as Prime Minister, both in 1996, represented a major turning point in Greek politics. His personality and political platform, both represented a significant change. The hugely charismatic, and populist, Andreas Papandreou was the founder and leader of the party after the fall of the Colonels in 1974 and had served as Prime Minister for 11 years (1981–9; 1993–5). PASOK had been

Table 1.3 Relative performance of the 15 member states according to the structural indicators on the Lisbon Programme shortlist

Levels		AT	BE	DE	DK	ES	FI	FR	GR	IE	IT	LU	NL	PT	SE	UK	EU15
GDP per capita in PPS (EU 15 = 100)	2003	110.9	106.5	99.3	112.6	87.3	101	103.5	73.5	121.9	98.4	186.5	109.4	69.2	101.4	108.7	100
Labour productivity (EU 15 = 100)	2003	97.9	118.5	95.7	98.3	95.7	100.1	113.6	91.8	120.4	106	129.7	95.6	63.8	96.1	97	100
Employment rate (%)	2002	69.3	59.9	65.3	75.9	58.4	68.1	63	56.7	65.3	55.5	63.7	74.4	68.2	73.6	71.7	64.3
Employment rate of older workers (%)	2002	30	26.6	38.6	57.9	39.7	47.8	34.8	39.7	48.1	28.9	28.3	42.3	50.9	68	53.5	40.1
Educational (20–4) (%) attainment	2003	85	81.1	73.3	74.4	63.4	86.2	81.1	81.7	85.7	69.9	69.8	73.3	47.2	85.6	78.2	74
Research and Development expenditure (% of GDP)	2002	1.9	2.2	2.5	2.4	1.0	3.5	2.2	0.6	1.2	1.1	1.7	1.9	0.8	4.3	1.8	2.0
Business investment (% of GDP)	2002	20.9	18.3	16.9	17.8	21.8	16	16.4	20.1	17.7	17.8	17.9	17.4	21.6	13.5	15	17.2
Comparative price levels (EU15 = 100)	2002	102	99	104	131	82	123	100	80	118	95	100	102	74	117	107	100
At-risk-of-poverty rate (%)	2001	12.0	13.0	11.0	11.0	19.0	11.0	15.0	20.0	21.0	19.0	12.0	11.0	20.0	10.0	17.0	15.0

Indicator	Year																
Long-term unemployment	2002	0.8	3.5	4	0.9	3.9	2.3	2.8	5.1	1.3	5.3	0.8	0.7	1.8	1	1.1	3
Dispersion of regional employment rates	2002	2.4	8	5.9	n.r.	9.2	7.8	6.2	4.2	n.r.	16.6	n.r.	2.2	3.9	4.6	6.6	12.6
Greenhouse gases emissions (Index base year = 100)	2001	110	106	82	100	133	105	100	126	131	107	56	105	136	97	88	98
Energy intensity of the economy	2001	146	228	168	125	227	263	189	261	161	188	191	201	238	229	225	194.2
Volume of transport	2002	120	100	102	85	137	95	96	127	133	103	110	97	126	90	85	102.4

Source: European Commission (2004a), Report from the Commission to the Spring European Council: Delivering Lisbon, Reforms for the Enlarged Union, p. 61. *Notes:* (1) The analysis of the comparative price levels takes into account the relation between GDP per capita and comparative price levels; (2) The analysis of greenhouse gases emissions is based on the distance-to-target indicators for the Kyoto Protocol and burden-sharing targets of the EU member states; (3) n.r. stands for non-relevant.

Table 1.4   Attitudes towards EU/EC membership 1980–2005 (per cent)
I feel that my country has benefited from EU membership

Country	1985	1990	1995	2000	2005
LU	69	72	73	70	75
IRL	67	84	87	86	86
NL	67	75	68	61	61
IT	70	65	52	49	49
GR	42	78	72	72	67
EC 12	53	58	—	—	—
EU 15	—	—	46	47	—
EU 25	—	—	—	—	52

Sources: (1) European Commission (1985a), Eurobarometre No. 24, December; (2) European Commission (1990), Eurobarometer No. 34, December; (3) European Commission (1995), Eurobarometer No. 43, Autumn; (4) European Commission (2001), Eurobarometer, No. 54, April; (5) European Commission (2006d), Eurobarometer No. 64, June.

Table 1.5   Attitudes towards EU/EC membership 1980–2005 (per cent)
I think EC/EU membership is a good thing

Country	1985	1990	1995	2000	2005
LU	83	76	80	79	82
IRL	53	76	79	75	73
NL	77	82	79	71	70
IT	72	77	73	59	50
GR	45	75	63	61	54
EC 12	57	69	—	—	—
EU 15	—	—	56	50	—
EU 25	—	—	—	—	50

Sources: (1) European Commission (1985b), Eurobarometer No. 23, June; (2) European Commission (1990), Eurobarometer No. 34, December; (3) European Commission (1995), Eurobarometer No. 43, Autumn; (4) European Commission (2006d), Eurobarometer No. 64, June; (5) European Commission (2001), Eurobarometer, No. 54, April.

moulded in his image and had adapted according to his direction. By 1995, however, his ill health meant that his demise was inevitable. After some delay, he resigned as Premier on 15 January 1996 (and died later on 22 June 1996), leaving the stage he had dominated. A few days later, on 18 January, Simitis defeated his rivals in a contest for the premiership. Simitis was the candidate that offered the greatest prospect for change. Akis Tsochatzopoulos and Gerasimos Arsenis were both, in varying ways, associated with the populist and clientelistic traditions of

Table 1.6 Support for single currency (per cent)

Country	1990 For	1990 Against	1995 For	1995 Against	2000 For	2000 Against	2003 For	2003 Against	2005 For	2005 Against
IT	72	11	76	13	79	17	70	26	64	NA
EL	64	10	67	19	70	21	64	33	46	NA
FR	62	19	63	31	62	32	68	28	78	NA
BE	61	16	67	22	72	24	81	15	83	NA
NL	61	25	61	28	64	31	62	34	71	NA
IE	58	17	68	18	69	20	79	14	87	NA
PT	55	16	52	28	57	26	69	25	67	NA
ES	53	10	58	20	68	24	70	25	61	NA
DE	50	27	38	50	47	44	60	33	66	NA
LU	47	26	72	20	75	20	83	15	89	NA
UK	38	43	38	55	21	63	23	65	28	NA
DK	35	50	30	66	41	55	52	43	50	NA
AT	—	—	35	51	53	38	24	67	67	NA
FI	—	—	32	59	45	49	70	27	79	NA
SE	—	—	32	57	26	64	41	54	44	NA
EC 12	55	23	54	35	62	31	67	28	—	NA
EU 15	—	—	52	36	55	37	59	35	—	NA
EU 25	—	—	—	—	—	—	—	—	60	NA

Sources: (1) European Commission (1990) Eurobarometer No. 34, December; (2) European Commission (1995), Eurobarometer No. 43, Autumn; (3) European Commission (2001), Eurobarometer, No. 54, April; (4) European Commission (2004c), Eurobarometer No. 60, February; (5) European Commission (2006d), Eurobarometer No. 64, June.

Notes: (1) The table follows the abbreviations applied in European Commission 2006d, Eurobarometer No. 64 (p. 4); (2) German percentage for 1995 depicts the average West and East German support; (3) data in the 2000 column depict percentage for Autumn 2000; (4) Greek support remains at the same level (64% for and 33% against) for the year 2004 (European Commission (2004b), Eurobarometer No. 61, July, p. B58); (5) Eurostat does not provide data for the negative attitudes towards single currency for the year 2005.

PASOK.[5] Tsochatzopoulos, in particular, was seen as the leader of the *proedrikoi* (leader's faction) protecting the inheritance of Papandreou. They would continue to be an oppositional faction more or less throughout Simitis's period as Premier. The election by MPs was in fact a close-run affair.[6] But on 1 July 1996 a party congress elected Simitis as PASOK's new leader (by 53.8% to Tsochatzopoulos's 45.7%). Simitis's position was further legitimized when he led his party to victory in the October 1996 parliamentary elections (PASOK won by a margin of 41.4% to 38.1% over the centre-right New Democracy party (ND/ΝΔ: Νέα Δημοκρατία) (Featherstone and Kazamias, 1997). Simitis's second election victory in April 2000, however, was much closer: PASOK led ND by just 43.8% to 42.7%.

Politically, Simitis's *mantras* were 'modernization' and 'Europeanization'. 'Modernization' involved a package of economic, social, and political reforms that sought to mix liberalization (a shift from statism) with a new social solidarity (Simitis, 2005). Simitis led a faction within PASOK comprising rising personnel such as Theodoros Pangalos, Giannos Papandoniou, Vasso Papandreou, and George Papandreou (Andreas's son). Their modernization agenda was defined within the frame of 'Europe': it had little meaning without reference to the need to adapt to the EU. Simitis's modernization project was both bold and comprehensive in intent. It began with a sense of urgency. Greece needed to place itself at the core of the EU, which meant that entry to the single currency had to be secured. In the mid-1990s, the performance of the Greek economy remained the most divergent in the EU from the Maastricht convergence criteria. The New Democracy government of Constantinos Mitsotakis (1990–3) had been over-optimistic in believing that it could establish a rapid convergence. In reality, it failed to meet the conditions for the EU aid provisionally allocated to Greece. It had also been thwarted by strong union opposition to its neoliberal reforms. Andreas Papandreou reaped the benefit at the 1993 election, promising an easier path to EMU. By contrast, Simitis stressed the urgency of his modernization project. Greece had a historic opportunity to fulfil its European interests, but this would not last.

Thus, Greece had to undertake a big leap forward by following a new national development strategy. This had to entail structural economic reforms to introduce greater flexibility and competitiveness, an agenda that foreshadowed, in inspiration, the EU's Lisbon 2000 project. It was evident that these reforms had to embrace further privatization, greater liberalization of the labour market, and a more just and efficient pension system. While the state's economic role had to be leaner and more efficient, at the same time it had a basic responsibility to build a 'new social state', a theme that was shared elsewhere in Europe, not least in Romano Prodi's Italy (Simitis, 2005: 125–49). In politics, Simitis and his supporters advocated a greater separation of the 'party' from the 'state': a break with the incestuous 'rousfetti' politics or bureaucratic clientelism of the recent past. The 'clean hands' and modesty of Simitis were extolled. Simitis's modernization project also embraced the reform of the Greek constitution, continuing a momentum established by the ND government of Mitsotakis. The latter had talked of the 're-foundation' of the state, while the Simitis Government inserted the principle of the 'social welfare state' into the Constitution.

The Simitis Government could claim a number of creditable policy achievements. Greece was a much more respected partner in the EU, typically a part of the prevailing majority on most major issues. Economically, it adopted the single European currency in 2001; it maintained a rate of economic growth well above the EU average for most of its period in office; it reduced Greece's inflation rate and brought it much closer to that of its EU partners. Other economic achievements proved more controversial. Notably, the reduction of the budget deficit – a crucial element in Greece meeting the Maastricht criteria for entry into the single currency – was later re-examined in 2004 by the EU Commission (European Commission, 2004d). The deficit was recalculated according to a different set of rules. Simitis and his supporters claimed they had not contravened any rules, rather that new ones were being applied after the event. Opponents felt that they had manipulated the data for political purposes, hiding expenditure commitments.[7] More generally, while the Simitis Government had had perhaps unprecedented courage to confront an agenda of structural reform, its substantive progress in implementation was disappointing even to many of its supporters. In 2002, a report for the World Economic Forum examined the record of EU countries in implementing the Lisbon Programme and it reported that Greece was consistently the worst performer across the eight dimensions it had defined (2002).

By the end of its period in office, the Simitis Government looked tired and somewhat disoriented. It even looked less 'clean', with allegations of corruption giving the sense that it had stayed too long in power. In January 2004, Simitis announced he would resign as PASOK leader, allowing his successor to lead the party into the next election. George Papandreou was soon anointed and he embarked on a fresh approach, to appeal to the disaffected. But PASOK's position in the polls was too low to turn around so quickly.

The elections in April 2004 were a clear victory for New Democracy. It defeated PASOK by 45.4% to 40.5%, gaining a parliamentary majority of 15% over all other parties. The new government of Costas Karamanlis – the nephew of the former premier – proclaimed a fresh start, reforming the state and creating a more competitive economy. The programme again seemed very much in line with the Lisbon Programme on structural reform. Yet Karamanlis and his colleagues had learnt from the demise of the Mitsotakis Government of the early 1990s. The strategy was to be more sensitive to what was politically feasible. It also adopted the language of inclusiveness and consultation. The government would reach out to opponents and endeavour to create a new consensus for reform.

What was striking was the narrowness of the ideological differences between the two major parties, compared to their differences in the 1980s and early 1990s. Simitis had led PASOK towards a more market-oriented social democracy, shedding the statism of the past. Karamanlis talked more of competition and the private sector, but his approach was to be moderate, gradualist, and inclusive. The policies and priorities had converged. Election campaigns lacked the emotion of the past and more attention was paid to competence and achievement. The task of governing – steering reform to implementation – still looked daunting, however. The domestic constraints seemed very powerful. Indeed, the track record of structural reform suggested that the domestic system was structured in a manner that appeared to militate against consensus and delivery.

1.4   Where the book fits in

This book seeks to build on the existing literature on Greece and to fill in some notable gaps. Lavdas's book (1997) on the Europeanization of Greece was an innovative study when it was published, but it is now somewhat dated: it covered the period prior to Costas Simitis becoming Prime Minister, and the conceptual literature on 'Europeanization' has been further developed since then. His book focused on government–business relations and domestic policy patterns, focusing in particular on regulatory change (privatization) and the EU structural policy. The general argument was compatible with that developed here: while the direction and content of EU influence on Greek policy was evident in this period, such 'external' pressures were mediated by domestic 'arrangements and coalitions' (Lavdas, 1997: 6). Pagoulatos's study (2003) was groundbreaking, though its conceptual and historical focus was very different from the present volume. A study in political economy, it charted Greece's gradual shift from a 'developmental state' to a 'stabilization state' in the post-war era, focussing on the state and finance. It made little direct reference to the literatures on 'Europeanization' or on 'varieties of capitalism', two major approaches taken up here. The present volume seeks to provide a conceptually informed study of the public policy process in Greece, incorporating the dimensions of agenda setting, actor strategies, interest mediation, and implementation. As such, it hopes to complement earlier work and close some of the gaps in the literature. The book draws on some previously published work. The themes of governability and of the limits to Europeanization were signalled in Featherstone (2005). The empirical case study on pension reform extends earlier coverage in Featherstone, Kazamias, and Papadimitriou (2001) and Featherstone (2005). The case study on labour market reform builds on the work of Papadimitriou (2005). The study of Olympic Airways (OA/OA: Ολυμπιακή Αεροπορία) draws on Featherstone and Papadimitriou (2007), broadening its coverage. While building on this earlier work, the present volume extends the empirical coverage, broadens the conceptual discussion, and develops themes only lightly touched upon previously.

The research for the empirical chapters involved extensive searches of relevant documents and of news coverage. Altogether some 3000 newspaper reports have been consulted in order to trace the domestic debate on structural reform over the past decade. In addition, over 50 personal interviews (see the appendix) have been conducted with key actors in Greece. These included all of Simitis's heavyweight cabinet Ministers involved in the three policy areas covered in the book as well as a number of junior Ministers, prime-ministerial and ministerial advisers, managers of state-controlled companies, and high-ranked civil servants in the ministerial bureaucracies. The range of government officials interviewed gave the opportunity to cross-reference the information provided and build an accurate picture of the constraints under which the Simitis Government had to operate. A number of opposition politicians were also interviewed, some of whom were subsequently allocated key ministerial portfolios in the Karamanlis Government (2004–7). These interviews helped in identifying some of the structural issues of Greek public policy that cut across party politics and have shaped the agendas of successive governments, irrespective of their ideological predisposition and profile.

In addition to the above, leading officials from Greece's social partners were also interviewed. They included the leadership of the main trade union confederation (GSEE: General Confederation of Greek

Workers / ΓΣΕΕ: Γενική Συνομοσπονδία Εργατών Ελλάδος), the main employers' organizations (SEV: League of Greek Industries / ΣΕΒ: Σύνδεσμος Ελληνικών Βιομηχανιών and ESEE: National Confederation of Greek Commerce / ΕΣΕΕ: Εθνική Συνομοσπονδία Ελληνικού Εμπορίου) as well as representatives from many unions of Olympic Airways/Airlines. Their views were invaluable in understanding the strength of opposition to the 'modernization project', as well as the accumulated grievances of social partners over the way in which successive governments have sought to pursue structural reform. The interviews were conducted on a confidential basis and their anonymity in the narrative that follows has been respected.

1.5   The core questions and argument

This book examines the relevance of EU stimuli and processes to domestic reform in Greece. In doing so, it asks four basic questions:

- To what extent have EU commitments shaped the domestic reform agenda in Greece?
- How far have these commitments empowered the government in the reform process?
- What reforms have been achieved?
- What explains the limits of the reforms implemented to date?

The responses to these questions require a discussion that links the conceptual and the empirical dimensions. Alternative conceptual approaches are considered to frame the policy case studies. Theory helps to structure a clear empirical explanation. Thus, a comparison is drawn between an explanation based on the Europeanization approach and that on 'varieties of capitalism'.

The three sectoral case studies display differences of type. The relevance of EU commitments to domestic choices varies across the sectors. Each is affected by general EU pressures, notably fiscal constraints. All three are related to the Lisbon Programme of reform that signalled priority concerns, but involves 'soft processes' of benchmarking and sharing best practice. In addition, privatization involves direct regulatory intervention by the Commission to guard against unfair state subsidies and sweeteners. Domestically, the three sectors comprise both distinct and common actors and processes. All three sectors pose tests of the will and capability of the national government to deliver on an agenda it has signed up to, negotiating and overcoming domestic opposition.

In general, the book argues that EU commitments have indeed significantly shaped the domestic reform agenda in terms of its normative content and priorities. In doing so, they strengthened what already existed at the member-state level – in the name of 'modernization' – but were too weak to establish dominance in the relevant discourse. The national government leadership willingly embraced this European empowerment, finding legitimacy for itself in it. Yet this will was not shared across the government: internal divisions of interest and preference dissipated the reform initiative. An uncertain will undermined the capability to deliver. Both would be needed in abundance if the government was to negotiate reform successfully through the minefield of domestic opposition, overcoming 'veto points' with antagonistic interests. The achievements of reform in all the three policy sectors will be shown to be limited over successive governments. This pattern of outcome points to *systemic* features that resist the adaptation of the domestic model towards a liberal state–economy relationship. The EU stimulus in this regard challenges embedded norms and interests at home. At the same time, the domestic tension remains and even grows as a 'Europeanizing' elite defines reform as an essential development priority and fears what the alternative path of its opponents will mean for the national interest. At present, both the proponents and the opponents of reform lack the political strength – the necessary constituency – to be fully successful in their strategies. 'Europeanization' highlights the systemic pressures, but the EU's instruments are too weak to overcome the inertial tendencies. To explain the latter, the particularities of the Greek 'model' must be brought into the picture.

The Greek model – the political system, the economy, and the 'welfare' system – displays both tension and inertia. These are the result of a complex pattern of embedded and conflicting interests and, to some extent, identities. The blockages to EU adaptation can be identified by reference to distinct literatures that frame the domestic conditions. 'Europeanization' approaches highlight, for example, the nature of the 'misfit' between the EU and domestic policies, the weakness of reform coalitions, the prevalence of 'veto points', and the limitations of the domestic discourse. Conflicting interests arise from conditions rooted in the system. An alternative approach – based on the 'varieties of capitalism' literature – highlights the limitations of the domestic welfare regime, the pattern of relatively high employment protection, the stable product demand, the strong barriers to market entry, and a set of cultural attitudes that mix an aversion to risk and the protection of distorting privileges. These produce a set of rational interests among the key actors that lead to blockages to reform. The book examines the relevance and compatibility of the different conceptual frames to examining the problem of Greek adaptation to EU stimuli.

The case studies and the country selection add up to something more, however. They raise important questions about the ability of the EU to manage and implement a programme of structural reform. This agenda has importance because of the recognition by EU leaders of the increasing economic and social threats to the European order posed by globalization and the competitive challenges emanating not only from the US and Japan but also now from new economic powers such as China and India. The ineffectiveness of the EU in implementing a reform agenda would question the ability of Europe to adapt and secure its well-being in the future. At the same time, low 'reform capacity' on the part of a member state would prompt doubts about Europe's ability to remain cohesive and question the participation of the particular nation in the EU's core. Indeed, the problem of adaptation may also highlight one of governability. Why is reform so difficult? How can government steer its agenda?

1.6   The structure of the book

The conceptual framework adopted in this book is outlined in Chapters 2 and 3. Chapter 2 clarifies the relevance of 'Europeanization' to the study of domestic reform, defining its usage and elaborating its logic. Chapter 3 then contrasts this with other conceptual frameworks focussing on domestic regimes – notably, 'varieties of capitalism' – that posit the resilience and path-dependence of the domestic system in the face of external pressures. Thus, the two sets of framework facilitate a study of the significance and limits of 'Europeanization': the case studies become an evaluation of the relevance of each theoretical perspective. The combination, more generally, helps in the understanding of the impact of the EU on its member states, clarifying the conditions facilitating or blocking domestic adaptation to 'Europe'. Ultimately, the frameworks of 'Europeanization' and 'varieties of capitalism' are seen as expanding the perspective of each other in a manner that is complementary.

The main empirical analysis of the book is to be found in Chapters 4, 5, and 6. They examine, in turn, the impact of the EU on the domestic reform process in Greece in three key sectors. Chapter 4 focuses on the extent to which EU pressures – the entry criteria for the single currency, the Lisbon Programme on the reform of the social model, and the OMC inspiration for shared learning – have shaped the domestic reform process on pension reform. Chapter 5 similarly examines EU stimuli for the reform of the labour market. The external stimulus from the EU existed: Greece was intent on securing 'euro' entry, albeit a little late; the constraint of the Stability and Growth Pact was felt on fiscal policy; and the Lisbon Programme had referred to an active employment policy and flexible working patterns. Chapter 6 refers to the single market and Lisbon stress on liberalization, on the one hand, and the EU's prohibition of state aids, (under its 'Competition Policy') on the other, as a basis for the EU stimulating a domestic process of privatization. The case selected here is that of Olympic Airways, a loss-making national carrier that successive Greek governments have endeavoured to restructure or sell off. The Commission was directly involved in the reform process by virtue of its monitoring of state aids, but it has also signalled its preferred solution of privatization on repeated occasions.

The three case studies thus cover a broad range of sectors. They constitute a test of the EU's ability to stimulate reform of the social model, of the labour regime, and of problematic state enterprises. They are the key aspects of the Lisbon Programme of creating a growing and adaptable economy across the Union. As such, they provide a test of the limits of Europeanization. The test is made increasingly relevant by the process of EU enlargement that has made the Union more heterogeneous in condition. The task of EU policy coordination is being made more challenging at the same time that questions arise as to its effectiveness in the older member states. Chapter 7 – the Conclusion – will return to this theme insofar as it reflects the overall concern of the book with the 'reach' of Europeanization: the nexus between EU developments and domestic political forces.

2
The Europeanization Process and the Greek Political System

2.1 Introduction

This study seeks to use the Greek experience as a test case. There are two major types of tests applied here. The first is of the extent to which EU membership has facilitated domestic economic and social reform. This is now commonly termed a test of the impact of 'Europeanization'. The conceptual framework for this test is the focus of this chapter. A second test – of the structures of the domestic system processing the external stimuli in a manner that produces limited, 'path-dependent' change – is discussed in the following chapter.

In testing the Greek case, the explanations that are developed in both chapters help to facilitate comparison with other national cases. The explanatory frameworks do not owe their origin to the Greek setting, but rather they are borrowed from comparative politics and political economy. This helps to illustrate similarities and contrasts: the extent to which the theoretical frames generate valid predictions about Greece and the degree to which Greece is found to be an exception from the 'norm'. In this way, the examination of the Greek case is brought firmly within a perspective of international familiarity.

By setting these alternative frames, the two chapters provide an analytical structure to the later case studies. These are not descriptive, empirical histories of various reform attempts; instead, they are structured as a set of test cases of relevance to wider political science concerns.

2.2 Adjusting to external pressure: The Europeanization of Greece

The previous chapter signalled the relevance of the European integration process to domestic change. The purpose here is to consider how the

'Europeanization' process can be conceptualized as a framework for the three case studies.

Academic study has given increased attention to the relationship between developments at the EU and domestic levels. 'Europeanization' has become an increasingly popular term for this interactive relationship.[1] The bibliographical survey in Featherstone and Radaelli (2003) reported only 5 academic journal articles referring to 'Europeanization' in the entire decade of the 1980s, but some 65 in the following decade. Moreover, the relevance of 'Europeanization' is likely to increase in the future. The expansion of policy competences at the EU level and their increasingly diverse form – from 'hard' law to 'soft' policy instruments – together with the extended heterogeneity of member states, consequent on an ongoing process of enlargement, are all features of an integration process that is likely to have more and more diverse ramifications at the domestic level. The study of Europeanization – and the asymmetries that it exhibits – will thus continue to be an important illumination of the evolving system of EU governance. It will also have a particular resonance for a member state like Greece with its combination of identities: a weaker economy in need of EU support, a distinctive southern European state tradition, a position typically of a 'policy-taker' rather than a policy initiator vis-à-vis the EU, and a country with a risk of peripheralization in the context of further enlargement.

Inevitably, however, with 'Europeanization' becoming a more fashionable term, there is a risk of stretching the concept beyond meaningful limits, as Radaelli has noted (Featherstone and Radaelli, 2003). It is useful to set limits on its definition. Thus, it ought not to be seen as a synonym for 'integration': there is no distinctive need to apply it to the creation of new policies at the EU level. Moreover, 'Europeanization' should not be assumed to automatically involve convergence between member states. If the outcome of EU impacts was near uniform, there would be much less value in studying them. It is precisely the apparently asymmetrical effects of Europeanization, which can also be temporary and reversible, that prompt the interest in examining its processes. There is therefore the need to differentiate the impacts of 'Europeanization' across policy sectors and geographic regions. Moreover, these impacts can be distinguished according to their penetration of the domestic setting in their depth and breadth, as well as the 'time, timing and tempo' associated with them (Featherstone and Radaelli, 2003: 48).

As is already clear, the nature of Europeanization produces a complex ontology. It refers to the relationship between EU-level commitments and participation, on the one hand, and the domestic politics, polity, and processes of EU member states, on the other. Thus, the direction of change may be either 'top-down' (the EU to the domestic level) and/or 'bottom-up' (the domestic level to that of the EU). With this complexity, simple definitions appear elusive. Ladrech was one of the first to offer an explicit definition. Europeanization, he argued, was 'a process reorienting the direction and shape of politics to the degree that EC political and economic dynamics become part of the organisational logic of national politics and policy-making' (1994: 69). This appears too limited a definition, however, in that it requires further elaboration to *operationalize* its terms and to gauge impacts.

There is some degree of consensus over the need for the definition of 'Europeanization' to be broadly set. Radaelli sought a synthesis with the following definition:

> *Processes of (a) construction, (b) diffusion, and (c) institutionalisation of formal and informal rules, procedures, policy paradigms, styles, 'ways of doing things', and shared beliefs and norms which are first defined and consolidated in the making of EU public policy and politics and then incorporated in the logic of domestic discourse, identities, political structures, and public policies.*
>
> (Featherstone and Radaelli, 2003: 30)

This appears all-encompassing, though some may feel its direction of influence is too 'top-down'. A further synthesis is given by Dyson and Goetz:

> *Europeanisation denotes a complex interactive 'top-down' and 'bottom-up' process in which domestic polities, politics and public policies are shaped by European integration and in which domestic actors use European integration to shape the domestic arena. It may produce either continuity or change and potentially variable and contingent outcomes.*
>
> (2003: 20)

This is consistent with all that has been claimed here so far. Moreover, they attempt to embrace the directions of influence rather more than hitherto. As such they go beyond Goetz's previous concern to clarify the 'missing link' between EU stimuli and domestic outcomes (2000: 222). Earlier, Knill and Lehmkuhl (1999) had identified three mechanisms of Europeanization: positive integration (where the EU prescribes policy model), negative integration (where EU commitments dismantle national regulations), and framing integration (where EU involvement alters beliefs, expectations). Each of these had a 'top-down' direction. Dyson and Goetz introduce much more sensitivity to cater for more varied conditions linking the EU and the domestic levels. Specifically, they argue that three dynamics link the domestic and the EU levels. These are dynamics of coexistence (where both levels exhibit high mutual autonomy and there is little effective impact) co-evolution (where there is mutual interaction leading to accommodation between the two levels), and contestation (involving a clash of beliefs and preferences between the two levels). Clearly, the latter two offer the greatest interest: both involve a degree of change, rather than 'no effect' (though this might involve surprises of its own on a comparative basis).

More latterly, Bulmer and Radaelli (2005) identified three modes of governance in the EU, associated with distinct types of policy, to produce different mechanisms of Europeanization. These range from the hierarchical and coercive – where EU competence is strong and enforcement mechanisms limit the scope for 'cheating' or non-compliance, though their exact nature varies between 'positive' and 'negative' integration – to the competitive and horizontal – involving regulatory competition between states and actors where the EU plays a very limited role – and the non-hierarchical/voluntary nature of facilitated coordination, as in the OMC linked to the Lisbon Programme. The empirical application of such a framework is not unproblematic; as Bache and Jordan (2006: 25) point out, not all EU policies can be singly and neatly categorized in this fashion. They themselves suggest a matrix distinguishing the intended 'direct Europeanization' from the inadvertent 'indirect Europeanization', and 'voluntary' and 'coercive' Europeanization according to the acceptance or resistance of domestic actors to EU stimuli (2006: 24). The Bulmer and Radaelli typology seems more nuanced and, like Dyson and Goetz, conveys the main theme of relevance here: that the linkages between EU stimuli and domestic politics vary, in part, according to the type of governance existing at the EU level.

Definitions are critical in setting out the meaning of 'Europeanization' within an EU context. But 'Europeanization' does not constitute an independent theory to underpin empirical analysis. Europeanization is not so much a theory as a distinct set of processes in need of explanation (Featherstone and Radaelli, 2003: 333). It is an 'attention-directing device' (Olsen, 2002). A researcher needs to support the definition of the focus within an established conceptual framework, albeit adapted to the EU-domestic setting. The test of 'Europeanization' thus becomes enwrapped in that of the borrowed theory.

Most writers on the subject have followed some variant of 'new institutionalism' for their studies of Europeanization (Hall and Taylor, 1996;
see also Bulmer and Lesquene, 2005: 7–9; Bulmer, 2007). As is well established, the three main variants of the approach define 'institutions' differently.[2] The conception of the institutional setting is broadest for
'sociological institutionalism' (or 'social constructivism'). It includes not
only formal rules, procedures, or norms but also symbols and cognitive
and normative beliefs that provide 'frames of meaning' guiding actors.
The divide between 'institutions' and 'culture' is broken down (Hall and
Taylor, 1996: 947). Thus, institutions affect not only the strategic calculations of actors but also their basic preferences, beliefs, understandings,
and identities. 'Institutions' are therefore a very strong independent variable (Checkel, 1999). Actors here follow a 'logic of appropriateness' and
'rule-governed action', involving the internalization of norms (March
and Olsen, 1984; 1989). The approach is compatible with studies that
focus on shifts of loyalty, the cognitive and affective response to integration, and the role of ideas in shaping negotiations.

For 'historical institutionalism', the understanding of 'institutions' is
less broad. The impact of the institutional setting develops over time,
evolving from a calculus into a more cultural form as actors become
locked into the institutional setting (Checkel, 1999: 547). Institutions
can therefore be both an intervening and an independent variable.
Institutions possess asymmetries in the power of actors and their access
to the policy process. The 'historical' aspect is reflected in the attention
given to path dependency – with specific contextual features of the
institutional setting guiding development along a set of 'paths'. Such
development involves both intended and unintended consequences
and inefficiencies. The continuity of this path dependence is punctu-
ated, nevertheless, by 'critical junctures' in which substantial change
occurs and history moves onto a different course (see Hay and Wincott,
1998). The approach lends itself to studies of how institutions have
an intervening effect on actor preferences and interests in the short-
term and a stronger longer-term impact to establish distinct paths of
development, involving incremental change (see Bulmer and Burch,
1998; 2000b).

For rational choice institutionalism, 'institutions' are seen in the most
narrow and minimalist sense. The actor-centred approach follows a
methodological individualism. Drawing on rational choice assumptions, actors are assumed to behave rationally on the basis of fixed preferences, seeking to maximize their interests. Yet institutions structure
the interactions – or the bargaining game – between actors, with their

preferences defined endogenously. Indeed, actors 'select their best available course of action under the circumstances, given their (institutionally shaped) preferences and perceptions' (Scharpf, 1997: 32). Actors follow a 'logic of consequentialism': the strategic opportunities and constraints faced within institutional settings. The latter affects the choices on the agenda, provides information, and offers enforcement mechanisms that reduce the uncertainty about the behaviour of others. This allows 'gains from exchange' and potentially better social outcomes (Hall and Taylor, 1996: 945). The approach may be reflected in studies of EU negotiations or of domestic bargaining between key actors in response to EU pressures of adjustment.

The assumptions of each variant of 'new institutionalism' differ. They each assume that 'institutions' are an independent factor affecting political behaviour. But they interpret agency and structure differently, positing contrasting constraints on actors and how their preferences are formed. Different lenses will capture different aspects of what are large and multifaceted subjects (Checkel, 1999). Parsimony can stem from a narrow interpretation of institutions and the strategic interactions of actors, but a broader notion will be required to account for cognitive and normative elements. Boerzel and Risse similarly argue that rationalist and constructivist logics can occur simultaneously or sequentially in reality.

Borrowing the theoretical framework of 'new institutionalism' in order to gauge 'Europeanization', leaves the latter open to the criticisms of the former, however. Critics of institutionalism assert that the specification of the independent variable in terms of institutional setting is too broad an amalgam, hiding a variety of causal mechanisms and interactions (John, 1998: 63–4). There are many causes of public policy: John asserts that the availability of resources can be an independent factor in decisions on energy policy, for example. Moreover, in comparative studies account needs to be taken of the fact that societies and sectors do not begin from similar starting points. The response to external shocks may be affected by different circumstances, independent of institutions. At the same time, comparative studies need to allow for differences that are unique to particular sectors and those that are unique to individual societies. The present study sees such points as offering words of caution rather than being a basis for rejection of 'new institutionalist' research designs.

The particular focus of 'Europeanization' presents problems of its own. There is the task of distinguishing the domestic effects of EU membership from other external impacts. 'Globalization' is a potential independent variable that looms to varying degrees over a number of policy sectors and would compete with a causal explanation focussed on the EU (see Hennis, 2001). Moreover, in applying an institutionalist perspective, there is the problem of clarifying the interaction between two levels of institutional properties – the EU and the domestic – posing issues of identifying the relevant structures and agents. The task is to understand what was transmitted and understood between the EU and the domestic levels: how, why, and by whom.

Turning to the particular case of Greece and the issues involved in applying 'Europeanization', Ioakimides (1998, 2001) has written authoritatively on Europeanization in the Greek context. He rightly stresses the relevance of different domestic situations to the experience of Europeanization. The geopolitical calculations of France or the UK affecting the motivations for EU participation contrast with the weaker position of Greece. While the latter sought EU entry on grounds of political interest – the consolidation of democracy, regional advantage – the routine experience of membership has been one of *importing* norms, patterns of behaviour, and even the culture of integration. 'Downloading' from the EU has been much more relevant than 'uploading' for Greece. Moreover, such importation has been seen as synonymous with domestic 'modernization', as noted here in Chapter 1. According to Ioakimides, the Europeanization pattern can be distinguished between the 'responsive' and 'intended'. The former involves passivity on the part of domestic elites: EU impacts occur without the intent to transpose them into a wider reform paradigm. By contrast, 'intended' Europeanization involves an activism by domestic actors to use the EU as an ideological force for modernization.[3] Greece experienced the shift between the two types in the 1990s and especially with the rise of Simitis in 1996. Ioakimides distinguishes the EU's impact on Greece across four dimensions: market regulation, functional competences, territorial decentralization, and institutional adaptation (and the strengthening of democratic institutions and civil society). The cumulative effect has been the rebalancing of state–society relations in favour of the latter. That said, cleavages have been revised with the clashes of modernity and traditionalism.

Ioakimides is undoubtedly correct to map out the effects of EU membership in the context of long-established systemic traits in Greece. Critical changes clearly occurred by the end of the first Papandreou governments in the 1980s. The focus of the present study is different, however. It is primarily focussed on the EU's policy impact in matters of structural reform in the context of the Lisbon Programme, a more recent concern. Moreover, it addresses the issue of why Greece has been slow to implement EU-inspired reforms relative to other member states. It questions the pattern of governance that links government and social actors. Crudely, 'Europeanization' can be intended yet still fail. The question here is, why?

The general literature on 'Europeanization' has confronted these analytical issues by focussing on the conditions affecting domestic adaptation. Early studies identified adaptational pressure arising from a 'misfit' between EU-level commitments and domestic practice (e.g. Knill 1998; Knill and Lenschow, 1998). If both EU commitments and domestic practice 'fit' (that is, they are complementary), then adaptational pressure is low and there should be little problem or delay with the implementation of EU rules. In cases of high adaptational pressure, the implementation of EU requirements is unlikely to be effective, since they challenge core structures and practices of domestic institutions. With more moderate pressure – where EU requirements demand changes, but do not challenge the core of the national tradition as such – the extent of adaptation is shaped by the preferences and resources of domestic coalitions, mediated by structures such as 'veto points' (on latter, see below). In this vein, Boerzel (2000) developed a 'push-pull model', where non-compliance is 'most likely if an EU policy causes a significant "policy misfit" and if there is no mobilisation of domestic actors pressurising public authorities to bear the costs of implementing the "misfitting" policy' (2000: 141). Haverland (2000) went further in his coverage of the domestic institutional opportunity structure: unwilling governments can be pushed to comply or governments may be willing but blocked by domestic actors able to veto.

The 'goodness of fit' between EU commitments and domestic conditions also needs to take account of the fact that the former vary in type (see also Heritier and Knill, 2001: 288). The EU stimuli to domestic change are a mix of the general and specific, the direct and indirect. A synoptic outline of two key EU sectors can highlight important contrasts:

- EMU: The Maastricht Treaty established a timetable tied to convergence criteria to govern which states could join in the single currency (the 'euro'). These were associated with a technocratic asymmetry of information and expertise to the advantage of a relatively closed policy community on monetary policy, buttressed by the pressure of credibility and reputation to comply. The threat of exclusion was real and keenly felt in states struggling to meet the criteria.

- The OMC and the Lisbon 2000 agenda: The policy objectives sustain conflicting interpretations on the basis of non-binding timetables, with member states at different stages in the reform process. Relevant policy communities are open, with a diffusion of expertise. Asymmetry of information and expertise is thus largely unavailable to any one group of actors. The normative acceptance of the adaptation of domestic policy regimes in line with the EU stimuli is contested, creating domestic veto points. The cost of non-compliance appears low. The OMC process appears distant and not easily understood.

The difference between the two policy areas is highly significant in terms of EU obligations serving as 'commitment devices' to aid domestic policy change. In the former, leverage is available to those domestic actors in charge of monetary policy once the political commitment to euro entry was made (Dyson and Featherstone, 1999). The position of the Ministry of National Economy in Greece (and that of the Central Bank) – like that of its EU counterparts – was greatly strengthened by this commitment. The Italian description of this reality was of EMU as a *vincolo esterno* (external tie), empowering domestic actors to pursue reform at home (Carli, 1993). Parallels exist here with aspects of the internal market programme and competition policy, insofar as the EU stimuli are clear (in content and timing) and based on 'hard' law. Again, the regulations governing access to EU structural funds may share some of these qualities and encourage domestic reform. Yet intersectoral and intrasectoral differences of EU commitment devices were all too apparent to the central European states in the process of accession (Grabbe, 2003). The prospective entrants faced strategic uncertainty, in terms of, *inter alia*, the singularity of EU policy models, policy priorities, and the measurement of compliance. Schimmelfennig and Sedelmeier (2004) in their study of central European accession have also stressed the importance of the credibility of the EU-level commitment to likely domestic responses. The limitations of EU leverage are even more apparent in the OMC process. With a 'soft law' process, leverage potential rests more squarely on peer pressure ('naming and shaming') and mutual socialization.

The variation in commitment devices may not necessarily be equated with the significance of EU effects, however. Privatization, for example, is an agenda where the EU has played only an indirect role. Single market legislation requires the liberalization of state monopolies in various sectors (e.g. telecommunications, transport), but it does not require a change in the ownership structure of the state enterprise itself. In the

Greek case, however, those identifying themselves as pro-EU 'modernizers' supported the privatization agenda. In the relevant political discourse, the two agendas became largely synonymous. The partial privatization of the state telecommunications corporation, OTE (Greek Telecommunications Organization/OTE: Οργανισμός Τηλεπικοινωνιών Ελλάδας) owed much to the EU, as Pagoulatos (2005) notes. In other words, the EU legitimized an agenda that it did not directly mandate. To some extent, similar pressures are relevant to the other sectoral case studies considered in the later chapters: pensions and labour market reform.

As these cases suggest, the focus on commitment devices helps to clarify the structure of EU–domestic linkage in the process. At the same time, the role of political and policy leadership must be explored and the relevant processes identified. The empowerment that may be gained from an EU obligation needs to be interpreted and deployed sensitive to the domestic context (Mörth, 2003). In Greece, as elsewhere, 'manipulation is the key to understanding the dynamics of policy-making' (Zahariadis, 2003: 2). EU stimuli may legitimize a domestic reform programme and the evidence for its use and effectiveness can be derived, in part, by an analysis of the policy discourse used by advocates domestically (Schmidt and Radaelli, 2004). Simitis's leadership of the modernization project is a relevant case here; his identification of the external imperative, his stress on a certain time frame affecting choices, and his interpretation of how EU pressures and domestic needs are to be made compatible are all crucial to an understanding of his mission. A focus on agency may focus on strategies, tactics, bargaining, and discourse.

The studies presented here place the analysis of 'Europeanization' within the conceptual framework of 'new institutionalism', as the most suitable. The major focus is of strategies and opportunity structures, following a rational choice variant, though the lens will widen to incorporate patterns of domestic discourse where these signalled a clear EU link. In the present volume, the *independent variable* is formed by common EU commitments or stimuli. The *dependent variable* is defined by the nature and extent of domestic shifts and adaptation. Their relationship may be affected by *intervening variables* constituted by the domestic 'institutional' setting, shaping the response to EU prompts. As noted above, the independent variable varies significantly in form, with variations in the types of EU obligation. Moreover, 'The same European policy may trigger fundamental reforms in one country, while having no consequence in others' (Heritier and Knill, 2001: 286).

A relevant vocabulary here is of the blockages to reform initiatives posed by 'veto players' and by 'veto points'.[4] 'Veto players', according to

Tsebelis, 'are individual or collective actors whose agreement (by majority rule for collective actors) is required for a change of the status quo' (1995: 289). He has argued that 'policy stability' – that is, no change – is more likely the higher the number of veto players and the greater the (ideological) distance between them (2002: 11–12). Knowing the number of veto players and their preferences leads to predictions of the outcome. He distinguishes between 'institutional veto players', established by a nation's constitution, and 'partisan veto players', such as political parties. He makes little reference to trade unions and employers' organizations, however, and regards corporatist arrangements as not requiring major adjustment to his focus on the passage of legislation (2002: 178–9). The perspective on 'veto points' is wider than that of 'veto players'. Drawing on Immergut (1992: 26) and Kitschelt (1986), Haverland (2000: 85) portrayed institutional veto points as referring to all stages in the decision-making process on which agreement is legally required for a policy change. Moreover, 'points are not physical entities but points of strategic uncertainty where decisions may be overturned' (1992: 27). Bonoli follows this definition, referring to the patterns of power distribution (2000: 42–3). The veto points are not random, but set by rules on representation and the process of coordination and decision (Immergut, 1992: 27). Veto points are distinguished using terms such as 'formal', 'informal', 'factual', and 'de facto'. Formal veto points are set by *de jure* rules – thus, 'many formal veto positions exist in federalist-decentralist political systems, with multiple-party coalition governments' etc. (Heritier and Knill, 2001: 258). By contrast, political practice and the interplay of institutions and interests give rise to *de facto* veto points (Immergut, 1992: 26–7). Though Immergut's focus is primarily electoral politics and party systems, it may be logically extended to organized interest groups and processes of social dialogue involving government, unions, and employers. Thus, Bonoli (2000: 43) and Heritier and Knill (2001: 258) regard trade unions and the interest mediation system as producing *informal* veto points. For the present study, the discussion will refer to *veto points* and will distinguish between *formal* and *informal* veto points for the Greek case studies.

The intervening variables affecting agreement (on policy reform) at the domestic level will vary between systems and sectors. Heritier and Knill refer to variations in the 'domestic constellation', which they distinguish across three factors: 'the specific stage of liberalisation [pre-liberalisation versus liberalisation] at which a country confronts the corresponding European policies; the sectoral capacity for regulatory reform (which includes not only the number of institutional veto points, but also the capacity to achieve political consensus); and the dominant belief system that affects the direction of potential domestic reforms' (2001: 288). They see 'reform capacity' as being 'determined by the number of formal and factual veto positions that need to be overcome in order to realise a decision, and by the degree to which that country enjoys politically integrated leadership' (2001: 258). They distinguish between member states with a high number of factual and formal veto points and countries with few. Schmidt also highlighted the institutional capacity of the state to respond to external pressures as a key intervening variable (Schmidt, 2002). Integrated political leadership can be provided by 'formal majoritarian hierarchical government or by a long-standing and successful practice of consensual bipartite, tripartite or multipartite decision making that incorporates or reconciles diverging interests' (Heritier and Knill, 2001: 258).

The nature and range of likely intervening variables has been usefully extended by Radaelli (2003: 46–50). He lists them as follows:

- The Institutional capacity to produce change
  - Veto players in the political system
  - Scope and type of executive leadership
- The Timing of European policies
- The Policy structure and advocacy coalitions
  - Technocratic capture potential
  - Adoption–implementation balance
  - Presence of a legitimating policy discourse
  - Impact of EU policy on domestic advocacy coalitions

This incorporates the earlier stress on institutional capacity and the timing of EU policies, with the conditions of domestic policy interaction – the role of expertise, the nature of the discourse, and the relevance of supportive coalitions. It also extends the coverage to matters of adoption and implementation – or compliance with the EU. It is therefore a guide that will be followed in this study.

With a focus on the conditions affecting national compliance with EU obligations, Falkner et al. (2005) have argued that differences of domestic culture will determine the degree of adaptation. They base their conclusions on a survey of cases in the area of labour law and they develop a general argument of the need to differentiate hypotheses according to domestic systems. They posit 'three worlds of compliance': a *world of law compliance* (in which priority is attached to law compliance above domestic concerns), a *world of domestic politics* (in which obeying EU rules is one goal among many and domestic concerns frequently prevail), and a *world of neglect* (in which EU compliance is not a goal in itself). They conclude that *culture* is a dominant factor in the world of law observance, while *interests* predominate in the other two worlds. Greece, they conclude, is part of the 'world of neglect', as are other southern EU member states. Dimitrakopoulos (2007) has argued for a more nuanced approach and one that recognizes differences between sectors and over time.

Patterns of 'non-convergence' between member states, despite a range of integration effects, are considered by Goetz in terms of 'clustered Europeanization' (Goetz, 2006). This involves differentiation between groups of states as a result of two variables: territory and temporality. For the former, Goetz refers to 'families of nations' and centre–periphery structures as points of contrast. Temporality matters in terms of the date a state acceded to the EU and the then context of domestic or EU-level reform. Goetz regards the southern European states as less of a 'family of nations' than the Nordic states – their mutual ties are looser. However, he suggests that their common peripheral status is of special importance. Greece, Portugal, and Spain joined the EU suffering economic backwardness and dependency. Nevertheless – and by contrast to the recent cases of central and eastern Europe – at the point of enlargement to the south, the 'core' EU states were both willing and able to share the costs of their adaptation. The southern European states faced policy misfits, lack of implementation capacity, and weakly organized civil society. The legacy is a combination of compliance problems together with elite-centred Europeanization.

The foregoing paints a complex picture of how Greece stands in relation to Europeanization. The degree of 'catch-up' for Greece suggests dynamics of co-evolution or contestation with EU obligations. Overwhelmingly, the process is likely to be 'top-down' rather than one of Greece being able to upload its preferences at the EU level. The OMC and the 'Lisbon process' may legitimize a process of domestic reform, but as a commitment device they will be weak in their domestic impact. Thus, the politics of adaptation will be shaped by the nature of the intervening variables found within the domestic system: the institutional capacity to produce change (veto points, nature of executive leadership), the timing of EU policies, and the structure of the domestic policy process (e.g. presence of a legitimating discourse, advocacy coalitions, the adoption/compliance culture). 'Europeanization' may be consequential or inconsequential depending on these domestic conditions.

2.3 Hypotheses for the case studies

The first focus here is of the nature of the EU-level stimulus, affected by different kinds of supranational governance. The Europeanization framework lends itself to the study of the domestic response to *external pressures for adaptation,* though the literature eschews a crude deterministic stimulus-response notion. Thus, the general hypothesis can be formulated as:

H1a. EU-level commitments provide a resource by which domestic actors in Greece can shape their environment, restructuring interests and/or ideas, but the outcome of this EU–domestic interaction will vary according to the type of EU pressure (hierarchical, facilitating) and the configuration of domestic conditions (institutional capacity, timing of EU policies, domestic policy structure).

Further,

H1b. The domestic impact of EU stimuli will vary according to the type of 'commitment device' involved. EU institutions will determine the nature of domestic change up to the limits of the 'coercion' available to them.

These two hypotheses emphasize the contingent nature of EU-domestic level interaction, with outcomes not predetermined in a uniform manner. The task is to confirm or refute these general propositions in the Greek case, specifying the factors that led to the observed outcomes. The focus here is the 'top-down' impact of the EU, given that this is most relevant to Greece in general and the case studies in particular. Moreover, the hypotheses are concerned with actor-responses: how EU stimuli affect their environment, interests, and ideational position. They recognize that EU commitments vary in their form, ranging from 'hard' to 'soft' and this is likely to affect their degree of domestic impact (Olsen, 2002; Knill and Lehmkuhl, 1999; 2002; Bulmer and Radaelli, 2005; Bache and Jordan, 2006). An implicit assumption is that without the threat of coercion, 'soft' EU processes such as OMC will prove an ineffective strategic lever to stimulate reform at the national level and change will depend on whether compensating domestic conditions exist or not (e.g. a legitimizing discourse, a relevant advocacy coalition).

This latter aspect leads to the second theme: of the *reform capacity* of the system. This is an explicit and central theme in the Europeanization literature. Applying the conventional framework to Greece, it appears as a surprising or paradoxical case. Its tradition of unitary and single party government would suggest 'integrated political leadership'. Moreover, its constitutional structure (a unitary and largely centralized state, with a politically limited head of the state and a unicameral legislature displaying weakness in relation to the executive) would also suggest few formal veto points. Yet these expectations of a relatively high 'reform capacity' are contradicted by the number of pressure groups as 'informal veto points' in relevant policy sectors (Heritier and Knill, 2001). Schmidt (2006) developed a typology of national system types in relation to Europeanization. Greece would probably fall closest to her notion of a 'simple polity' in which a unitary state faces disorganized interests (and produces 'statist' policies, with restricted access of social interests to policymaking). Yet in Greece interests are 'disorganized' insofar as they fail to sustain social concertation and corporatist pacts – it is a matter of disorganized power (and informal veto points). According to Schmidt, unitary states with disorganized interests find it harder to adapt to EU policies and practices.

Thus, the Europeanization hypotheses here would be

H2a. The extent of domestic adaptation will depend on (a) the degree of 'policy misfit' with respect to the content of EU stimuli, and (b) the availability of a domestic coalition pressing for such reform.

H2b. In the absence of formal veto points and with an electoral system strongly biased in favour of single party governments (with comfortable parliamentary majorities), effective opposition (informal veto points) will be found among those stakeholders with accumulated privileges, and it is the strategic interaction between government and the latter, and the relative resources of each, that will determine the outcome of reform.

Hypothesis 2a is drawn from the earlier works on Europeanization of authors such as Boerzel, noted above, and attempts to sustain a general rule. Hypothesis 2b is more nuanced to the prevailing conditions of veto points within the domestic system and the paradox identified within the Greece. It seeks to identify the blockages.

The third theme follows on from this and concerns actor interests and strategies. Here, the Europeanization approach has limited specificity, leaving it to borrow from other literatures. The approach highlights the aspects of 'misfit' and of 'timing'. In these respects, Greece will typically be seen as a laggard, due to its embedded statism and 'pre-liberalization' stage of reform. The degree of misfit will thus be relatively high. However, time, timing, and tempo (Goetz, 2001) will also be a strategic tool for manipulation by domestic actors, as they attempt to sequence, delay, or advance reform. The culture of compliance is itself problematic (Falkner et al., 2005). Thus, the following can be derived:

H3a. Where regulatory compliance is an issue and domestic opponents are entrenched, reform actors will define their interests in terms of manipulating the timing of compliance with EU obligations and postponing effective implementation.

With respect to the policy process, Greece again exhibits a contrast. On the one hand, there is the strategic isolation of government actors advancing reform (with weak institutional resources and circumspect political support from party colleagues), the relative absence of independent 'think tanks' to come to their aid, and the limited policy role of the party structures themselves. On the other hand, public opinion is generally very supportive of deepening European integration. Thus,

H3b. In the absence of a clear EU obligation to comply (or a strong 'commitment device'), an individual Minister will be left politically isolated to battle reform against domestic opposition and his/her success will depend on the availability of a legitimating public discourse of the risk of Greece's marginalization from 'Europe'.

2.4 Conclusions

The hypotheses developed here – and in the following chapter – will structure the empirical case studies. The empirical analysis will lead to conclusions as to the relevance of these frameworks in a 'problematic' setting like that of Greece, a severe test of the Europeanization approach.

The Europeanization framework is used to highlight a distinctive independent variable – pressures emanating from the EU and felt within the national system – as an explanation of domestic policy change (the dependent variable), based on a series of potential intervening variables (or 'mediating conditions'). The assumption is *not* that EU pressures will necessarily determine the domestic outcome. Indeed, the Europeanization perspective assumes that the pattern of outcomes will vary across member states. Therefore, the task is to clarify the conditions within the domestic system that lead to this set of divergent outcomes. The hypotheses elaborated above will help to show the relevance or non-relevance of the EU stimulus and how it has been interpreted at the domestic level.

The more that the attention shifts to the domestic conditions, however, the greater is the impetus to reverse the lens on the inquiry. To do so, the logic is to examine the relevance of other conceptual frameworks that seek to characterize the crucial features of the domestic polity. That is the task of the following chapter.

3
The Domestic Constraints on Reform

The previous chapter examined the external stimulus to reform represented by the pressures of the EU. The Europeanization literature delves into the domestic conditions that might affect the processes of adaptation to such stimuli. Yet the further such a search progresses, the greater the need to consider different literatures that focus on the domestic system. A number of approaches support a shared claim that domestic politics matters, but they stress different explanatory variables. This chapter considers a broad range of 'domestic' approaches to embrace the major lines of enquiry in comparative politics and political economy. It then proceeds to select from these approaches the most relevant aspects to build a hypothesis for the later case studies. The discussion is intended to deepen the understanding of the previous chapter, to enrich and to extend beyond the limits of the Europeanization perspective. It discusses the relevance of political culture, the nature of the party system, the existing form of interest mediation, and the prevailing models of capitalism and welfare provision. The starting point for each is the 'domestic' and none prioritizes the EU. Ultimately, however, it is argued that both sets of approaches – those of Chapters 2 and 3 – need not be seen as incompatible; rather, one compensates for the limitations of the other in the development of a more rounded explanation.

The focus of each approach considered here is that the domestic structures will absorb external pressures for reform and shape the domestic response to them. Change will likely be incremental, path dependent, and confined.

3.1 Political culture

The broadest perspective on the domestic context of any system is to begin with the most prominent features of its political culture. In the recent political science literature this has become less fashionable as the elaboration of specific hypotheses accounting for change appear problematic. Here, it is accepted that long-term patterns of culture shape attitudes and agendas and are relevant to understanding the structure of beliefs and interests of key policy actors. A brief survey will suffice to set the context.

The introduction of liberal ideas and institutions into the modern Greek state, after its establishment at the start of the 1830s, proved problematic.[1] Tsoukalas highlighted the contradictions between imported liberal norms and the pre-liberal social structure (Tsoukalas, 1991). The liberal model of society assumed a Western rationality of depersonalized legal norms, individual human rights, free markets, and free competition. Nineteenth-century Greece had difficulty in assimilating pure, undiluted individualism and the associated depersonalization of behavioural codes. Traditional Greek moral standards were not centred on the individual, but on the group: a hierarchy of reciprocal bonds involving the extended family, the village, the region, and the Greek 'race'. Internal group morality and solidarity are important. Attitudes towards corruption have been shaped by competing notions of group loyalty. Clientelism and political patronage are similarly grounded in group values. Further, the new Greek state had no bourgeoisie to promote a minimal state and no organized social force to oppose the extension of the role of the state. The liberal state model, argues Tsoukalas, was thus there 'for the taking' by such indigenous social norms. Liberal modernizers, such as Premier Trikoupis, at the end of the nineteenth century suffered as a result. Similarly, Mouzelis (1996) argued that the crucial feature for Greece's development has been the failures of the state, which stem from the endogenous culture.

These historical features still have relevance, though how far is debateable. The traditional view of Greece interprets 'civil society' as being very weak, with little space left between the state and the society. Fundamental liberal concepts did not penetrate very deeply. Pollis (1987) emphasized that 'privacy', 'civil society', and 'inalienable rights' are foreign concepts for Greek culture. 'They have no language . . . and no meaning,' she argued. Political culture has been traditionally 'overpoliticized' – a permanent characteristic according to Tsoukalas (1991). Politics is everywhere, politics has no limit, and politics is a bid for social power. The state has favours to be distributed to those connected to power. The noun 'afilos' [ἄφιλος] – he who has no friends – is used to characterize politicians who refuse to use their influence to help their friends. Political nepotism is still evident in the reproduction of political elites. The Anglo-Saxon notion of freedom *from* the state, of liberty resulting from anti-statism, has been an alien notion. The state was to dominate an underdeveloped economy and society. A more recent literature has challenged these perspectives, however (Mouzelis and Pagoulatos, 2005: 87–103; Sotiropoulos 2004; Voulgaris 2006). Over the last decade or more, it is claimed that civil society has been strengthened with activity expressed on various social issues, such as the environment. Greek society has undergone significant change – it has become a country of immigration; a cultural 'Europeanism' has affected attitudes; and a new weight has been given to civil liberties.

The depth and extent of these changes – in particular, their impact on the role of the state – is difficult to determine. The context remains, at least, one that reflects a cultural dualism, as Diamandouros (1994) has outlined. This dualism has deep roots, reflecting split identities and interests between 'modernizers' and 'traditionalists' in the path of development. In the nineteenth century, leaders such as Adamantios Korais preached the need for Greece to imitate Europe and study Europe. Europe *was* modernization, as it has been again more recently for Premier Simitis. However, not all Greek leaders welcomed 'Europeanization' or 'Europeanism'. Some saw the Western culture as alien and decadent and believed that an imitation of it would prove fatal for Greece. Anti-Europeanism went with national independence and Greek irredentism. Such attitudes find partial resonance in the recent campaigns of Archbishop Christodoulos and the LAOS party, noted in Chapter 1.

These historical traits – of the weakness of a 'liberal' state tradition; of the embedded culture of clientelism, patronage, and group solidarity; and of a strong elite desire to imitate 'Europe' being qualified by populist reservations – are important in defining the structural legacy affecting the mindset of contemporary actors. They paint the social context of where the actors are 'coming from'.

3.2 The party system

It is almost trite to assert that, in Greece, parties matter. The deeply ingrained culture of clientelism has evolved with changes in society. In the post-1974 system, clientelism took on a bureaucratic character with parties as the agents of patronage (Lyrintzis, 1984). Displaying parallels to Italy, Greek politics became marked by the 'party-state', especially when Andreas Papandreou became Premier in 1981 (Featherstone, 1990). The clientelistic distribution of favours lays itself open to corruption.

More typically, the allocation of posts and resources to 'our' people eschews those with opposing party affiliations and favours incumbent interests. Prior to the election of Costas Simitis, parties stressed the charisma of the leader. Party rallies in Athens at election time were huge, for example, with voters coming to hear 'Andreas' (Papandreou). While cultural traits have evolved and voters appear to be less loyal and less ideological (Nikolakopoulos, 2005), the importance of party and clientelism remains seemingly immutable in public life. This militates against liberal norms of the separation of the party and the state and favours group identities and reciprocal obligations.

The context here is of the consolidation of the post-1974 democratic regime in Greece, with the endurance of the contemporary political parties (Gunther et al., 1995; Pappas, 1999, 2003; Lyrintzis, 2005). Since 1981, the party system has essentially been based on three blocs: left, centre-left, and centre-right (Lyrintzis, 2005). With one brief interlude, due to exceptional circumstances, the Left (in the main, KKE: The Communist Party of Greece / KKE: Κομμουνιστικό Κόμμα Ελλάδας) has been excluded from government and it has consistently been the smallest bloc. This has left a two-party contest for office between PASOK and ND. With the exception of two brief coalition governments in 1989–90, all governments after 1974 have been formed by single parties. Moreover, the system has displayed stability: there have been 11 elections since 1974, 14 governments,[2] and just 9 individuals serving as prime minister (or 11 governments and only six prime ministers if the caretaker governments of 1989–90 are excluded). The results of the recent national parliamentary elections are given in Table 3.1.

Yet the Greek party system continues to display a high level of conflict. It has fallen well short of the conventional classifications of consensual systems. Since 1974, it has not emulated a 'politics of accommodation' (Lijphart, 1975) the settlement of divisive issues, on which there is little consensus, on the basis of elites engaging in compromise to find pragmatic solutions in a climate of depoliticization and proportional rewards (Lijphart, 1975: Chapter 7). Rather, since the restoration of democracy in 1974, Greece has generally sustained a majoritarian, adversarial, and polarized two-party system (Pagoulatos, 2004). In the emotive clashes of the late 1970s and the 1980s, politics in Greece was highly charged. By the 1990s, it had undergone a shift towards being more result oriented, not least as voters could judge domestic performance by increasingly relevant EU benchmarks. But major issues of policy reform – such as pensions or state administration – on which there is a substantial convergence of position by a large proportion of political and technocratic leaders, escape resolution by cross-party consensus as strategic calculations are made in a climate of conflicting interests and exclusivity. Little cooperation has been sustained between the major parties. Even the 'rules' can be part of the 'game'. The electoral system has undergone frequent adjustments, apparently to advantage the incumbent party. The Constitution has been reformed (1985, 2001), upholding majoritarian principles of competition and lacking cross-party support (Eleftheriadis, 2005).

Ideological distances have narrowed, however. They have long seemed flexible and malleable. KKE is the one major party that maintains a strongly ideological and 'rejectionist' stance. It has often been dubbed a 'hardline' orthodox communist party, though it has also displayed its own twists and turns. For its two larger rivals, the ideological labels of 'Left' and 'Right' have been manipulated for seemingly opportunistic electoral reasons. PASOK, in particular, under its first leader Andreas Papandreou, practically demonized the Right for its historical crimes against the 'people'. Constantine Karamanlis, the first Premier of the transition to democracy, defined his party ideology as one of 'radical liberalism'. The reference was loose and shallow (Loulis, 1981), no doubt an attempt to broaden the appeal and to avoid being tarnished by the allegedly 'dark' histories of the Right. When ND encountered electoral failure (in 1993) with a somewhat 'neoliberal' appeal, it reverted to a more centrist and less purist stance. For its part, PASOK shifted from a neo-Marxist rhetoric of denouncing world capitalism in which Greece was the victim of various forms of imperialism. Its initial purpose was defined as a 'national liberation' struggle (Featherstone, 1987; Lyrintzis, 1984). In office, after a crushing victory on a populist appeal for 'Change' ('αλλαγη') in 1981, it gradually accepted identification as being social democratic, eventually joining in 1989 its peer parties in the 'Confederation of Socialist Parties of the EC' and the Socialist International (Featherstone, 1988; Pagoulatos, 2004). This reached its natural conclusion with the 'modernization' project advanced by a new party faction headed by Costas Simitis in the 1990s. By the 1996 election, the ideologies of the two main contenders for power had very substantially converged: both sought general liberalizing reforms in the economy and society and both were strongly pro-European.

Crucially, both major parties had come to advocate privatization of, at least, some state enterprises: ND, by ideological conviction, sought to implement a radical programme when in government in 1990–3; PASOK by a combination of an ideological shift and an acceptance of an EU-related fiscal constraint, prior to EMU convergence. The strategy of selling off state assets allowed the option of reducing the government's borrowing requirement and thereby helping to meet one of the Maastricht Treaty's convergence tests. The combination of motives – ideological and instrumental – is, indeed, typical as Pitelis and Clarke (1993: 6) have noted: 'There are various reasons that governments privatize and usually it is not only one, but a combination of them together.' Nevertheless both parties now shared an ideological stance that embraced privatization, at least on pragmatic grounds and with varying degrees of enthusiasm. The reconfiguration of the party system was crucial to the policy.

Yet governments cannot expect cross-party support or independent legitimation of their reform initiatives. Moreover, the flow of technocratic expertise into the elaboration of policy content is normally structured by party identity: individuals attach themselves to one side or the other and expect their careers to be dependent on whether their party is in power or not. Though individual experts of different parties often share basic cognitive and normative beliefs, the party embrace, rather than scientific knowledge, differentiates their position. To a significant extent, this has been evident in the area of macroeconomic debate over the last decade or so and the agenda for the Greek economy, with the apparent proximity of stance taken by some of Greece's leading economists. In any event, the discontinuity of personal expertise between governments – all senior policy posts are party appointees and permanent civil servants have little policy input – is matched by the relative absence of independent policy think tanks dealing with domestic policy issues, as previously noted. Ministers surround themselves by their own personal advisers in order to acquire expertise. The party structures themselves play no significant role in the elaboration of government policy. Internal processes are heavily centralized and 'top-down'.

Thus, a party system approach to the Greek case studies would stress the clientelistic nature of political life, affecting party strategies and interests; the conflictual nature of interparty relations and the two-party polarization of socio-political life; the absence of consensual mechanisms and practices; the distance of the internal party structures from policy-making; the 'colonization' of the state apparatus by the governing party; the personalistic nature of technocratic input into the elaboration of policy; and the power of the party leader to determine options and strategy. These are important contextual features for the later case studies. Moreover, a party focus can illustrate the shifts in policy stance – as with the case of privatization – but the Greek context does not suggest that parties themselves should be seen as a part of a causal chain to explain the changes.

Moreover, recent literature on party systems has considered the extent to which the nature of parties is changing and how far this is contributing to 'state failure'. Here 'failure' is cited as a weakening capacity of democratic systems to manage social change and to meet voter preferences. The main responsibility for such outcomes lies with political leaders and bureaucrats exploiting the system to maintain their wealth and power. Such actors operate in a monopoly situation, with voters unable to exit and find alternatives; interparty cooperation sustains cartel-like behaviour; and systemic competition induces ideological convergence. Katz and Mair (1995), while not addressing state failure directly, wrote of similar trajectories as parties were increasingly becoming 'cartel parties'. Kitschelt (2000) has offered a thorough critique of such depictions in general. In some respects, it is tempting to refer to 'state failure' in the Greek case, given the problems encountered in introducing structural economic reforms. While the party system has shown stability and parties have become more professional, displaying some innovation in technique, other traits associated with the 'state failure' thesis are either nonexistent or part of a traditional pattern (cf. Lyrintzis, 2005). Interparty cooperation is minimal. The marginalization of local organizations and the autonomy of party leaders are part of a long-term pattern. Thus, it is difficult to highlight a relevant dynamic here.

Moreover, Greek governments encounter 'failure' more emphatically due to problems beyond the party system. Prime Ministers have to manage party factions and rivalries, while also being sensitive to their electoral base. But blockages to reform are more clearly evident in the wider arena of government-union-employer relations.

3.3 Neo-corporatism: Explaining the Greek shortfall

The complexity of relations between the government, unions, and employers in Greece lends itself to explanation on the basis of a 'neo-corporatist' approach. This refers, at a minimal level, to the ability of a government to negotiate sustainable bargains (e.g. on wages, employment, and/or social policy) with unions and employer organizations (Schmitter and Lehmbruch, 1979; Berger, 1981; Goldthorpe, 1984; Alvarez et al., 1991).[3] The model posits a small number of organizations possessing a representational monopoly within their own area of interest that are then incorporated into policymaking as co-responsible partners (Schmitter, 1977: 9; Sargent, 1985: 232; Cawson, 1986). The 'political exchange' also depends on incentives from the government and the discipline of unions to establish reciprocal agreements (Scharpf, 1987; 1991).

The approach was particularly popular in the 1970s, helping to explain the various forms of concertation that were then evident across the west European states. In more recent years, however, it has encountered a paradox: the existence of neo-corporatist type agreements in systems apparently lacking the organizational preconditions for successful concertation. The emergence of various kinds of social pacts appeared related to the external discipline of the EMU (Hancke and Rhodes, 2005). In any event, there is the more immediate problem of identifying the extent to which Greece fits the neo-corporatist model.

At least until recent years, Greece did not approximate to the typical neo-corporatist model. Instead, in the post-war period it has usually been seen as constituting a 'state corporatist' model of some type, emphasizing the reach of the state. Mavrogordatos (1988) outlines the history of state corporatism in Greece. State interference in the trade union movement began under the premiership of Venizelos, with a package of legislation in 1910 and subsequent political interventions, was greatly extended by the authoritarian Metaxas regime (1936–41), and was reinforced by the Colonels' junta (1967–74) (Featherstone, 1987; Leon, 1976). Greece sustained a very fragmented, highly regulated structure of trade unionism that can easily appear opaque to the outsider. Collective bargaining has been subject to extensive state regulation, with various forms of bilateral ('collective') agreements being signed between unions and the employers on an annual and, more recently, biennial basis. Trade union density (that is, the size of union membership) is relatively low. Estimates of trade union density place Greece alongside the UK, Germany, and The Netherlands in the 20–29% range (see Table 3.2). Large numbers of small enterprises are largely unaffected by the collective agreements of the corporatist structures.

However, Pagoulatos (2003) argues that the notion of 'state corporatism' belongs in the era of the 'developmental state', pre-1974; latterly, the term overstates the scope for state control over organized interests and of the possibility of state-imposed concertation. He stresses, instead, the fragmented and rent-seeking character of interest mediation. Thus, he prefers the identification of the system as one of a unique type of 'parentela pluralism' (2003: 162). Lavdas had earlier depicted the Greek system as one of 'disjointed corporatism' – a pithy term, but one defined rather cumbersomely as where there is 'a combination of a set of corporatist organisational features and a prevailing political modality that lacks diffuse reciprocity and remains incapable of brokering social pacts' (1997: 17). The enclaves of sectoral corporatism 'have been the result of mutations' of the state corporatist tradition (1997: 17).

By contrast, Pagoulatos wishes to give more emphasis to the 'generally pluralistic group setting' (2003: 162).

The extent of recent change is disputable. In the 1990s, Pagoulatos argues, government and party intervention in trade union organization and activity had been 'relaxed, financial autonomy of labour unions was increased, the General Confederation of Greek Workers (GSEE) acquired significant political autonomy, and collective bargaining was liberalised' (2003: 167). Further, 'consensus-oriented, neocorporatist-type procedures and institutions were strengthened, centralised collective bargaining and the pursuit of social pacts coexisting with highly decentralised company-level agreements' (2003: 167). This seems to exaggerate the degree of consensus and the significance of the pursuit of social pacts, however. The rhetoric on the importance of social dialogue only emerged gradually in the late 1980s and the early 1990s (Ioannou, 2000). Since then, it has been marked by a 'stop-go' character, discrediting it as a process and creating further mistrust. Moreover, the agenda of social dialogue has been inconsistent and fragmented, resulting in *ad hoc*, partial bargaining. Thus, Lavdas's earlier pessimism was not fundamentally overcome. Before returning to power, PASOK in 1993 had assailed the Mitsotakis Government for the absence of social dialogue. In the government, its strategy was attacked for being *ad hoc* and opportunistic (Ioannou, 2000). It created several bipartite and tripartite bodies to facilitate dialogue (most notably, OKE: Economic and Social Committee / OKE: Οικονομική και Κοινωνική Επιτροπή in 1995), but it then neglected and bypassed them, creating a new 'National Social Dialogue' in 1997 with a different structure and an inconsistent purpose (Featherstone and Tinios, 2006).

The attempts at 'tripartite social dialogue' in 1997 and 2000 were widely regarded as failures (Zambarloukou, 2006: 220–3). The unions had initially shifted ground by supporting dialogue because of the transformation of the economic setting (increased unemployment, declining union density, privatization, the opening to foreign competition, technological change, and the abolition of compulsory arbitration) (Zambarloukou, 2006). Yet the dialogue broke down. Zambarloukou argues that this was due to long-term problems of a lack of trust and the absence of a culture to support dialogue, as well as the internal structural problems of the unions. More specifically, the unions came to view government initiatives on pension and labour market reform as a 'zero-sum' agenda, involving costly losses and few gains.

What the neo-corporatist focus suggests for the Greek case studies – with the 'disjointed' or 'parentela' character of interest mediation – is the structuring of conflict, with coordination and consensus extremely difficult to manage in a climate of antagonism and mistrust. Indeed, Greece is typically depicted as exhibiting low 'social capital' (Putnam, 1993; Lyberaki and Paraskevopoulos, 2002). Moreover, the structure of conflict is strongly marked by the mode of representation *within* the major bodies. Both the union (GSEE and ADEDY) and employers' (SEV) federations have internal representation that is skewed towards certain groups, overplaying their interests. Among the union confederations, disproportionate strength has been enjoyed by employees of the broad public sector, affecting the stance of the leadership on key economic and social issues. At the same time, the employers' federation has displayed the predominance of the few very large firms (some ex-state monopolies). This has favoured the distinctive interests of those who have benefited from the prevailing market regulations, barriers to entry, and stable product demand. Moreover, the membership of Greek firms in the major employers' organizations is relatively low in European terms. The representation balance is tipped away from those with interests in more open, competitive private markets. Interest representation tends to reflect the legacy of the risk-averse, statist, and anti-competitive traditions of the 'developmental state'.

This contextualizes the bargaining interests and strategies of the key social partners, and these features will be taken up again at the end of the chapter.

3.4   Models of capitalism: Greece as an outlier

Recent scholarship has shifted away from neo-corporatist frameworks to develop a rather more holistic approach on the nature of the domestic economy. Hall and Soskice (2001), in particular, broke new ground with their 'varieties of capitalism' approach, and it has encouraged a burgeoning literature in comparative political economy. Hall and Soskice set out to answer how different models of capitalism, defined by their institutional characteristics, shape economic performance. In particular, 'It provides a new analysis of the pressures governments experience as a result of globalisation and one capable of explaining the diversity of policy responses that follow' (Hall and Soskice, 2001: vi).

The basic idea is that national economies can be modelled in terms of their institutional frameworks and that the behaviour of these economies can be explained by reference to the propositions of rational interest derived from the models. While the perspective accounts for different kinds of actors, the models are strongly focussed on the behaviour of firms as 'companies [are] the crucial actors in a capitalist economy' (2001: 6). They are the key agents of change within systems. This represented a clear attempt to shift the focus of the 'neo-corporatist' literature beyond the stress on the state's relationship with organized labour. The Hall and Soskice models see firms as being engaged in a set of strategic interactions. Critical here is the relationship that the firm is able to establish internally with its employees and externally with a range of other actors (including 'suppliers, clients, collaborators, stakeholders, trade unions, business associations, and governments' (2001: 6)). These relationships are problematic in various ways, and a firm's success depends greatly on its ability to coordinate effectively with a wide range of actors. Hall and Soskice highlight five spheres in which firms must develop relationships to resolve their coordination problems: *industrial relations* (how to coordinate bargaining over wages and working conditions with the labour force), *vocational training and education* (how to secure a workforce with suitable skills), *corporate governance* (providing satisfactory access to finance and return to investors), *interfirm relations* (particularly with suppliers and clients to secure demand, supply, and access to technology), and, finally, *employees* (how to ensure employees have required competencies and cooperate well to advance the interests of the firm). Economic growth depends, in large part, on the efficiency with which capital and labour are deployed. Hall (2007) refers to 'total factor productivity' to reflect this efficiency. On the basis of their institutional infrastructure, national economies can derive comparative advantages affecting their performance.

With respect to types of national setting, Hall and Soskice draw a central distinction between *liberal market economies* (LMEs) and *coordinated market economies* (CMEs). The former comprise nations such as the USA, the UK, Australia, Canada, New Zealand and Ireland. Here, a market-friendly economy structures interactions: firms coordinate with an 'arm's length exchange in a context of competition and formal contracting', responding to market signals in the manner described by neoclassical economics (2001: 8). The supply of finance and the system of industrial relations are dominated by market mechanisms. By contrast, in *coordinated market economies* (such as Germany, Japan, the Netherlands, and Sweden) firms rely more on non-market relationships to resolve their coordination problems (including finance and industrial relations). Economies are structured by an embedded network of corporate institutions and collective organizations, which encourages collaborative relationships and sensitivity to the interests and strategies of other actors.

The general approach is not without its critics (Morgan et al., 2005). Three concerns can be highlighted. Firstly, the institutional arrangements posited by these models are said to be more mutable and more internally diverse than assumed. The responses of firms to their institutional environment appear more dynamic and innovative. As Morgan notes, 'firms are rarely limited in their choices of strategy and structure to a single model of "rules of the game"' (Morgan et al., 2005: 5). Firms are active participants in their own fate, learning and responding (Hancke and Goyer, 2005). Rationalist approaches may neglect this 'actorness' (Streeck and Thelen, 2005). Secondly, national systems cannot be seen in isolation: their variability is 'interdependent with, and mutually constitutive of, the international context' (Morgan, et al., 2005: 4). Indeed, the 'varieties of capitalism' approach does not easily differentiate between types of external pressure or the means by which these are conveyed into the domestic system. It is structured to model rational behaviour within a particular national setting and it emphasizes the domestic path dependency of change. Recent scholarship in this genre has grappled with the mutability of domestic structures in the context of exogenous shocks, recognizing that it challenges the limits of the approach (Hancke et al., 2007).[4] But the basic approach has difficulty in accounting for how specific EU policies and pressures may enter the domestic arena and shift agendas and interests: the framework is not geared up to identify such linkages or to recognize their potential importance in particular areas of the domestic setting. Thirdly, the approach is systemic: it is not attuned to explaining specific policy outcomes in particular sectors. It argues that the institutional structures of different models of capitalism influence not only the actions of firms and governments but also the response of the political economies to socioeconomic challenges. Indeed, with these responses, trajectories are established involving path-dependent incremental change. However, as Hall notes, these structures 'never fully determine that response' (2007). General propositions of actor rationality in the economy can be derived, but the approach is removed from the internal dynamics that determine the specific policy content and outcomes: public policy analysis. To overcome this limitation, the 'varieties of capitalism' approach would need to be extended and to follow other conceptual contributions with which it is intellectually consistent – primarily rational choice.

Of more immediate relevance to the present study is that Hall and Soskice left explicitly outside either of their models France, Italy, Spain,

Portugal, Greece, and Turkey (2001: 21). The southern European states are seen as 'ambiguous' cases falling between the two ideal types. Intuitively, specialists on southern Europe were left uncomfortable – though to varying degrees – with an approach that

- is centred on the firm and its myriad of relationships, seeing them as the key agents of change, contrasting with the distinct market structures and histories of southern Europe, and tending to downplay the centrality of the state in the domestic economy;
- neglects other forms of non-market relationships (to those found in *coordinated market economies*), such as clientelism and corruption;
- has difficulty in fully accounting for the distorted (or disjointed) nature of the parallel welfare regimes of southern Europe; and
- understates the relevance of the EU dimension to domestic reform and development in small, marginal economies (see Thatcher, 2004, for a related argument on external pressure overcoming domestic institutional inertia).

It is not surprising, in this context, that France – the home of étatisme – could not be neatly fitted into the two models of Hall and Soskice. Moreover, to underplay the role of the state in southern Europe is to take the 'politics' out of the model, leaving a partial and abstract notion.

The tradition of state-driven development in southern Europe is central to Greece's economic history (Diamandouros, 1994: 11, 1993; Tsoukalas, 1993: 62). Pagoulatos, for example, identifies Greece in the post-war period as a weak and incomplete 'developmental state', based on a 'state-driven policy pattern' with a protected market and a deeply underdeveloped civil society (2003: 47). The late (or 'late-late') industrialization of Greece, and its dependence on the Greek Diaspora and on foreign capital, meant that the state filled a domestic vacuum (Demertzis, 1994; Mouzelis, 1978; 1993). The state exercised disproportionate influence over the economy, through extensive regulation, protectionist measures, transfers, and subsidies. Moreover, these instruments were applied in a particularistic manner, with the state subject to a pervasive 'rent-seeking' behaviour and favouring certain sectors and interests (Sotiropoulos, 2004). The foreign origin and deployment of capital became associated with a semi-peripheral, underdeveloped form of capitalism (Diamandouros, 1994: 23; Giner, 1982: 176; Mouzelis 1978). Rather than manufacturing, these capital funds were directed by a 'comprador' bourgeoisie (serving foreign interests) towards activities such as banking, commerce, and shipping (Mouzelis, 1978: 20–1).

A large agrarian and service sector, alongside a limited manufacturing base and an economy structured on small- and medium-sized enterprises that were predominantly family owned, shaped the economy. Yet while the state was omnipresent, it was also fundamentally weak (Tsoukalis, 1997). 'Its pervasive influence', notes Tsoukalis, 'is intimately related to a clientele system, which it has been precisely intended to serve' (1997: 169). State institutions are typically denoted as weak, inflexible, and inefficient.

To make the approach of Hall and Soskice more relevant to Greece, therefore, the typology would need to be adapted. Several authors have attempted to do so, for different purposes. Some recent literature has suggested important similarities between central and southern Europe. McMenamin compared 22 states across 62 political, social welfare, and economic variables (2004). Accepting that capitalist democracy can vary, he argues that 'East-Central Europe is to be found with the four European "cohesion" countries, suggesting a relatively coherent peripheral status, in spite of radically different histories' (2004: 269). Schneider and Panuescu also identify similarities between the Mediterranean and east European systems (2004). But the present task is to identify the distinctiveness of southern Europe, in general, and Greece, in particular. Three such approaches can be highlighted that help in this regard: 'state capitalist', 'mixed market economies', and a more holistic representation.

Schmidt has elaborated a 'state capitalist' model, with which she approximates France and Italy (2002). She contrasts this model with the 'market capitalism' of the US and the UK and the 'managed capitalism' of Germany, the Netherlands, and Sweden. She outlines the 'ideal-typical' characteristics of state capitalism as follows:

> In state capitalism, the business relationship tends to be state-organized. Inter-firm relations are mediated by the state, while interaction between firms when not mediated by the state is generally as competitive and distant as in market capitalism [e.g. the US, the UK] except where there are ties through cross-shareholding akin to the managed capitalism model. Industry–finance relations are similarly state-mediated. Industry is more dependent on the state than the banks or the markets for financing and takes a more medium-term view due to the state's greater focus on national politico-economic priorities than on firm value or profits per se. Therefore, business–government relations tend to be state-directed, with the state influencing business development through planning, industrial policy,

or state-owned enterprises. It often picks winners and losers rather than only arbitrating among economic actors or facilitating their activities. Government relations with labour also tend to be state-controlled although more distant than its relations with business. Wage bargaining is largely determined by the state, which often imposes its decisions on fragmented unions and business, while labour-management relations are mostly adversarial.

(2002: 116)

This ideal model is closer to the Greek reality than either of the Hall and Soskice categories. Schmidt suggests that the 'state capitalist' countries are being transformed in their economic practices as a result of the retreat of the state and towards the lesser depiction of 'state-enhanced' capitalism (2002: 141) and even more recently 'State-influenced market economies' (2007). While the Greek economy – and the role of the state within it – has undergone various and significant changes over the last two decades, its distinguishing features remain significant. Moreover, a challenge for any depiction of a more statist model than that advanced by Hall and Soskice is that the state is important in different systems in different ways (Hancke et al., 2007). The particular structure of the Greek economy and the position of the state within it do indeed display some distinctive characteristics. It is not clear if Schmidt's formulations help very much in modelling the interests and behaviour of the state, firms, and unions in Greece. The theoretical interpretation of their interaction appears somewhat limited.

A second approach is the more holistic one of Amable (2003), who deploys cluster analysis (and principal components analysis) to investigate a range of prevailing empirical conditions across 21 OECD countries. He offers a typology of five ideal types: the market-based (akin to a LME for Hall and Soskice), the social democratic, the continental, the Mediterranean, and the Asian. A summary of his Mediterranean type is given in Tables 3.3 and 3.4.

The portrayal of the southern European conditions reflects a number of important realities. The depiction recognizes the extensive regulatory role of the State and it usefully broadens the picture to incorporate the institutional complementarities with welfare and education. These complementarities help to highlight a likely pattern of interests held by actors: for example, limited welfare provision increases the attachment to job security. This point is taken up later.

Amable's methodology here displays a distinctive purpose: it garners the quantitative data to offer a picture of the empirical reality. Its validity depends on how well the data reflect that reality. It is not an 'ideal-type' modelling strategic behaviour as such, rather it is a categorization of prevailing conditions, lacking strong theoretical support (Hancke, et al., 2007: 23). Its depiction is close to the conditions evident in Greece, but an interpretation has to be added of actor interests and behaviour before explanations of outcomes may be developed.

A third alternative formulation for the Mediterranean states is provided by Molina and Rhodes (2005). Working within the framework of Hall and Soskice, they propose an additional model, that of *mixed market economies* (MMEs). In MMEs, unions and employers have stronger organizational structures than in LMEs (such as the US, the UK), but they are more fragmented and have more problems in articulating their interests than in CMEs (such as Germany, Sweden). They have difficulty in delivering collective goods and in sustaining autonomous coordination in collective bargaining. However, they do have the strength to veto reform: indeed, the political system is marked by a capability problem in responding to reform pressures. Reform is arduous and depends greatly on the leadership of government actors in being able to overcome the coordination problems and to manage domestic veto points. The creation of reform coalitions is more prolonged and problematic than in LMEs or CMEs. The MMEs exhibit some stability: they are more than 'a cluster of countries in transition with only partially-formed institutional ecologies' (Hancke et al., 2007). Moreover, MMEs are hybrid systems: southern European states have low social protection and high employment protection. The depiction of MMEs appears more conducive to developing theoretical explanations of interests and behaviour.

The model differs from that of Hall and Soskice who posited the complementarity of production and welfare regimes and see them as being essential for efficiency.[5] By contrast, Molina and Rhodes see the hybrid of MMEs as potentially having greater scope for adaptation and compromise. Other writers have also challenged the 'functionalist' assumption that complementarities will lead to higher systemic performance (Boyer, 2005; Crouch, 2005). Soskice has now himself examined other types of system, as in Latin America, where institutional complementarities produce suboptimal Pareto outcomes.

As a model, the MME depiction supports an explanation of the problems of Lisbon-type reforms being enacted in Greece, especially with respect to many of the problems of social concertation. Coordination problems and veto points abound. The reform task is daunting: a number of important features are strongly embedded. Moreover, the 'hybrid' character is reflected in skewed and limited social provision, which affects the rational self-interest of key groups affected by economic reform.

3.5 Welfare regimes: Greece's skewed and embryonic provision

As the MME model refers to welfare politics and the economic-social policy linkages are recognized here as very important for the case of Greece, it is appropriate to turn to the comparative literature on welfare regimes. The linkage between capitalist models and welfare regimes is an important one for political economy approaches and it has been the subject of much debate. The focus of contention is whether complementarities lead to optimal outcomes or whether they sustain inefficiencies. Either way, as Pierson has argued, analysts need to consider how different national patterns of social policy are 'embedded in and help to shape distinctive national "varieties of capitalism"' (2001: 5).

The focus on social models, in fact, pre-dates that on varieties of capitalism. Esping-Andersen's groundbreaking analysis of 'three worlds of welfare capitalism' depicted liberal, Christian democratic, and social democratic welfare regimes (1990). The extent to which this typology reflected conditions in southern Europe was taken up by Ferrera (1996), who argued that there was a distinctive type of welfare regime in the region. With respect to the specific pension provision, a conventional distinction is that drawn between 'Bismarckian' social insurance schemes and the 'Beveridge' poverty-prevention model. The former are found in Germany, France, and Italy, while the latter are found in Denmark, Sweden, and the UK. Different types of provision carry distinctive risks. The 'pay-as-you-go' pension schemes are more vulnerable to demographic and political changes; the 'funded' insurance schemes are subject to capital market vicissitudes (Boersch-Supan and Miegel, 2001). Such features suggest that 'policy makes process': the nature of provision affects the reform process. Moreover, Europe's 'welfare states' have reached different stages of development; these raise different issues for a reform agenda (Pierson, 2001: 431n). The objectives of reform must thus be placed within the domestic context of provision: a politics of retrenchment (Pierson, 1998) is distinct from an agenda of varied policy objectives (Pierson, 2001; Natali and Rhodes, 2003). In some contexts, the agenda on pensions must be directly related to wider issues of welfare, employment, education, taxation, and wages.

The politics of welfare reform are complex. Pierson (2001) has seen welfare system reform as being 'path dependent' and his analysis places them within a frame of historical institutionalism (see above). Thus, welfare institutions are 'sticky', immovable objects. The capability of government to achieve (e.g. pension) reform will be circumscribed by the political power of blocking constituencies formed by those regarded as the current 'winners' of the system; the latter will act defensively, fearful of incurring 'losses'. Similarly, Esping-Andersen referred to a 'frozen welfare landscape'. In this view, reform initiatives are likely to be seen as involving 'zero-sum' outcomes: with clear winners and losers. Hence political leaders will display 'blame avoidance' tactics, to cut their political costs. By contrast, Natali and Rhodes (2003) have argued that the constraints on reform may be relaxed by a tripartite social dialogue (government-unions-employers) committed to considering a wider agenda and a new mix of policy instruments. The bargaining outcome could thus be seen as 'positive-sum', with the benefits distributed evenly. Reformers would thus be ready to claim credit for such outcomes. Alternatively, domestic reformers might be empowered to act domestically on the basis of an accepted EU commitment. The objective of meeting the convergence criteria for participation in the single European currency, for example, entailed fiscal constraints with indirect consequences on state welfare expenditures. Priority to 'euro' entry prompted attempts at pension reform (Featherstone, 2004). Yet, apart from the EMU entry test, EU obligations in this area depend on 'soft policy' instruments. Thus, reformers in states dependent on external empowerment do not receive it, while those in states that do not need it resist a stronger EU role (De la Porte and Pochet, 2002).

The Greek 'model' follows that of the Mediterranean welfare state (Ferrera, 1996).[6] It is marked by a highly fragmented system of income maintenance, with peaks of generosity and major gaps in provision (e.g. pensions); a shift towards universalistic principles in healthcare (albeit with major problems of adaptation and funding); a low degree of state provision in social assistance (and a reliance on other sources of non-state support); and the persistence of clientelism affecting the selective distribution of benefits and privileges. The major gaps in the provision are left for other structures to fill: traditionally, the extended family. From the inauguration of compulsory social insurance in 1934, the Greek system has been anarchic, separating social need from a rational allocation of scarce resources and struggling to develop notions of solidarity and citizenship (Venieris, 1996). Indeed, social policy has been subordinate to 'social politics'. Katrougalos and Lazaridis (2003) distinguish the systems of Greece and Italy from those of Spain and Portugal: the former are more fragmented in structure and more costly as a percentage of GDP.[7] But alongside matters of cost are major issues of the coverage and equity of provision, as the later case study will examine.

Social conditions in Greece reflect its relatively late economic development, a labour force more skewed towards agriculture and services,

and continuing poverty relative to the EU averages. Successive governments have given higher priority to redistributive policies at various
times from the 1970s onwards. In parallel there has been increased
debate in Greece over the effectiveness, efficiency, and equity of social
provision, in the context of deepening concerns over the failings of the
domestic state. The Greek agenda on pension reform has not been one
of simple retrenchment, but rather of reordering privileges and coverage
alongside rationalization. It is a variant of the 'late-comers' agenda recognized by Pierson, where welfare provision is in some respects still
being created. The institutional setting is critical to the explanation of
reform (or its failure) – composed apparently of 'immovable objects'
and 'irresistible forces' (Pierson, 1998). Successive reform initiatives
on pensions have faced powerful veto points, with current stakeholders defending entrenched and highly iniquitous privileges and
other groups being squeezed out, while political leaders have also been
constrained by the pervasiveness of clientelistic interests.

Few would argue that the linkages between the Greek economic and
welfare regimes produce Pareto optimal outcomes. The welfare system
is expensive, wasteful, and socially exclusive. There is much concern
that it fails current and future needs. Similarly, the economic system
displays inefficiencies and dysfunctionalities. It is a juxtaposition of
over-regulation and a large black economy, of business collusion and
dependence on the state, of strong labour protection and high structural unemployment. Finding Pareto optimality across these regimes
for a majority seems an illusion. Instead, there are blockages and vetoes
on behalf of minority interests as the later studies of reform initiatives
will show.

3.6   Distinguishing the Greek case: An empirical check

The discussion so far has been largely concerned with conceptualiza-
tions. It is now appropriate to consider those conditions that appear to
reflect the essential Greek 'reality'. A brief survey of the empirical data
is in order to indicate the goodness of fit with the conceptual models of
the economy.

The problems of the Greek state, of the economy and of clientelism,
noted above, continue today. In international comparisons of 'government effectiveness', Greece scores relatively low to other EU states (see
Table 3.21). The problems of state inefficiency are evident, for example,
from the fact that Greece has had a poor record in the transposition of
the EU's single market rules and has had a high rate of infringement

cases (see Tables 1.1 and 1.2). And while it has been inefficient, the Greek state is not small. Total public spending in Greece (as a percentage of GDP) was 49.8% in 2004, a little higher than the EU 25 average whereas in 2006 it dropped to 46.1%, a bit lower than the EU 25 average (Eurostat, 2006). Of a more local character, successive governments have struggled to assert state authority over illegal building by 'land-grabbers',[8] to establish a first-ever land registry to help in this regard (a problem that also involves arsonists and summer forest fires), to stamp out petty corruption in countless everyday state transactions (in which, for example, the citizen is obliged to provide *fakelaki* or envelopes of money to secure a public service), or to end the practice of party appointees even at the lowest level of the public sector to jobs with little function or application. The state remains inefficient, obese, and often corrupt.

With respect to the economy, the key characteristics in this regard are the following (for the specific data, see Tables 3.4–3.21):

- *The structure of the economy* is marked by very few large enterprises and very many microfirms and small firms and this affects the state's position.

  Characterizing 'statism' in Greece – the state's relations with the private sector – must reflect this juxtaposition and the contrasting influence that follows it. On the one hand, there is the pre-eminence of a small number of enterprise networks, and especially their individual heads who possess a strong public profile and have privileged access to and influence over the 'party-state', which in turn affects the policy, planning, and allocative decisions of relevance to their particularistic interests. By contrast, there is the relative political weakness of the vast majority of Greek enterprises vis-à-vis the state and the impact of the latter in terms of the regulation and availability of resources, though this is tempered by problems of local implementation.

- *The employment structure* reflects this pattern and Greece's late industrialization. It is based on
  - o the importance of services, the disproportionate size of agriculture, and the relatively low importance of industry;
  - o low rates of employment for women, low numbers of part-time workers, and, a very high percentage of unemployed;
  - o a problem of long-term structural unemployment, with relatively high numbers unemployed for a prolonged period and high youth unemployment.

- *Patterns of interest representation are somewhat skewed: Union member-ship* is quite high (predominantly in the public sector) while the coverage of the major *employers' organizations* is very low.

   Thus, the market conditions the interests represented by the unions and business. The interests of women, part-time, and temporary workers – and, of course, the (long-term) unemployed – have a weak voice, as do those in the very many micofirms and small firms in the service sector. The voice of large manufacturing firms is much larger, but also distinct and unrepresentative.

- *The Greek market* shows a relatively low cost for labour, extensive state regulation, low competitiveness, burdens on enterprise, and a large black economy:
   o Labour costs, relative to hours worked, are comparatively low.
   o International comparisons of competitiveness, the extent and quality of state regulation, and burdens on doing business indicate structural disadvantages.
   o The size of the black economy (informal sector) is exceptionally big.

The conditions identified by Amable (2003) are relevant here: high state regulation and low competitiveness While job protection is strong, labour is relatively cheap and flexibility is available via a range of mechanisms (e.g. compulsory overtime), business activity can circumvent state regulation via the black economy.

- The effectiveness and efficiency of the *Greek state* is comparatively low:
   o The size of government administration, as a proportion of GDP, is relatively high;
   o Measures of government effectiveness show Greece scoring relatively low.

The Greek case reflects a 'statism' but it is one of weakness, poor coordination, limited resources, and low skill. Managing the state machine to enact and deliver reform is thus an exceptional challenge.

- Perceived *corruption and tax evasion* is very high.
   o Greece scores poorly on comparative international indices of corruption
      • Irregular payments by businesses in tax collection is reportedly one aspect of the problem of corruption.

The cultural phenomenon of corruption is anti-competitive: it imposes costs and distorts the market, whilst offering privileged contact via enclosed networks. It is evident at all levels and across sectors. Tax evasion indicates the problem of the state administration in maintaining an appropriate revenue base.

- State spending on *social protection* is relatively high, but skewed:
  - Public expenditure on social provision, as a percentage of GDP, has increased over the long-term and compares favourably with other EU states.
  - However, the coverage of state provision is relatively limited: that spent on families is low while the cost to the state of pensions is high.
  - Other provision is patchy: unemployment benefit is low and limited in scope and duration.

This regime structures interests, as actors respond to 'complementarities'. The welfare 'deficit' is made up by families, where possible. Yet the deficit undermines job mobility and flexibility. The inequity in benefit entitlement creates problems of social exclusion, while those covered by pension funds act as veto points to reform.

The data shows the relevance of the literature considered here. The highlighted characteristics reinforce and also deepen the depiction of Amable (2003), who examined cross-country data. They qualify the picture of 'statism' offered by Schmidt. State-economy relations are differentiated by the former's obsesity and weakness and by the skewed structure and representation of the latter, affected by the mode and timing of economic development. They add empirical detail to the explanatory model of MMEs advanced by Molina and Rhodes. It is the latter that appears most promising, from this literature, to a modelling of the key Greek conditions and the domestic blockages to reform. That said, the depiction of actor interests will need to take account of the distinctive economic structures and practices of the Greek setting.

3.7   Research hypotheses for explaining policy outcomes

Where is the hypothesis here that might help explain policy outcomes in Greece? Linking the various approaches, there are several steps to take to derive a hypothesis of the rational actor interest. These involve consideration of the political system, the domestic economy, and the interests of the individual voter.[9]

A stylized model of the political system can be created to define actor interests and to test the propositions empirically. The prevailing culture is marked by clientelistic practices and attitudes, militating against liberal norms and showing the resilience of 'statism' in attitudes and practices. The party system is majoritarian, with two highly competitive (duopolistic) parties needing to concentrate power. A centre-left and a centre-right party compete for the support of the median voter. Both are 'leadership parties' (Iversen and Soskice, 2006), with party leaders acting via a small coterie of personal advisers. The political style traditionally is defensive and wary of open, non-partisan public debate. The mass party lacks input, 'think tanks' are limited and underdeveloped – both features being a consequence, not a cause, of the other attributes.[10]

The labour and product markets define the economic interests of the relevant actors. A 'varieties of capitalism' perspective – the MME model is closest – would focus on the rational interests of the 'median voter' towards policy reform and assume their representation through the labour mediation process. However, in the Greek context, the interests of voters show a marked contrast. Katrougalos and Lazaridis identify Greece (and other southern EU states) as having a division between the protected core of the labour market and the rest, especially those in temporary and irregular employment, those working in the informal sector and the unemployed (2003: 33–4). They term this division the 'Janus face' of the southern European labour market, where one side is characterized by rigidity and the other by flexibility and irregularity (2003: 42). This is directly relevant to the discussion here. Workers in the public sector enjoy high employment protection and seek to safeguard it. In the absence of high unemployment benefits and a developed system of vocational training, job protection is cherished. This indicates the close linkage between the labour market and the pensions system: heavy regulation and skewed welfare complement each other, as a 'varieties of capitalism' approach would expect. By contrast, workers in the private sector enjoy lower job protection, are often 'hidden' in a myriad of small family businesses, operate with lower unionization, and face the regulatory inefficiency of the state administration in enforcing legislation. Their regulatory benefits are fewer, though their material rewards are typically higher. Their 'voice' within the major unions is weaker. At the same time, the large firms leading SEV, the employers' association, have shown an attachment to the anti-competitive product regulations and barriers to entry, with stable product demand. By contrast, the 'voice' of the huge number of small and often microenterprises – a potential constituency for liberal market measures – is weaker.

Interest mediation is thus characterized by contrasting interests and strength of voice.

A general hypothesis can be derived (synthesizing the varieties of capitalism and neo-corporatism approaches) to explain (Lisbon-type) policy outcomes:

Market liberalizing reforms (e.g. employment flexibility, privatization) encounter a weak domestic constituency for support as the structure of interest mediation favours the interests of the public sector and the privileged position of the few large private corporations. As a result, the key social partners defend the current privileges and protection, fearing the risks of more open competition and the consequences of low state welfare provision. Similarly, pension reform will be resisted if it threatens current privileges or market stability, with workers anxious as to the lack of wider welfare support and firms as to the threat to current labour conditions. Stop-go incremental policy reform is the most likely outcome.

The general hypothesis seeks to build on a wider scholarship on interest mediation within Greece. A number of further assumptions can be derived:

- The institutional position of the major employers is marked by problems of representation. Major firms may tolerate lower efficiency in the deployment of labour and in the welfare regime at home in favour of the comparative institutional advantages that stem from the high level of regulation: stability and peace, barriers to market entry.
- Domestic firms lack the will or resources to accept the challenge of taking over inefficient and indebted state enterprises, requiring as it would the defeat of entrenched union power and a threat to the advantages noted above.
- Union confederations, dominated by public sector interests, resist greater labour market flexibility and pension reform for fear of loss of privileges and low welfare protection. They have little interest in a widening of employment protection (e.g. to part-time workers) if it risks opening up an agenda of reform threatening current job securities. The privatization of state enterprises will be similarly opposed: as a threat to current protection and privileges.

Each of these propositions reflects the rational economic self-interests of the key actors and they are endogenous to the system, highlighting the impediments to radical policy change. The model needs to be explored in the case studies; moreover, the 'static' picture needs to take account of variation and trends.

3.8 Conclusions

The previous and the present chapters have established two alternative frameworks by which the processes of continuity and change in structural reform in Greece can be gauged. The hypotheses that have been developed show a difference in their relevance. The Europeanization hypotheses have potentially general applicability, whereas those derived from the 'varieties of capitalism' apply at the level of firms and unions in particular sectors. Nevertheless to a considerable degree, they offer a coherent picture of what can be expected from the Greek case studies, stressing key themes:

- The *paradox of government capability*: concentrated authority (few formal veto points) but social weakness, given the ('disjointed') corporatist system and the entrenched interests of those with accumulated privileges;
- The potential gain for government – in terms of *external empowerment* – from strong EU commitment devices and/or a legitimating discourse fearful of Greek marginalization;
- The *problem of business representation* in Greece – stemming from the structure of the economy – and the relative weakness of a constituency for open, competitive markets, with major firms benefiting from barriers to entry;[11]
- The *skewed interests and representation of the major unions*, protecting accumulated privileges in an exclusivist manner

These are features that appear to define the problem of governance in contemporary Greece. This theme of constrained governance will be taken up in the Conclusion.

The approaches of 'Europeanization' and of 'varieties of capitalism' are drawn from distinct intellectual traditions. Moreover, they define different paths for European economic systems: crudely, one asserts the likelihood of increasing convergence, the other of sustained divergence – though both seek to allow for instances of the opposite. The 'varieties of capitalism' approach is not focussed to account for different kinds of external pressure influencing domestic change. Instead, 'globalization' is seen as confirming systemic differences and accentuating divergences between them. The international dimension is interpreted in terms of the comparative institutional advantages that remain after external pressures, more than as a specific causal explanation of general adaptation. Thus, the approach would support hypotheses of path dependency in relation to external pressure and would stress the resilience of the particular market model in interpreting such pressures. By contrast, 'Europeanization' seeks to account for domestic change as a result of pressures arising from EU membership. Here, the problem is not only to determine the relative significance of the external and the domestic, but also to disentangle the 'global' from the 'European'.

However, both approaches share more ontological similarities than is often recognized. Neither posits deterministic outcomes. 'Europeanization' recognizes divergent outcomes to common stimuli. 'Varieties of capitalism' has a 'strong, non-deterministic understanding of change, given its appreciation that the institutions that underpin coordination are subject to constant renegotiation' (Hancke et al., 2007). Both approaches are concerned with tendencies or trajectories. The clarification of independent and dependent variables is sometimes problematic with respect to positing a specific causality. Both depict system dynamics. Neither readily penetrates the internal processes that transmit stimuli to outcomes, in the sense of highlighting the intervening actors, actions, and mechanisms that link them. To overcome these limitations, both must borrow from other conceptual approaches and methodologies in order to provide greater empirical depth.

Moreover, recent work has considered the extent to which the 'Europeanization' and 'varieties of capitalism' approaches may be placed alongside each other. Menz (2005) suggests that the two approaches can be linked in order to explain particular empirical outcomes. His study asserts that it is possible to predict *ex ante* the way in which national systems will respond after the initial domestic equilibrium has been challenged by EU policies. Thatcher (2007) considered the impact of EU regulation that followed a 'liberal market economy' model on systems that equated with 'coordinated market economies'. He found that France and Germany needed EU regulation to legitimate reform and overcome domestic opposition to reforms such as liberalization and privatization. EU regulation helped national policymakers to break with previous institutional arrangements and to adopt sectoral arrangements very different from the prevailing national institutions. He concluded that the 'varieties of capitalism' approach was weak in accounting for the impact of EU intervention, but of high value in understanding cross-national differences in informal institutions and the processes of institutional change.

Such arguments are consistent with the thrust of this book. 'Europeanization' offers an account of agenda setting, of the availability (under certain conditions) of a legitimating discourse, and of strategic opportunities that appear beyond the reach of modelling capitalism.

At the same time, 'varieties of capitalism' helps to define actor rationality within the context of prevailing market conditions starting from the reverse vantage point to that of 'Europeanization'. As such, the two approaches can be viewed as two sides of the same coin: each is concerned with that not covered by the other. They are distinct rather than being necessarily contradictory.

Chapter 7 will consider how these alternative frames are best applied to explain processes of structural reform, in the light of the case studies. It will see these frames as the instrumental constructs they were designed to be, rather than as straitjackets or as catechisms to defend.

Table 3.1   Electoral results 1996–2007

Party	22/9/1996		9/4/2000		7/3/2004		16/9/2007	
	%	Seats	%	Seats	%	Seats	%	Seats
PASOK	41.5	162	43.8	158	40.5	117	38.10	102
ND	38.1	108	42.7	125	45.4	165	41.83	152
POLAN	2.9	—	—	—	—	—	—	—
KKE	5.6	11	5.5	11	5.9	12	8.15	22
SYNASPISMOS	5.1	10	3.2	6	3.3	6	—	—
SYRIZA							5.04	14
DIKKI	4.4	9	2.7	—	1.8	—	—	—
LAOS					2.19	—	3.80	10
Others	2.2	—	2.1	—	0.91	—	3.08	—
TOTAL	100.0	300	100.0	300	100.0	300	100	300

Source: (1) Ministry of Interior, http://www.ekloges.ypes.gr/pages/index.html, accessed on 14 October 2007; (2) Nikolakopoulos Ilias (2005), p. 49.

Table 3.2 Trade union density, 1999: Union membership as a percentage of total persons employed

Country	%
Denmark	87.5
Finland	79.0
Sweden	79.0
Cyprus	70.0
Italy	35.4
Greece	32.5
Portugal	30.0
Germany	29.7
The UK	29.0
The Netherlands	27.0
Spain	15.0
France	9.1
Weighted average for EU 15	30.4

Source: European Industrial Relations Observatory Online EIRO (2002): Industrial relations in the EU member states and candidate countries.

Table 3.3 Southern European capitalism: Amable (2003)

Institutional area	South European capitalism
Product-market competition	Price, rather than quality-based competition, involvement of the State, little 'non-price' coordination, moderate protection against foreign trade or investment, importance of small firms
Wage–labour nexus	High employment protection (large firms) but dualism: a 'flexible' fringe of employment in temporary and part-time work, possible conflicts in industrial relations, no active employment policy, centralization of wage bargaining
Financial sector	Low protection of external shareholders, high ownership concentration, bank-based corporate governance, no active market for corporate control (takeovers, mergers, and acquisitions), low sophistication of financial markets, limited development of venture capital, high banking concentration
Social protection	Moderate level of social protection, expenditure structure oriented towards poverty alleviation and pensions, high involvement of the State
Education	Low public expenditures, low enrolment rates in tertiary education, weak higher-education system, weak vocational training, no lifelong learning, emphasis on general skills

Sources: (1) Amable, Barré, and Boyer (1997); (2) Amable (2000).

Table 3.4 Institutional complementarities: South European capitalism

	Product markets	Labour market	Financial system	Social protection	Education system
Product markets		Low competitive pressure allows employment stability (large firms)	Low competitive pressure allows the establishment of stable finance–industry relations		Industrial specialization and structure (small firms) do not require a highly skilled workforce
Labour market	Formal employment protection prevents fast structural change (large firms)		Employment stability demands a lack of short-term constraints	De facto employment stability lowers the demand for social protection	Stability of employment prevents need for constant upgrading of the competences of the workforce
Financial system	Underdeveloped financial markets and stable bank–industry relations slow down structural change		Lack of short-term constraints enables employment stability		Weak individual risk-diversification possibility implies a higher level of social protection
Social protection	Low welfare expenditures imply lower tax distortions on the domestic market		Low welfare expenditures increase the demand for individual risk diversification		Low levels of social protection deter from investing in specific skills
Education system	The skill level of the work force prevents the need to engage in high-tech activities	The education system does not allow a large, highly skilled workforce		Low specific investments lower the demand for protection	

Sources: (1) Amable, Barré, and Boyer (1997); (2) Amable (2000).

Table 3.5 Trade union membership in Greece

	1993	1998	2003	% change, 1993–2003
GSEE	485,000	416,000	422,000	–13.0
ADEDY	236,000	240,000	217,000	–8.1

Source: From EIRO Online (2004): 'Trade Union Membership, 1993–2003', European Foundation for the Improvement of Living and Working Conditions.
Notes: (a) GSEE: General Confederation of Greek Workers; (b) ADEDY: Higher Command of Unions for Public Sector Employees; (c) The great majority of union members belong to the affiliates of these two confederations.

Table 3.6 Employers' organizations density, 1999*

Country	%
Germany	80
France	58
Denmark	44
Finland	36
The UK	38
Italy	23
Ireland	22
Greece	16
Weighted average for EU 15	30.4

Source: European Industrial Relations Observatory Online EIRO (2002): Industrial relations in the EU member states and candidate countries, 2002, derived from Commission-sponsored report of 1999.
* Estimate of percentage of total workforce employed by members of the employers' organizations affiliated to UNICE, the EU-level employers' confederation. In the case of Greece, the percentage refers to the total workforce employed by SEV-affiliated businesses.

Table 3.7 Employment by sector, 2005: Percentage of total employment

	Agriculture	Industry	Services
Italy	4.2	30.8	65.0
Spain	5.3	29.7	65.0
Slovenia	9.1	37.1	53.8
Portugal	11.8	30.6	57.6
Greece	12.4	22.4	65.2
Lithuania	14.0	29.1	56.9
Poland	17.4	29.2	53.4
EU 27	6.2	27.7	66.1

Source: European Commission (2007), Fourth report of economic and social cohesion, pp. 178–95.

Table 3.8   Male and female employment rates: Per cent

	Employment rates				
	Average 1985–7	Average 1995–7	2005	2006	2007
Ireland	53.0	57.5	69.3	70.3	71.0
Finland	72.4	61.5	68.4	69.4	70.2
Luxemburg	59.7	60.5	65.9	66.6	67.2
Greece	61.4	60.3	64.9	66.3	67.3
Spain	47.0	49.6	64.7	66.2	67.3
France	58.9	59.1	62.7	62.8	63.0
Belgium	55.9	58.6	62.2	62.2	62.6
Italy	54.4	51.3	57.7	59.0	60.1
Euro area	58.8	59.9	65.8	66.6	67.4

Source: OECD (2007b), Economic Outlook 81 Database and OECD Main Economic Indicators, table 20 – online database, http://www.oecd.org/document/61/0,2340,en_2825_32066506_2483901_1_1_1,00.html, 8 October 2007.
Note: Employment rates are calculated as the ratio of total employment to the population of working age. The working-age-population concept used here is defined as all persons of the age 15 to 64 years. For information about sources and definitions, see *OECD (2007a) Economic Outlook* 'Sources and Methods' *(http://www.oecd.org/eco/sources-and-methods)*.

Table 3.9   Male and female youth unemployment rates (age 15–24): Per cent

	1994	2003	2004	2005	2006
Portugal	14.1	14.6	15.3	16.1	16.2
Belgium	21.8	19.0	17.5	19.9	18.9
Sweden	22.7	13.8	17.0	22.3	21.3
France	27.5	21.5	22.7	22.8	23.9
Greece	27.7	25.7	26.5	25.3	24.5
Italy	30.5	26.3	23.5	24.0	21.6
Poland	32.6	43.0	40.8	37.8	29.8
Finland	34.1	21.6	20.8	20.0	18.8
Spain	42.9	22.7	22.0	19.7	17.9
EU 15	20.8	15.7	16.0	16.7	16.1
EU 19	21.4	18.2	18.3	18.6	17.4

Source: OECD (2007c), Employment Outlook, p. 249.

Table 3.10 Male and female long-term unemployment rates: As percentage of total persons unemployed

	1994		2003		2004		2005		2006	
	+6 mo.	+12 mo.	+6 mo.	+12 mo.	+6 mo.	+12 mo.	+6 mo.	+12 mo.	+6 mo.	+12 mo.
Portugal	57.2	43.4	57.8	32.8	65.0	43.2	69.3	48.6	70.5	51.8
France	61.7	38.5	62.0	42.9	61.3	41.6	61.2	42.5	62.6	44.0
Germany	63.8	44.3	68.5	50.0	67.6	51.8	70.9	54.0	73.1	57.2
Poland	65.2	40.4	70.2	49.7	68.7	47.9	71.6	52.2	69.1	50.4
Greece	72.8	50.5	74.3	56.3	74.4	54.8	72.6	53.7	75.2	55.6
Spain	73.4	56.2	59.6	39.8	58.0	37.7	47.7	32.6	44.4	29.5
Belgium	75.2	58.3	64.7	46.3	68.9	49.6	68.3	51.6	69.0	55.6
Italy	79.5	61.5	74.1	58.2	65.5	49.7	67.7	52.2	68.5	52.9
EU 15	67.6	48.4	61.5	43.4	60.4	42.4	60.5	43.5	60.9	44.2
EU 19	66.9	47.0	63.7	45.1	62.5	44.1	63.1	45.7	62.8	45.9

Source: OECD (2007c), Employment Outlook, p. 265.

Table 3.11 Employment by professional status: Per cent

	Greece		Spain		Italy		Portugal		UK		EU 15	
	'98	'06	'98	'06	'98	'06	'98	'06	'98	'06	'98	'06
Employees	56.4	63.6	77.2	81.8	71.3	73.4	70.9	75.2	87.3	86.7	83.3	84.1
Employers	7.3	8.2	5.2	5.5	12.4	7.3	6.2	5.5	3.1	3.0	5.6	4.9
Self-employed	25.0	21.6	14.7	11.1	12.0	17.4	19.7	18.1	9.0	9.8	9.2	9.9
Family workers	11.3	6.5	2.7	1.4	4.3	1.9	2.3	1.2	0.4	0.3	1.9	1.2

Source: Politis (2007).

Table 3.12 Employment by economic activity: Per cent

	Greece		Spain		Italy		Portugal		UK		EU 15	
	'98	'06	'98	'06	'98	'06	'98	'06	'98	'06	'98	'06
Agriculture	17.9	12.0	7.7	4.9	5.8	4.2	13.8	11.9	1.7	1.3	4.7	3.7
Industry	23.2	22.0	30.5	29.5	32.7	29.8	35.1	30.4	26.7	22.0	29.7	26.5
Services	58.9	65.9	61.8	65.6	61.5	66.0	51.1	57.8	71.6	76.7	65.7	69.8

Source: Politis (2007).

Table 3.13   Cost of labour: Ratio of total cost of labour to total hours worked, 2003

Country	%
Portugal	9.56
Greece	13.37
Spain	14.75
Italy	19.99 (2002)
EU 25	20.95
EU 15	24.32

Source: Ministry of Development (2005), Annual Competitiveness Report 2005, p. 130.

Table 3.14   Global corruption index: 2006 rank

	2006	2005
Finland	2	2
Sweden	3	7
Denmark	4	3
Spain	28	28
Portugal	34	31
Italy	34	31
Greece	47	47
Poland	48	43
Croatia	51	42

Source: World Economic Forum (2006), Global Competitiveness Report 2005–6, p. xvii.

Table 3.15 Product market regulation (Index scale of 0–6 from least to most restrictive)

	1998	2003
The United Kingdom	1.1	0.9
Denmark	1.5	1.1
Austria	1.8	1.4
Portugal	2.1	1.6
Spain	2.3	1.6
Greece	2.8	1.8
Italy	2.8	2.9
Czech Republic	3.0	1.7
Poland	3.9	2.8

Source: OECD (2005a), Product Market Regulation in OECD Countries: 1998 to 2003, p. 59.

Table 3.16 Ranking on the ease of doing business

	2006 ranking	2007 ranking
The United Kingdom	5	6
Denmark	7	7
Ireland	10	10
Slovenia	56	61
Hungary	60	66
Poland	74	75
Italy	69	82
Turkey	84	91
Russia	96	97
Greece	111	109
Malawi	106	110
Honduras	107	111
Paraguay	110	112

Source: IBRD/World Bank (2007), 'Doing Business 2007: How Reform', p. 6.

Table 3.17 The size of the 'shadow economy' as percentage of GDP

	1999/00	2001/02	2002/03
Austria	9.8	10.6	10.9
The United Kingdom	12.7	12.5	12.2
Germany	16.0	16.3	16.8
Sweden	19.2	19.1	18.3
Spain	22.7	22.5	22.0
Italy	27.1	27.0	25.7
Greece	28.7	28.5	28.2
Slovenia	27.1	28.3	29.4
Lithuania	30.3	31.4	32.6
Bulgaria	36.9	37.1	38.3
Estonia	38.4	39.2	40.1
Latvia	39.9	40.7	41.3

Source: Friedrich Schneider (2005), 'Shadow Economies in 145 Countries All over the World: What Do We Really Know?', Centre for Research in Economics, Management and Arts, working paper no. 2005–13.

Table 3.18 Irregular payments in tax collection

Country	Score
Denmark	6.9
Spain	6.4
Portugal	6.1
Italy	5.7
Greece	4.0
Suriname	3.9
Sri Lanka	3.8
Pakistan	3.7

Source: Lopez-Carlos et al. (2006), The Global Competitiveness Report 2006–2007, p. 427.
Note: The score relates to the estimates of business leaders of the occurrence of undocumented extra payments or bribes connected with annual tax payments (1 = common, 7 = never occur).

Table 3.19 Public social expenditure

Country	Total public social expenditure in % of GDP				Public social expenditure for families in % of GDP				Total public social expenditure for old age in % if GDP			
	2003	2002	2001	2000	2003	2002	2001	2000	2003	2002	2001	2000
Austria	26.1	25.8	26.0	26.0	3.1	3.0	2.9	2.9	12.8	12.8	12.6	12.4
Belgium	26.5	26.1	27.2	26.7	2.7	2.7	2.7	2.6	7.2	7.1	7.0	6.9
Czech Republic	21.1	21.0	20.1	20.3	1.9	2.0	2.0	2.0	7.8	7.9	7.8	7.8
Denmark	27.6	29.6	29.2	28.9	3.9	3.9	3.8	3.7	7.2	7.1	7.1	7.1
Finland	22.5	21.9	24.8	24.5	3.0	3.0	3.0	3.1	5.8	5.6	5.4	5.3
France	28.7	27.9	28.5	28.3	3.0	3.0	3.0	3.0	10.5	10.3	10.4	10.5
Germany	27.3	27.0	27.2	27.4	1.9	2.0	1.9	1.9	11.3	11.1	10.9	10.8
Greece	21.3	21.3	23.6	24.3	1.3	1.2	1.1	1.1	11.5	11.6	12.0	11.3
Hungary	22.7	21.9	20.1	20.0	3.5	3.3	3.2	3.2	7.5	7.6	7.0	6.9
Ireland	15.9	15.5	13.8	13.6	2.5	2.4	2.1	1.8	2.9	2.8	2.7	2.6
Italy	24.2	23.8	24.4	24.1	1.2	1.1	1.2	1.2	11.4	11.3	11.1	11.2
Luxemburg	22.2	21.6	20.8	20.0	4.1	3.7	3.3	3.2	4.5	4.3	4.0	7.2
Netherlands	20.7	19.9	21.8	21.8	1.6	1.6	1.4	1.5	5.4	5.3	5.2	5.3
Poland	22.9	23.0	23.0	21.9	1.5	1.5	1.5	1.5	11.4	11.2	10.8	9.9
Portugal	23.5	22.2	21.1	20.5	1.6	1.5	1.1	1.1	8.8	8.3	7.7	7.3
Slovak Republic	17.3	17.9	17.9	18.3	1.9	1.9	1.9	2.1	6.4	6.6	6.6	6.5
Spain	20.3	20.2	19.6	19.9	1.0	0.9	0.9	0.9	7.9	7.9	8.0	8.2
Sweden	31.4	30.4	29.5	29.8	3.5	3.5	3.4	3.3	10.1	9.5	9.4	9.3
The United Kingdom	20.6	20.1	21.8	21.7	2.9	2.7	2.7	2.6	5.9	5.8	5.8	5.6

Source: OECD 2004, Social expenditure database.

Table 3.20 Expenditure on general public administration: General government sector, in per cent of GDP, 2004

Country	%
Ireland	10.4
Great Britain	10.9
Spain	12.5
Germany	12.9
Portugal	13.3
France	13.8
Italy	18.4
Greece	19.7
EU 19	14.2

Source: OECD (2007d), OECD Economic Surveys: Greece, p. 50.
Notes: (1) General public services comprising executive and legislative organs, financial and fiscal affairs, external affairs, foreign economic aid, general services, basic research, research and development, public debt transactions and other general public services; (2) The EU 19 aggregates are unweighted averages. EU 19 covers all EU members that are also OECD members.

Table 3.21   Governance indicators

	Government effectiveness	Regulatory quality	Rule of law	Control of corruption
The United Kingdom	1.83	1.76	1.73	1.86
Germany	1.52	1.39	1.77	1.78
France	1.20	1.06	1.31	1.44
Spain	1.05	1.06	1.10	1.18
Portugal	0.95	1.00	0.97	1.11
Greece	0.62	0.79	0.64	0.39
Poland	0.49	0.64	0.25	0.14
Italy	0.38	0.84	0.37	0.31
Bulgaria	0.14	0.54	−0.17	−0.05

Source: Kaufmann et al. 2007.

4
Whose Benefits? The Elusive Reform of the Greek Pension System

4.1 Introduction

Pension reform has proved to be difficult and controversial in many European countries in recent years. The EU's attempts to coordinate a reform programme in this area face major challenges at the national level: not least, differences of model and of opposition from current stakeholders. At the same time, there are strong fiscal imperatives for reform as pension costs seem set to spiral. These features are reflected in the Greek case. Yet the problem appears more acute in Greece. The current welfare regime has not just proved to be 'sticky', but rather to be a quagmire (Pierson, 2001). The projected deficits of the pension system have been the worst in Europe; at the same time, there are gross inequalities of benefit provision. Unions and current stakeholders have provided very strong opposition to reform attempts. The government's reform capacity has been in doubt. Strategically, any government in Greece should welcome an external leverage for pension reform.

This is a case study that serves to widen the lens beyond matters of economics – privatization, labour markets – to the area of welfare regime. It offers the opportunity to examine the relevance of 'Europeanization' in a critical sphere: one at the heart of debates on the 'social state' and one into which the EU has entered only recently. The EU's initiatives are 'soft' in form, as well as new, and the case is a relevant test of its claims to a coordinated agenda of reform for the future.

4.2 The EU stimulus to domestic reform

The relevance of the EU to the process of pension reform in the member states can be best understood as emanating from two closely interconnected sources: the adoption of the single European currency (the euro) and, more recently, the launch of the EU's Lisbon Programme.

The first such pressure relates to the fiscal constraints affecting government budgets in the run-up to (and in the aftermath of) membership of the Eurozone. The Maastricht Treaty provisions on the EMU set clear fiscal rules for *euro* entry. Member states should have a budget deficit equivalent to no more than 3% of their GDP and debt levels no greater than 60% of GDP. While the decisions on *euro* entry made at the Brussels European Council in May 1998 displayed much flexibility of interpretation on the public debt rule, the 3% budget deficit limit was adhered to more strictly and was replicated in the Stability and Growth Pact adopted at the Amsterdam summit in June 1997.

These rules posed major problems for Greece. Government borrowing had reached 19% of GDP in 1990, with pensions payments alone accounting for 15% of GDP (Featherstone et al., 2001). Deficits remained high – 13.4% in 1993, 10.2% in 1995 – until they reached 2.5% in 1998 when the *euro* decision was due (Eurostat, 2003). Debt levels proved more intractable: 110.1% of GDP in 1993, 105.8% in 1998, and not falling below 105% until 2002 (Eurostat, 2003). Successive Greek governments – under Mitsotakis, Papandreou, and Simitis – affirmed their commitment to reforming public finances in order to gain entry to the *euro* system. Indeed, during the EU-level negotiations on Greece's entry into the *euro*, pressure was placed on the Simitis Government – notably by the Germans – to make more substantive progress on pension reform as a specific means of promoting Greece's convergence.[1] Such a direct focus must have strengthened the understanding of the relevance of reform to Greece's European credibility. More generally, the relevance of European stimuli to domestic change in Greece has often been cited (Diamandouros, 1994; 2000; Ioakimides, 1998; Pagoulatos, 2003).

Following closely on the heels of EMU as a test of EU membership came the latter's move into the area of structural economic reform and a shift to 'soft' law as a decision-making style. The EU agenda on structural economic reform has developed apace in recent years culminating in the launch of the Lisbon Programme (March 2000) aiming to make the EU '. . . the most competitive and dynamic knowledge-based economy in the world' (European Council, 2000a). In order to pursue this ambitious objective, a new instrument for orchestrating and coordinating reform across the member states was introduced: the OMC. The launch of the OMC marked a radical departure from the classic 'Community Method' which was centred on the production of EU legislation which was legally binding for the member states. The OMC approach is essentially an intergovernmental forum of consultation. The purpose of the exercise is not full-scale harmonization or the production of 'hard law'. Instead the OMC aims at spreading the best practice across member states and assisting the emergence of national policies on the basis of agreed EU goals (European Council, 2000a). The OMC was initially employed as a tool of economic surveillance within the context of EMU (e.g. the Broad Economic Policy Guidelines – BEPG) and later utilized in the European Employment Strategy (EES). Following the launch of the Lisbon Programme, the use of OMC operations was extended to more areas including, among others, social inclusion, healthcare, education, and pensions (see below).

The EU's commitment to competitiveness (as reflected in the Lisbon Programme) coupled with the macroeconomic constrains enshrined in the Stability and Growth Pact (1997) underpins much of the debate on pension reform in Europe. The first explicit EU reference to this direction can be found in the conclusions of the Cologne European Council (1999) which urged the member states to review their pension systems '. . . in order to be able to cope with the financial burden on welfare spending of the ageing population and the need to influence future labour supply' (European Council, 1999). Moreover, the coming into force of the Amsterdam treaty with its new chapter on employment made further calls for the development of employment-friendly welfare provisions in the member states.

The need for the development of a coherent policy mix between employment and social protection policies was also recognized by the Commission in its 1999 *Concerted Strategy for Modernising Social Protection*, which stressed the importance of welfare state provisions that encourage and facilitate the return to work as the only effective means of combating long-term social exclusion and addressing the financial strains caused by demographic ageing. With particular reference to pensions, the Commission's proposals called for the reform of the financing of national pension policies involving elements of both funded and pay-as-you-go (PAYG) systems. It also argued for the need to extend the participation of the older workers into the labour market by measures to discourage early retirement schemes (European Commission, 1999b: 14).

During the first half of 2000, the commitment of the Portuguese Presidency to pursue its agenda on competitiveness (that gave birth to the Lisbon Programme) provided further impetus for an orchestrated reform of the European social model. As far as pensions were concerned, the decisions of the European Councils in Lisbon (March 2000) and

Santa Maria da Feira (June 2000) supported the Commission's ideas and urged for the development of more effective means of coordinating national pension policies aiming '. . . at improved forecasting of future trends and at obtaining in-depth knowledge of recent, actual or expected national pension reform strategies' (European Council, 2000b). To this end, the Lisbon European Council called for the creation of a High Level Working Party on Social Protection within the Economic Policy Committee (later to be replaced by a separate Social Protection Committee)[2] with the task of '. . . preparing, on the basis of a Commission communication, a study on the future evolution of social protection from a long-term point of view, giving particular attention to the sustainability of pensions systems in different time frameworks up to 2020 and beyond, where necessary' (European Council, 2000a).

A first progress report – focusing in particular on the public finance and economic consequences of ageing – of the High Level Working Party on Social Protection was presented in November 2000 (EPC, 2000). The progress report concluded that in the majority of EU member states the effects of ageing over the next few decades will add roughly 3–5% of GDP to pension expenditure, which '. . . even if spread out over several decades, poses a considerable challenge for the sustainability of public finances and the debt burden' (EPC, 2000: 7). The report, however, also recognized that more work was needed in reviewing existing national expenditure projections using common macroeconomic indicators and demographic assumptions. For that reason, the Nice European Council urged a final version of the report to be submitted by June 2001.

The progress report by the Working Party on Social Protection was supplemented by a Commission Communication (European Commission, 2000b), outlining the main principles for coordinated reform across the Eurozone. The Commission proposals did not differ substantially from those presented in its 'Concerted Strategy' in 1999, making references not only to the long-term sustainability of public finances, the need for greater flexibility to accommodate professional and geographical mobility but also to gender equality and the need to enhance the redistributive element of public pension systems in favour of those with poor labour market opportunities (European Commission, 2000b: 14). Here too, the Nice European Council instructed the Commission to submit a new Communication by September 2001 aiming to develop common objectives guiding the reform of pension systems across the EU.

The decision of the Laeken European Council in December 2001 to extend the OMC to the area of pensions was another indication of its commitment to establish EU-wide mechanisms of surveillance and coordination in this field. To this end member states were asked to present 'national strategy reports' along 11 commonly agreed objectives structured around the themes of (a) adequacy of provision, (b) financial sustainability of pension systems, and (c) responsiveness to changing needs.[3] The evaluation of national pension strategies was published in a joint report by the Commission and the Council in March 2003. The report identified a number of 'horizontal' priorities for action, including

- ensuring the financial sustainability of pension systems by extending the working life of employees and improving overall employment rates in the EU
- ensuring better protection of older people from poverty and social exclusion
- making pension systems more responsive to flexible working patterns and reducing inequalities of pension provision between men and women (European Commission/Council, 2003).

With regard to the Greek strategy paper, submitted in the immediate aftermath of the 2002 Reppas reform (see below), the European Commission/ Council report identified a number of major problems, including

- the precarious financial position of the Greek pension system
- an increased risk of poverty and social exclusion for older people
- significant discrepancies of pension provision between and within different generations of pensioners
- poor employment rates and short (and decreasing) working lives.

In the second round of the EU's benchmarking exercise for pensions, which was conducted in 2006, many of the criticisms contained in the 2003 report remained (no new reform initiative had taken place in the meantime). Even the diplomatic language normally used in these reports could not disguise the EU's sense of urgency in its 'encouragement' of the Greek government to pursue reform:

> In order to meet the financial challenge of ageing, the process of pension reform needs to continue with financial consolidation in due course, building on the modernisation that started with the 2002 reform ... Significant further efforts will be needed to stabilise expenditure growth in order to ensure the long-term financial sustainability of the pension system
>
> (European Commission/Council, 2006: 177)

The trajectory of the EU's involvement in the area of pensions pointed to an increasing Europeanization of the pension reform agenda across the member states. Greece too had not been immune from this process. In this sense European pressures reinforced already powerful domestic incentives for reform. These are explored in the next section of this chapter.

4.3   The wrong kind of mushroom: The key features of the Greek 'pension problem'

The many different facets of the Greek pension system make it an extremely difficult 'problem' to unpack. The problematizing of the issue of pensions in Greece (as indeed in any other country) cuts across a number of traditional disciplines and the normative, methodological, and conceptual tools they offer for its study. In this sense pensions can be viewed as an issue affecting economic stability and performance; as a social policy arena underpinned by notions of citizenship and inter-generational (and intragenerational) solidarity, or, more broadly, as a public policy puzzle reflecting wider issues of political culture, institutional constraints, and constellations of power within a given society. This section seeks to identify the key features of the Greek pension system as a means of contextualizing the process of reform that is discussed in the rest of the chapter. The time frame that informs this overview is the late 1990s, the period immediately preceding PASOK's major reform initiatives in the field of pensions.

Financial sustainability

The 'welfare state' has been only limitedly developed in Greece. Provision is very patchy. Social benefits are low and restricted. The health service – though upgraded in the 1980s – remains problematic. The one area that stands out in this context is the public provision of pensions. The centrality of pensions in the context of social policy in Greece is a key issue for understanding the strength of opposition to its potential reform. In 2000 public expenditure on pensions accounted for 12.6% of GDP (EU = 10.4%), representing more than 50% of the country's entire social spending (European Commission/Council, 2003). The ratio between social/pension spending was the second highest in the EU (behind Italy).

The Greek pension system is a predominantly Bismarckian model (pension entitlements connected to contributions through work) financed on a (PAYG) basis whereby those currently at work cover the pension costs for those who have retired. The financial pressures to the system emanate from many different sources, including

- high replacement ratios (pension relative to 'exit salary'), particularly in the public sector and state-controlled companies (Mylonas and De la Maisonneuve, 1999)
- a relatively low average labour-market exit age of 59.6 (EU = 59.9), particularly among women (Greece = 57.7; EU = 59.1)
- very low employment rates (affecting 'the base' of those who can support pensioners). In 2001 Greece had the worst record of employment in the EU at 55.4% (EU = 64.1%).
- a very low fertility rate (at 1.3), expected to produce one of the worse old-age dependency ratios – population aged over 65 as a percentage of the population aged between 15 to 64 – in the EU by 2050 (Greece = 54%; EU = 49%) (European Commission/Council, 2003).

The combined force of these pressures was expected to produce the worst 'pension scenario' in the EU, in which a narrow base of future employees will be called to support an increasing 'mushroom' of pensioners. By 2050 public expenditure on pensions was projected to double, reaching 24.8% of GDP (EU = 13.3%). This was despite the fact that Greece had the second highest (behind Italy) rate of social security contributions (at 26%) for private sector employees in the Organization for Economic Cooperation and Development (OECD) (European Commission/Council, 2003; OECD, 1997).

Institutional structure

The Greek pension system is one of the most fragmented in the EU. It is typically organized along occupational lines and is structured around 'primary' and 'auxiliary' pension funds, both of which come under what the EU terms as the 'first pillar'. Primary funds are financed from contributions by employers, employees, and the state and typically account for 80% of total pension entitlements. Auxiliary funds are financed by employers and employees only and typically account for 20% of total pension entitlements. In effect pension entitlements deriving from both primary and auxiliary funds are guaranteed by the state. In the absence of common rules governing retirement ages and replacement ratios (or indeed any other organizational aspect of the Greek pension system), the retirement arrangements provided by these funds vary to an astonishing degree (see below). In 2001 there were over 200 auxiliary pension funds and 27 primary pension funds (O'Donnell and

Tinios, 2003). The basic structure of primary pension funds was as follows:

- IKA (Social Security Foundation / IKA: Ίδρυμα Κοινωνικών Ασφαλίσεων), covering most of the salaried private sector employees, with the exception of
  - o employees in the banking and press sectors as well as seamen who had their own separate funds.
  - o OAAE covering the self-employed, with the exception of
  - o 'Liberal professions' such as doctors, lawyers, and engineers who had their own separate funds.
- Civil servants did not have a separate fund, but their pensions were paid directly from the government's budget. However,
  - o employees in state-controlled companies had own separate funds.
- OGA (Agricultural Social Security Fund / ΟΓΑ: Οργανισμός Γεωργικών Ασφαλίσεων), covering farmers.

The legislative framework governing the operation of 'second pillar' of occupational pensions was, in 2001, non-existent and as a result very few such schemes existed. Private pension schemes ('third pillar') were also limited and in most cases they came in the form of a lump sum (rarely as an annuity).

Distribution of pension entitlements

The presentation of the Greek 'pension problem' in averages hides one of its most important features: the widespread inequality of pension entitlements across and between generations. These discrepancies can be best understood within the context of Greece's well-documented history of clientelism in which societal groups with privileged access to the government were able to acquire and preserve a much better 'pension deal' for their members. In terms of cross-generational equity of pension entitlements, Matsaganis (2002) makes the following observations:

- Employees of the civil service, the state-controlled companies, and the banking sector enjoyed considerably lower retirement ages and received muchhigher pensions (relative to their contributions) than employees in the private sector. Replacement ratios of primary pensions in the former averaged at over 90% (in some cases reaching 108%) as opposed to 60% in the latter.
- The retirement age for the self-employed was similar to that of private sector employees, but replacement ratios of primary pensions averaged at 54% (albeit with smaller pension contributions).

- Liberal professions (doctors, lawyers, engineers) paid disproportionately low pension contributions to their income and enjoyed high replacement ratios from their primary pensions (around 90%).
- Farmers paid minimal social security contributions and received small pensions (with replacement ratios at 20%).
- There was no universal basic pension. The minimum pension granted to employees of the private sector with 15 years service stood, in 2001, at €364 with a supplementary €82 through a means-tested benefit known as EKAS. However, a large number of people had no pension rights at all (e.g. those with a fragmented career history or those who had never worked).
- The problems of adequacy of the Greek pension system were vividly reflected in the fact that, in 1999, 33% of the Greek population aged over 65 was at a risk of poverty. This was the worst record in the EU where the average share was 17% (European Commission/Council, 2003).

Moreover the system had produced significant discrepancies of pension entitlements between generations. The 1992 pension reform, for example, had significantly tightened retirement ages and replacement ratios for private sector employees who entered into the labour market after 1993 (see below). In more general terms, institutional fragmentation, the gross inequalities in coverage, and the PAYG-funding principles of the system had structured perceptions in a defensive way and encouraged 'the passing of the buck' to future generations (O'Donnell and Tinios, 2003; Featherstone and Tinios, 2005).

Hence, by the late 1990s the Greek pension 'problem' had produced powerful domestic incentives for reform: the system was not only financially unsustainable, but it failed the tests of adequacy and intergenerational (and cross-generational) equity. The impetus for reform was further enhanced by the increasing Europeanization of the pension 'problem' and the EU's growing involvement in setting the an overarching reform agenda. Yet domestic opposition to change in Greece remained formidable. This will be chartered in the following sections of this chapter.

4.4   Between appeasement and reform: Tackling the Greek pension 'problem' in the early 1990s[4]

The restoration of democracy in 1974, and the subsequent expansion of the welfare state provision as a means of consolidating Greece's new and fragile democracy, came to add new financial pressure (previously unfelt due to its relative immaturity and limited provision) to the Greek pension system's endemic imbalances. The aftermath of the 1981 electoral victory of the Pan-Hellenic Socialistic Movement (PASOK) brought a substantial rise in social expenditure and, in particular, pensions, which for the period 1980–5 rose in real terms by 11.3% (OECD, 1997: 22–3). Nevertheless by the mid-1980s the long-term sustainability of the Greek pension system had begun to cause serious concern. In October 1985 the PASOK government, fresh from its second successive electoral victory and confronted with a growing economic crisis at home, announced its 'Stabilization Programme' designed by the then minister for National Economy, Costas Simitis, aiming at reducing some of the most glaring imbalances of the Greek economy. Pension reform did not form a part of Simitis's Stabilization Programme. Nevertheless, in keeping with its reformist spirit, a committee of experts was appointed by the then Minister of Health, Welfare, and Social Insurance, George Gennimatas, to work in secret, exploring the possibilities of change in the Greek pension system. The committee was initially headed by Evaggelos Tsoukatos, a former (1963–4) governor of IKA, the country's largest pension fund. Following disagreements with his political masters, however, Tsoukatos was soon forced to resign and was replaced by George Kremelis, a professor of the Panteion University in Athens. In a practice that was to become all too familiar in the future, the confidential report was leaked to the press igniting stiff opposition by the trade unions. Responding to the pressure, Gennimatas refused to acknowledge the existence of the Kremelis committee and its report. The pension system was to remain untouched for the lifetime of PASOK's second administration.

The need for reform of the pension system entered forcefully the political agenda in 1990 amid a climate of severe economic crisis and political uncertainty (for a full chronology of pension reform in Greece look at Table 4.1). Following the collapse of the all-party-coalition government headed by technocrat Xenophon Zolotas in early 1990, a new election was announced for April 1990. The Conservative New Democracy (ND) party achieved a Pyrrhic victory in the polls, forming a single-party government, but with a parliamentary majority of just one seat. The new government was soon confronted with the country's dire economic straits. In 1990, the government's general borrowing requirement reached 19% of the GDP and with pension payments alone amounting for the same year to 15% of the GDP,[5] fears began to emerge that the Greek state would soon be unable to pay pensions and salaries for its public sector employees. Against this background, Prime Minister Constantinos Mitsotakis instructed the preparation of swift legislation in order to address the most pressing problems of the pension system. The overall responsibility of the reform process was allocated to the Minister of National Economy, George Souflias, who, working closely with his adviser Platon Tinios, partially sidelined the inexperienced Minister for Health, Welfare, and Social Security, Marietta Giannakou-Koutsikou. In an attempt to overwhelm the unions and neutralize the opposition to his reform agenda, Souflias insisted on a very speedy conclusion of the whole process with plans to have the draft law debated with the social partners over the (politically) quite summer holidays. Indeed the new law (1902/90) was passed through the Greek parliament on 28 September 1990 with a majority of just one vote (Keesing's Record of World Events *37721*).

Law 1902/90 was a mixture of 'housekeeping' measures and provisions to strengthen the financial position of the pension system. It provided, among others, for

- the gradual increase in pension contributions by 3%, from 27% to 30%[6]
- increases in the retirement age for men and women to 60 and 58, respectively
- the indexation of pensions to the salaries of public sector employees and not to the minimum wage of non-qualified industrial workers
- a series of measures for combating the widespread contributions evasion
- the tightening of the rules governing the granting of incapacity pensions
- the abolition of some of the most dazzling privileges for the public sector employees (Provopoulos and Tinios, 1993: 338–9).

Despite its positive short-term effects, however, law 1902/90 lacked a long-term perspective and avoided tackling the fundamental structural deficiencies of the pension system. Much of this hesitation can be explained by the magnitude of domestic opposition. During the two weeks that the law was debated in the Greek Parliament (13–28 September), Athens came to a standstill on four occasions following massive demonstrations by the private (GSEE) and public (ADEDY) sectors unions. Against this background the government was forced to concede much ground, particularly to the employees in the state-controlled companies (e.g. DEI: Public Enterprise of Electricity / ΔΕΗ: Δημόσια Επιχείρηση Ηλεκτρισμού and OTE) and banks. Moreover, some of the most highly indebted funds (such as the Seamen Fund – NAT: Ναυτικό

Απομαχικό Ταμείο – and the pension funds for the self-employed) were excluded from the reform altogether. In fact, Souflias himself recognized that reform was indeed incomplete and that the 1902/90 law was to be just the first step, simply ensuring the short-term viability of the system until a more radical shake-up of the system was introduced after the general election planned for 1994. Yet, despite its moderate changes, law 1902/90 proved politically costly for the Minister of National Economy. Days before the law was adopted by the Greek Parliament, Souflias announced his temporary retirement from the government due to ill health. Though he later returned to Mitsotakis's cabinet, he was never given an economic portfolio again.

Souflias's incomplete task of 1990 was taken on by Stefanos Manos, the third successive Minister of National Economy of the Mitsotakis's government, in 1992. Manos's appointment (February 1992) came at a critical stage for the Greek economy. In January 1991 the government had turned to the EC for a 2.2 billion ECU loan to support the Greek balance of payment. The new loan however, payable in three instalments, was made conditional on the imposition of strict austerity measures based on a Stabilization Programme drafted jointly by the Greek government and the European Commission. Despite its promises for sweeping reforms, however, the record of Mitsotakis's Government was indeed poor with economic indicators for 1991 falling well short from the targets set by Stabilization Programme. Economic underperformance and the subsequent EC refusal to release the second instalment of the 1991 loan caused major embarrassment to the Mitsotakis Government. Immediately after his appointment, Manos sought to reverse the negative climate by announcing the speeding up of the reform process with plans for widespread privatizations, a five-year pay freeze in the public sector and radical reform of the pension system (*Financial Times*, 10 March 1992). To this end the government appointed a committee of experts under the chairmanship of Professor Rossetos Fakiolas with a mandate to provide a study of the pension system which would then be used as the basis for the government's dialogue with everyone concerned. The composition of the committee was indeed wide with representatives from all social partners, including the two biggest trade unions, ADEDY (representing public sector employees) and GSEE (representing private sector employees).

Nevertheless the work of the committee was soon discredited and so was its report that was published on 20 May 1992. For its opponents, the report was not only far too cautious and generally worded, but also very hastily prepared. Moreover, the trade unions walked out of the committee, accusing the government of using it as a smokescreen for the promotion of a different agenda, and proceeded with the publication of their own alternative report (*To Vima*, 15 July 1992 and 9 August 1992).[7] In fact, the proposition that the Fakiolas committee was used as a smokescreen was not far from the truth: Manos himself later revealed that, in parallel with the proceedings of the Fakiolas committee, the government had secretly commissioned the IMF to produce its own, more 'technical', report on the reform of the Greek pension system. The content of the IMF report was, nevertheless, leaked to the press[8] personally by the Minister of National Economy, Stefanos Manos, in an apparent attempt to use its bleak predictions in order to strengthen the government's position in the dialogue with the trade unions which had begun since mid June.

By the end of the summer of 1992, however, the dialogue between the government and the unions became increasingly unsustainable, with the latter walking out of the talks on 13 August. The unions promised to resist, at any cost, the government's plans to introduce legislation on the matter (*To Vima*, 16 August 1992). Indeed, following a one-day strike by more than 100,000 public sector workers, further strikes in state banks, transport organization, and public utilities continued for more than three weeks causing widespread disruption in the capital, Athens (*Financial Times*, 14 September 1992). The government found itself under more pressure following reports that, in addition to the fierce attacks by all opposition parties, senior members of the ND party (among them, former Foreign Minister Antonis Samaras and former vice president of the government Athanasios Kannelopoulos) were threatening to overturn the government's slim parliamentary majority, voting against a number of provisions included in the draft bill. Concerns against the government plans were also voiced by the Governor of the Bank of Greece, Efthimios Christodoulou (a former Minister of National Economy in the Mitsotakis Government), who reportedly appeared sceptical about the impact of the proposed increases of national insurance contributions on inflation.

The law on pension reform (2084/92) was eventually passed by the Greek Parliament in the second week of September 1992. Its content, however, bore little resemblance to the ND's pre-election promises for a radical shake-up of the pension system or to the neoliberal profile of the government's Chief Economic Minister, Stefanos Manos. Under pressure, Manos was forced to cede much ground in the orchestrating of the reform to the more 'consensual' Minister for Health, Welfare, and Social Security, Dimitris Sioufas.[9] Tactically, this decision was perhaps a wise one, considering that Manos's radicalism and aggressive style would have impeded the chances of the 2084/92 law overcoming the opposition within the ND, let alone the fierce attacks by the opposition parties and the trade unions. Yet at the end the whole process lacked conviction and a clear sense of direction (some argued it also lacked a clear economic rationale).

The new legislation did, indeed, introduce some radical changes for all new entrants into the labour market from 1 January 1993, including, among others,

- an increase of retirement age to 65 for both men and women
- a 3.65% increase (from 30% to 33.65%) in the total national insurance contributions paid by all employers and employees
- a reduction of the 'ceiling' of the primary pension/exit salary ratio from 80% to 60%.

Nevertheless the structural deficiencies of the Greek pension system were left, once again, largely untouched. The fragmentation of the system and the significant differences in the pensions provided by different funds also remained. More importantly, the new law created a two-tier system with a major element of intergenerational inequity: those who have entered the labour market prior to 1993 (whose privileges were not affected) and those who entered after 1993 (whose pension entitlements were considerably curtailed). The horizon of the 2084/92 law was also limited, ensuring the system's financial viability for just 20 years – a short period of time for a legislative arrangement of its kind. Finally, law 2084/92 preserved most of the privileges enjoyed by strong sectoral groups. To this end, special exemptions were given to the employees of the electricity company (DEI) and state-owned banks, while the so-called noble funds (e.g. engineers, doctors, lawyers, military) retained in full their controversial benefits and were essentially exempted from the provisions of the 2084/92 law.

During the turbulent period between the fall of the Mitsotakis Government in the summer of 1993 and September 1996, pension reform almost disappeared from the agenda of the PASOK government. Andreas Papandreou, the victor of the elections of October 1993 was physically weak and preoccupied with other, more pressing problems. When Costas Simitis succeeded him in January 1996, he had an uphill struggle to assert his authority in the party (and indeed the government), and this left little scope for any serious attempt to tackle a matter as difficult and politically costly as pension reform. It was only after

Simitis had been firmly established both within PASOK and in government (following his electoral victory of September 1996) that he was in a position to begin considering possible solutions for longer-term problems such as the pension reform. It was in this context that the Spraos committee was established.

4.5   Having one's fingers burned: The 1997 'Spraos report' on pensions[10]

The Spraos committee (its official name was 'Committee for the study of the long-term economic policy') was an ad hoc committee of technocrats established in October 1996, initially for one year. It was set up by Prime Ministerial Decree 967 on the basis of which its remit was to examine the medium- and long-term development of the Greek economy and submit reports to the Prime Minister aiming to assist Greece's economic convergence with the rest of the EU's member states (*Efimerida tis Kyverniseos*, vol. B, 18 October 1996). The Committee produced seven reports in total with that on social security and pension reform eliciting the greatest interest from the public.[11] The idea for the committee originated within the close circle of Prime Minister Simitis, who warmed to the idea of a technocratic committee (broadly on the model of British royal commissions) that would provide objective advice on the main problems of the Greek economy. The committee's reports would be made public, almost immediately upon completion. Giannis Spraos, Professor Emeritus of the University of London, a person with close personal links with both Costas Simitis and some of his collaborators, was chosen to head the committee. Spraos had lived away from Greece for most of his adult life. However, he was now given a very public, frontstage role that included liaison duty not only with the top government echelons but also with the media. Ominously, Spraos had little prior experience of performing such a role in the Greek context.

The committee itself had no direct link with government Ministers or specific ministries and departments; neither was it expected to report its findings (at least formally) to a Minister or department. The members of the committee reported to Spraos; Spraos himself reported to the Prime Minister and also liaised with Ministers as and when this was required. The committee was empowered to access and seek information from any source it needed to and could co-opt any expert it wished. It met at regular intervals, usually every two to four weeks, in premises made available to it by the National Bank of Greece, to discuss draft reports prepared by its members.

The seven members of the committee were of varied 'origins': two (Giannitsis and Tinios) were advisers to the PM; one (Kousoulakos) was the Secretary-General of the Ministry of Finance; another (Stournaras) was an adviser to the Minister of National Economy and chair of the prestigious Council of Economic Advisers; another (Garganas) was a Vice-Governor of the Bank of Greece; one (Droukopoulos) was an academic and a member of KEPE (a government-linked economic and social think-tank); another (Glynos) was a close associate of Vasso Papandreou, the powerful Minister for Industry. The choice of members was decided after informal consultation with the ministries on whose terrain the committee would be operating. Platon Tinios, had links with Miltiadis Papaioannou, the Minister of Labour and Social Security. Kousoulakos was a nominee of Alekos Papadopoulos, then Minister of Finance; Stournaras and Glynos were nominated by Giannos Papandoniou (Minister of National Economy) and Vasso Papandreou (Minister for Industry) respectively; Droukopoulos was an 'independent'; while Giannitsis and Garganas were both close to the PM (*Ta Nea*, 4 July 1997).

The report on pensions, formally published on 13 October 1997, was drafted by Platon Tinios, a key figure in the PM's Economic Office who was long associated with the process of pension reform in Greece. Long before its official presentation, however, aspects of the report have been leaked to the press.[12] This had led to damaging speculation that the report was advocating cuts in existing pension rights and privileges, thus threatening the interests of politically powerful social groups. Such attacks contradicted the report's own claim that it merely sought to 'shed light on the array of options so as to make it possible for the right social choice to be exercised' (Committee for the Study of Long-Term Economic Policy, 1997). Further, the report noted that 'it deliberately does not suggest a complete model of reform . . . it neither contains nor adopts specific proposals . . . (on) the most crucial points, which are left open to be decided through the process of social dialogue' (Committee for the Study of Long-Term Economic Policy, 1997). The report emphasized the urgency of reform, and its narrative clearly pointed to certain courses of action being necessary to achieve desirable goals (30 priority areas were identified for this purpose).

According to the authors of the report, the Greek pension system's main problem was its 'overblown promises', which were naturally impossible to be put into effect (*Eleftherotypia*, 14 October 1999). The report attacked the safeguarding of privileges and of clientelistic relations, and described the 'absurdity' of the accumulated segmentation of the pension system (Committee for the Study of Long-Term Economic

Policy, 1997). Moreover, the report was very critical of the fact that often pensions accounted for more than 100% of the exit salary. Despite the positive effects of an increasing number of women and immigrants contributing to the Greek pension system, negative demographic developments, combined with the 'maturing' of some of the most striking privileges agreed in pervious decades, meant that the system would be rendered unsustainable by 2010. According to the author of the report, by 2005 the retirement would begin of 'the largest generations of pensioners with the highest accumulated rights in the history of Greece', while by 2030 'a thin and fragile trunk of workers' would be forced to support a 'mushroom' of pensioners (Committee for the Study of Long-Term Economic Policy, 1997).[13] As Spraos put it when he presented the report, 'We [Greeks] grow old[er] and reproduce less' (*Eleftherotypia*, 14 October 1999).

While the diagnosis of the problem emphasized indigenous factors, the report made repeated reference to the exogenous pressures of the EMU. The reform of pension funds could help Greece meet the Maastricht convergence criteria, in which 'General Government' was defined as including such funds. Savings in social security would have contributed to fiscal improvement in the same way as an increase in VAT revenue. Moreover, the public debt criterion in the Maastricht Treaty limited the options for pension reform, if these involved increased state expenditures in a transition to a new system. The report recognized that the Greek social security system had 'a fourty-year . . . history of reports which, in amazing unison, have identified the same problems and have proposed the same solutions'. It rejected the political expediency of 'reform by instalments'. Nevertheless, in skirting round advocating any complete package of reforms of its own, the report was content to support, implicitly or explicitly, individual components of reform. It included proposals for 30 areas requiring action and gave backing to a range of policy options, including measures to rectify the fragmented nature of the social security system and ensure its long-term financial viability (for more details, see Committee for the Study of Long-Term Economic Policy, 1997).

The public reaction that followed the official publication of the report was yet another clear manifestation of the variety and magnitude of the sectoral interests opposing a meaningful reform of the pension system, as well as of the uninviting social, political, and institutional setting in which the Spraos committee had to pursue its objectives. Arguably, Spraos's openness towards the media impeded the committee's ability to handle the effects of the report's publication more effectively. Spraos's style left the report vulnerable to a long and sustained attack originating from all corners of the political spectrum. While the criticisms against the committee members were in most cases unsubstantiated, the coverage of the report created the impression that radical and painful reforms were not only imminent but also likely to produce only 'losers'. The vulnerability of the committee against populist and distorted criticisms was further increased by the fact that, despite being written by technocrats, the report was not very technical and thus failed to 'shield' its conclusions with irrefutable hard evidence.[14]

The reaction to the report revealed a conspicuous absence of supporters and an abundance of critics. The two largest trade unions (GSEE and ADEDY) rejected the findings of the report, with differing degrees of ferocity, depending on the political affiliation of the representative responding to the report's publication (*Avgi*, 14 October 1997; *Eleftheroptypia*, 14 October 1997). The Athens Labour Centre (ALC; Εργατικό Κέντρο Αθήνας, EKA), several of the unions of retired workers, and the Union of Postal Workers, all rejected the report as did all political parties to the left of PASOK, including the KKE and DIKKI (Democratic and Social Movement/ΔΗΚΚI: Δημοκρατικό Κοινωνικό Κίνημα) (*Athinaiki,* 14 October 1997; *Avgi*, 14 October 1997). While ND refrained from official reactions, DAKE (Democratic Independent Workers' Movement /ΔAKE: Δημοκρατική Ανεξάρτητη Κίνηση Εργαζομένων), its trade union affiliate, openly rejected the report (*Eleftheros Typos*, 14 October 1997). The reactions by the government-appointed managers of pension funds were muted or non-committal: the Governor of IKA declared that 'the government is responsible to judge and decide', while the governor of TEVE (Greek Social Security Fund for Craftsmen and Small Traders/TEBE: Ταμείο Επαγγελματιών και Βιοτεχνών Ελλάδας) said that the report touches the problem areas that have been long demonstrated and that reform should take place before 2005 (*Apogevmatini,* 14 October 1997). Ironically, the findings of the report were openly supported only by a former ND Minister George Souflias and the League of Greek Industries – SEV – (though both expressed reservations over certain aspects) (*Avgi*, 16 October 1997).

Within the government, on the day of the publication of the report, Miltiadis Papaioannou, Minister of Labour and Social Security initially declared his support for its findings; however, the next day (14 October 1997) Nikos Farmakis, deputy Minister for Health (whose brief included social security) declared that 'any report or proposal is not binding for the government'; the same day the government spokesman, Dimitris Reppas, said that 'the government does not adopt the Spraos report, but considers it a contribution to the processes of the social dialogue' (*I Niki,*

14 October 1997; *Avriani*, 14 October 1997). In short, despite the fact that both friends and foes acknowledged that its conclusions varied little from what was already known (from previous IMF and OECD studies) about the Greek pension system, the report was savaged by the press which ascribed to it (and to the government) a number of ulterior motives and creeping suggestions for radical reform. Once this happened and once the scale of the reaction became clear, the attitude adopted by the government was no surprise: the government distanced itself from the findings of the hybrid consultant it had itself appointed; it also postponed reform until after the next election. In the meantime, a 'mini pension' law, dealing with essentially procedural aspects of the pension system, was passed in 1998.

4.6   The road to hell: Giannitsis's 2001 pension reform initiative

PASOK's third consecutive victory in the April 2000 election created new opportunities for the reform of the Greek pension system. Despite the very small margin of its victory in the polls, PASOK enjoyed a comfortable majority in parliament. Simitis's own position was also strengthened as a result of PASOK's election victory. Dominant in his own party and with high approval rates across the electorate, the PM pledged that during his second term in office he would extend and complete his modernization agenda. Labour market regulation and pension reform stood at the top of this agenda. To oversee the process of reform in these two policy areas, Simitis appointed one of his closest associates and a personal friend to the Ministry of Labour, Tasos Giannitsis.

Soon after his appointment in the new government, Giannitsis sought to reassure the social partners that the process of pension reform would be consensus driven and that the government would not seek to surprise anyone (*in.gr*, 11 May 2000). A few days later, the Minister commissioned (to the British government-run firm Government Actuaries) an actuarial study on the Greek pension and its financial prospects for the next 30 years. For the government, the study served a twofold purpose. The first was one of substance. The report was the first attempt to analyse (at this depth) the provisions of the hugely fragmented Greek pension system and make medium- and long-term projections about its financial viability. In addition, the report served as a strategic recourse for the government. To begin with, the time needed for the preparation of the report (initially thought to be completed by January 2001) (*in.gr*, 25 November 2000) offered the government enough breathing space to prepare its strategy and test the intentions of the social partners. Most importantly – unlike the Spraos report where number crunching was deliberately kept to a minimum – the new report was meant to offer 'irrefutable' hard evidence about the state of the Greek pension system and, thus, provide a 'technocratic shield' to the government's reform proposals. It was this 'technocratic shield' that the government hoped to utilize during the social dialogue (due to begin in Spring 2001) before the new pension law went through parliament in Summer 2001.

Despite the fact that the social dialogue was yet to begin, the period between May 2000 and March 2001 saw a great deal of interest, speculation, and alleged revelations over the pending reform of the Greek pension system. During this period, the main protagonists of the process were engaged in a constant battle to win public support and gain the initiative. While the government's proposals to the social partners had not yet been officially unveiled, a constant string of leaks to the press revealed the main thrust of the government's plans. While the precise content of these proposals remained vague and varied depending on the source of the leak,[15] the government appeared determined to tackle both the fragmentation of the Greek pension system and revisit some key issues affecting pension entitlement such as the retirement age, the length of social security contributions, and the salary/pension replacement ratios.

With regard to the organizational shake-up of the pension system, the government was reported to favour a three-pillar structure (*Ta Nea*, 27 December 2001; *To Vima*, 26 November 2000 and 11 March 2001):

- A first pillar of compulsory 'primary' pension financed by employers, employees, and the state (although the extent of the latter's role in this scheme remained unclear). The existing multi-fragmentation of primary pension funds (estimated to be over 100) was to be replaced by the creation of a small (as low as four)[16] number of 'super-funds'.
- A second pillar of compulsory 'auxiliary' and 'supplementary' pensions organized along occupational lines and financed by employees and employers alone.
- A third pillar of optional and individually funded pension schemes provided by private pension funds and supported by the government through tax breaks.

In addition, newspaper reports made reference to the government's intentions to implement a series a measures, including (*Ta Nea*, 27 December 2000)

- the universal application of the retirement age of 65 for both men and women to all employees in the public and private sectors (along the lines of the 2084/92 law applicable to those employed after 1993)
- the capping of replacement rates (of both primary and auxiliary pension) to 80% of the exit salary
- the calculation of the exit salary on the basis of the average earnings during the last five years of employment (instead of the last salary as was the practice for public sector pensions)
- the redefinition of the term 'arduous and unhealthy occupations' (applicable to more than 40% of the private sector employees) which allowed the bringing forward of retirement by five years
- the encouragement of participation in the labour market even after the retirement age and the discouragement, across the board, of early retirement[17]
- the introduction of a means-tested 'national' or 'basic' pension (irrespective of contributions) which would be funded by the state through general taxation.

Much of the speculation over the government's intentions in the forthcoming social dialogue revolved around the 'implementation timetable' and 'time depth' of the suggested reform. Since its re-election in April 2000, the PASOK government reassured the public that the forthcoming reform would not affect 'mature pension rights' (i.e. those employees close to retirement) and sought to quantify the term as meaning three-four years (*Ta Nea*, 27 December 2000). Subsequently, however, the government's position appeared to have softened, and by late March 2001 leaks to the press suggested that the government was ready to accept a ten-year definition of the term (*Kathimerini*, 20 March 2001; *Eleftherotipia*, 1 April 2001). The government's suggested time frame made it clear that the main group likely to be affected by the reform would be that which entered the labour market between the early 1980s and 1993,[18] which would also form the main body of pensioners over the next decade. This target group of over one million employees was highly significant for PASOK's electoral fortunes. Many of these people had benefited greatly from extensive clientelistic channels in the 1980s and had secured employment either in the central administration or the 'wider' public sector (public utilities, nationalized companies, and state-controlled banks) where pension entitlement was far more generous than the private sector. Giannitsis's plans threatened to disturb this status quo. Former patrons were now turning against their clientele. The battle over PASOK's soul was about to begin.

During the winter months of 2000 both private (GSEE) and public (ADEDY) sector unions mounted a remarkably coordinated attack on the government's alleged reform plans. Despite the potential for disagreements (fuelled by the highly uneven pension provision for private and public sector employees), both GSEE and ADEDY adopted a similarly rejectionist position towards the government. In particular, GSEE's decision to support the powerful banking sector union (OTOE: Greek Federation of Banking Unions / OTOE: Ομοσπονδία Τραπεζοϋπαλληλικών Οργανώσεων Ελλάδας) in its militant opposition against the government's plans to integrate all banking sector pension funds into IKA was a crucial factor in upholding the unions' united front. Much of the union opposition to the government's plans was communicated by the GSEE's scientific advisory body, the Institute of Labour (INE/INE: Ινστιτούτο Εργασίας) and its energetic head, Professor Savvas Robolis. In February 2001, in an attempt to pre-empt the findings of the actuarial study commissioned by the government, INE/GSEE published its own proposals for the future of the Greek pension system. In its assessment, INE/GSEE argued that the reduction of salary/pension replacement ratios or/and increases in contributions and retirement ages would have little effect in alleviating the bleak financial position of most pension funds. Instead, the report argued, attention should be paid to the reduction of unemployment rates, the better management of the funds' reserves, and, above all, the honouring of the government's financial commitments to the pension funds (*To Vima*, 18 February 2001).

Indeed, the issue of the so-called tripartite financing of the pension system was elevated to a top priority by GSEE's President Christos Polyzogopoulos. The principle of tripartite financing (2/9 from the employees' contributions, 4/9 from employers' contributions, and 3/9 form state funds) was enshrined into 2084/92 law for all those who entered the labour market after 1993. However, the level of the state's contribution to the pension of older employees (i.e. those who entered the labour market before 1993) was never codified in law. Instead the state intervened on an ad hoc basis to finance the huge deficits of all major pension funds (many of which were technically bankrupt), thus making possible the disbursement of pensions to those who were entitled to them. For the unions, this rather 'messy' arrangement was always a source of irritation, leaving them vulnerable to what they regarded as constant government interference and potential blackmail. On their part successive governments (including Simitis's) insisted that the state's financing of the pension system would only be set in stone as part of an overall reform package which would tackle the country's 'pension crisis' for the long run.

In addition to the bitter disagreements over 'tripartite financing', the unions also defended the principle of retirement after 35 years of employment (irrespective of age) and resisted any move for the reduction of salary/pension replacement ratios. GSEE's President also dismissed the idea of involving private insurance schemes in the second pillar of the pension system as '. . . coming from another planet' (*Imerisia*, 19 February 2001; *Kathimerini*, 21 February 2001). Similar attacks on the government's plans were reiterated by all (party-affiliated) fractions of GSEE during the proceedings of GSEE's tirtieth congress (*in.gr*, 15 March 2001). Astonishingly, GSEE's positions very much paralleled those of the League of Greek Industries (SEV). In a press conference soon after the publication of INE/GSEE's proposals on pension reform, the President of SEV, Lefteris Antonakopoulos, stated his support for GSEE's proposals on the triparty funding of the system and on the need for more effective measures to combat unemployment, while he reserved SEV's right to respond to GSEE's proposals on the management of the pension funds' reserves (*in.gr*, 22 February 2001).

The government's reported plans received a hostile reception from all opposition parties, albeit with different degrees of ferocity. On the left, KKE's Secretary General Aleka Papariga expressed her party's dismay at what she called the 'forthcoming [pension] storm' and called on the unions not to engage in any discussion with the government and the employers (*in.gr*, 28 February 2001). The President of the leftist Synaspismos (SYN: Coalition of the Left, Movements and Ecology/ΣΥΝ: Συνασπισμός της Αριστεράς, των Κινημάτων και της Οικολογίας), Nikos Konstantopoulos, described the existing pension arrangements as 'non-negotiable' and urged the government to support the pension funds' growing deficits through taxation (*in.gr*, 28 February 2001). On the right, the ND, which during its time in office in the early 1990s initiated two pension reforms, refrained from announcing its position on the future of the Greek pension system prior to the official launch of the social dialogue on this issue. However, the government's plans were criticized by a number of prominent figures of the party, including former Minister of Social Security Dimitris Sioufas who warned that the new law would '. . . be detrimental to the well-being of employees and pensioners' (*Kathimerini*, 12 February 2001).[19] Even the President of the Hellenic Republic, Constantinos Stefanopoulos, took the unusual step (given the non-party political nature of his office) of intervening to the debate on pension reform. Speaking to the GSEE's thirtieth congress, the President urged the government not to raise NI contributions and retirement ages and to find 'new resources' for the support of the pension system (*Kathimerini*, 16 March 2001).

Much of the opposition to the government's reform initiative, however, came from within the governing Socialist party (PASOK). Soon after Simitis's re-election in the April 2000 election, PASOK's 'traditional' left-wing, led by Akis Tsochatzopoulos, demanded that the government should strengthen its social profile by engaging in large-scale redistributive policies in order to 'return the cost of convergence with the EMU criteria back to the working classes' (*To Vima*, 5 November 2000). At the forefront of the traditionalists' demands stood the introduction of a 'minimum income guarantee' for combating poverty as well as 'soft' labour market and pension reforms. On the other side of the fence, the reform-minded Minister of Labour, Tasos Giannitsis, had found himself at the centre of much controversy at the end of 2000 over his handling of the labour market reform (see chapter 5) which had stained his relationship with the powerful Minister of Economy, Giannos Papandoniou and the formidable Minister of Culture, Theodoros Pagalos, who was eventually dismissed from the government in November 2000.[20] Pagalos's dismissal was meant to provide a powerful message that Prime Minister Simitis was determined to back Giannitsis and his reform agenda. Yet, despite the PM's support, the Minister of Labour was fast running out of friends in his own party.

Giannitsis's precarious position became apparent on 19 April 2001 when he announced the government's official position with regard to pension reform. These included

- the introduction of a uniform retirement age of 65 applicable to all employees (implemented gradually within a transitional period of ten years)
- the capping of replacement ratio for primary pension to 60% of the exit salary (implemented gradually within a transitional period of ten years)
- full pension entitlements after 40 years of employment irrespective of age
- the calculation of the exit salary on the basis of the average earnings during the last 15 years of employment (employees could choose the 'best ten years' during that period)
- the abolition of all 'pension benefits' for working mothers with children (allowing them to retire early on a full pension). Instead the state would subsidize pension contributions for two years for each working mother with a child under the age of 18

- the re-evaluation of the occupations termed 'arduous and unhealthy' (where retirement could be brought forward by five years)
- the restructuring of the pension system creation along eight funds: (a) salaried private sector employees (IKA), (b) public sector employees, (c) self-employed (OAEE: Social Security Organization for the Self Employed / OAEE: Οργανισμός Ασφάλισης Ελεύθερων Επαγγελματιών), (d) farmers (OGA), (e) employees in the banking sector, (f) employees in state-controlled companies, (g) professionals (doctors, lawyers, engineers, etc), and (h) journalists
- the administrative incorporation of all auxiliary pension funds into the eight primary pension funds that from then on would be responsible for the disbursement of auxiliary pensions
- a substantial, but means-tested, increase in the minimum pension available to those with a minimum of 15-year service (4500 days of work)
- the pension entitlements of those employees due to retire before 21 December 2007 would remain unaffected
- the extension of 'tripartite financing' to the entire pension system, under the following rules: (a) for the primary pension of salaried employees (employee 6.67%, employer 13.3%, state 10%), (b) for the auxiliary pension of salaried employees (employee 3%, employer 3%), (c) for the primary pension of the self-employed (employee 20%, state 10%), and (d) for the auxiliary pension of the self-employed (employee 6%) (*Ta Nea*, 20 April 2001; *Kathimerini*, 20 April 2001; *Eleftherotypia*, 20 April 2001; *in.gr*, 19 April 2001).

The range and intensity of the Giannitsis's proposals revealed his ambitious agenda for a radical shake-up of the Greek pension system. Against intense media pressure, the rather shy Minister of Labour sought to reassure the public that the government had opted for 'modest' reforms (*in.gr*, 19 April 2001). In his eyes, the decision not to increase contributions and guarantee all mature pension rights (i.e. for five years) as well as the government assurances over tripartite financing and the ten-year time frame for the full implementation of his proposals revealed the government's good will in tackling the country's explosive pension problem. But, how explosive was the problem? In an effort to shield the government from its critics, the Minister of Labour made public – on the very same day of his pension reform announcements – the actuarial study prepared on behalf of the government by the British. Indeed, the report made uncomfortable reading. Unless new sources of financing were to become available (either through increased contributions or through government financing) the Greek pension system would face total collapse within 15 years (*in.gr*, 20 April 2001). Against this background Giannitsis insisted that the government had no option but to act and urged union leaders and opposition parties to 'show responsibility' on the forthcoming dialogue (*in.gr*, 19 April 2001).

Giannitsis's hopes for a sober dialogue on this issue, however, were grossly misplaced. Almost immediately after the announcement of his proposals, GSEE and ADEDY issued a joint statement expressing their total rejection of the government's plans and called a general strike for 26 April. Following days of negative reporting in the media, a widespread perception was created that the government was about to privatize aspects of the Greek pension system and default on the commitments made by the Greek state to millions of employees. Despite subsequent attempts by the Minister of Labour to revisit some of his original proposals (i.e. over women's pensions and retirement ages), the government's public image was seriously wounded. For the opposition parties this was the time to make political capital. With both KKE and Synaspismos militantly opposed to Giannitsis's plans, the position of ND became critical for the government's reform agenda. However, Costas Karamanlis was in no mood to compromise his hard-earned centrist profile and throw the government a lifeline. In his meeting with GSEE President on 24 April, the leader of ND made it clear that he would support the unions in their opposition to the government's proposed pension reform (*in.gr*, 23 April 2001). Greece's former neoliberals were now attacking a PASOK-led government from the left!

The worst was yet to come, however. Two days before the day of general strike announced by GSEE and ADEDY, 63 members of PASOK's Central Committee wrote to the Prime Minister and demanded that the government withdraw its proposals on pension reform. The letter made reference to the 'vacuum between PASOK and its social base' and a widespread 'climate of anxiety and insecurity amongst the people' (*in.gr*, 25 April 2001). With the raw within PASOK growing out of control, the party's Secretary General, Costas Skandalidis, convened an extraordinary meeting of PASOK's parliamentary group on labour affairs and the party's trade unionists in order to agree to a common position on the government's proposals. After a highly charged meeting, the Minister of Labour was forced to announce that he would freeze his proposals and invite new contributions on the future of the Greek pension system with a view to new legislation been passed through Parliament before the end of 2001 (*Ta Nea*, 25 March 2001). Giannitis's u-turn, however, was not enough to satisfy his opponents. During the course of the following month, the government and the unions remained at loggerheads over the precise nature of the Greece's pension problem. GSEE, in particular, refused to accept the validity of the British actuarial study insisting that its own report (prepared by the Institute of Labour – INE) painted a more accurate picture of the problem. Without agreement on the basics, the unions refused to engage in any meaningful discussion over possible remedies and called for another general strike in May.

Having been cornered by the unions and the opposition within his own party, the beleaguered Minister of Labour was forced to concede, on 21 May 2001, that the government would engage in a dialogue with the social partners 'without preconditions' and with ample time to resolve the differences between the British actuarial study and the one produced by INE (*in.gr*, 21 May 2001). In truth his reform initiative was dead and buried. The British report was commissioned as a means of producing irrefutable evidence upon which the government's reform initiative would follow. Along the way, however, the report was transformed from a strategic resource in the hands of the Minister of Labour to the apple of discord between the unions and the government. Giannitsis himself acknowledged that the government had mishandled the issue of pension reform, but warned that the problem should not be swept under the carpet. Yet Giannitsis's credibility was so undermined in the aftermath of the 2001 'pension fiasco' that it was impossible for him to oversee a fresh government initiative on this front. This task fell on his successor to the Ministry of Labour, the softly spoken Dimitris Reppas.

4.7   Softly does it: The 2002 pension reform

Dimitris Reppas arrived in his new post in the aftermath of a major government reshuffle engineered by Prime Minister Simitis in October 2001 in order to reverse PASOK's slide in the opinion polls (attributed to a large extent to the 'pension fiasco' of 2001). Reppas's deputies in the Ministry of Labour, Lefteris Tziolas and Rovertos Spyropoulos, were also new to the job. The latter, a veteran trade unionist with a significant influence over PASOK's labour policies throughout the 1990s, was allocated the sensitive portfolio of social security. In the rest of the Cabinet important changes had also taken place, the most important of which was the departure of Giannos Papandoniou from the Ministry of National Economy and Finance after eight years as the 'Tsar' of the Greek economy. Papandoniou's replacement, Nikos Christodoulakis, was a low-key technocrat with a less abrasive style. Reppas too had developed a reputation as a consensual, yet smooth, operator. The chemistry between the two Ministers seemed better than that of their predecessors, Papandoniou and Giannitsis, whose dysfunctional relationship had cost dearly to the government's strategy on pensions a few months earlier. With new faces at the top jobs, the government was now seeking new ideas on how to tackle the Greek pension puzzle.

The new Minister of Labour moved quickly to bring back pension reform to the government's agenda, but dissociated himself from the strategy of his predecessor. Promising 'new money' for the pension system and no changes to pension entitlements for the following five years, Reppas went out of his way to reassure the social partners that the government, this time, was committed to a consensual pursuit of its pension reform agenda. Consultation was now the name of the game. 'The government would do nothing to trivialise or undermine . . . the moral demand of citizens for a solution to this problem', the Minister insisted (*Ta Nea*, 19 November 2001). To this end Reppas promised a new round of social dialogue early in 2002 with a view to new legislation been passed through Parliament by June of the same year.

In the run up to the opening of the social dialogue the Minister of Labour reiterated the government's commitment for 'realistic' reforms (*in.gr*, 30 November 2001), but kept the press at an arms' length in order to avoid the damaging speculation that had undermined Giannitsis's earlier reform initiative. Reppas had also to tread carefully with regard to his party's internal divisions. In January 2002, 45 'traditionalist' members of PASOK's parliamentary group (organized by Simitis's former 'lieutenant' and 'born again socialist' Theodoros Tsoukatos) made a big pitch to highjack the agenda for reform. In an open letter to Reppas and Christodoulakis they called for a swift resolution to the pension problem by (a) extending tripartite financing to all primary pensions, (b) allowing auxiliary pensions to become fully funded (thus reducing state control over the management of their assets), and (c) introducing new taxes in order to finance a range of pension benefits for working mothers and long-term unemployed (*in.gr*, 23 January 2002). The letter had the potential to destabilize PASOK as it challenged the authority of the two Ministers (and that of Prime Minister Simitis) and run against the government's commitment not to raise social security contributions (or any other taxes) in order to finance the deficits of the pension system. Reppas dealt with the unfolding crisis with considerable political skill. In a coded rebuke to the 'forty-five' he said that 'suggestions and opinions are useful to the extent that they contribute to the enhancement of understanding and the consolidation of a climate of trust [otherwise] . . . they can be damaging' (*in.gr*, 23 January 2002).

In the meantime the Minister of Labour continued to craft the government's proposals to the forthcoming social dialogue which included

- the gradual introduction of a uniform retirement age of 65 (for both men and women) in all pension funds of the private and public sectors. The issue of the length of service prior to retirement was left open for discussion
- the capping of the replacement ratio for primary and auxiliary pension to under 100% of the exit salary
- the acknowledgement that the tripartite financing of the pension system ought to be extended. However, the Ministry of Labour made no concrete commitment in this regard.
- the creation of a legal framework for separating the operations of primary and auxiliary funds with the latter gradually transformed into 'fully funded' systems (as opposed to PAYG) with significant autonomy from the state
- the restructuring of the pension system creation along six funds: (a) salaried private sector employees (IKA) which would also include those employed in the banking sector and state-controlled enterprises, (b) public sector employees, (c) self-employed (OAEE), (d) farmers (OGA), (e) professionals (doctors, lawyers, engineers, etc.), and (f) journalists (*Eleftherotypia*, 14 January 2002; *To Ethnos*, 30 January 2002).

To strengthen the government's hand in its dealing with the social partners, Reppas also asked Government Actuaries, the British-run firm whose report was a key point of friction during Giannitsis's reform initiative, to prepare 15 projections of the deficit of the Greek pension system based on different reform scenarios. This, according to the Minister of Labour, would help the social dialogue to focus on concrete cost-benefit calculations, rather than political expediency (*Imerisia*, 15 February 2002).

At this early stage of the process, the government's agenda seemed modest by comparison to the ambition and intensity of Giannitsis's earlier proposals. Reppas had opted for a sketchy outline of intentions rather than detail. By and large his proposals focused less on cost, prioritizing instead the structural/administrative weaknesses of the system. To this end, ambitious targets were set for the creation of six megafunds and for greater transparency and autonomy for auxiliary funds. The government's earlier alarmist rhetoric over the financial viability of the system (which shaped Giannitsis's agenda) was now all but forgotten.

The government's conciliatory (and modest) reform agenda paid off when, in March 2002, the Minister of Labour issued his official invitation to the social partners for a new round of consultation on reforming the Greek pension system. Unlike its rejectionist stance towards Giannitsis the year before, GSEE now seemed prepared to engage with the government's agenda as its President, Christos Polyzogopoulos, declared that the unions '. . . have no reason to be scared of the dialogue' (*in.gr*, 4 March 2002). The leader of ADEDY (the union of public sector employees), Spyros Papaspyros, also issued a cautious welcome to the process, but warned the government that he and his union would not accept any increase of the retirement age (which stood at 55 for public sector employees). Employers' organizations too welcomed the government's new reform initiative (*in.gr*, 5 March 2002).

In the weeks that followed the Minister of Labour engaged in a series of intense negotiations with the unions over three broad sets of issues: (a) the key determinants of pension entitlements (such as retirement ages, length of service, replacement ratios, special exemptions, etc.), (b) the organizational reform of the pension funds, and (c) the financing of the pension system.

With regard to the first set of issues, the overall financial impact of the agreed reform was modest. Despite its many exemptions,[21] the new system introduced a number of common rules regulating (full) pension entitlements for all major pension funds of the private and public sectors. These included

- the establishment of a common retirement age of 65 for a full pension;
- a full pension after 37 years of service irrespective of age;
- a ceiling on the replacement ratio of primary and auxiliary pensions which, combined, should not exceed 90% (70% primary, 20% auxiliary) of the exit salary;
- the granting of up to 4.5 years (one year for the first child, 1.5 years for the second, and two years for the third) of pensionable service for women with children who enter the labour market after 1 January 2003;
- the re-examination, by the end of 2004, of the list of 'arduous' and 'unhealthy occupations' where employees could bring forward their retirement (on a full pension) by five years (*To Vima*, 9 June 2002).

The new rules affected pre-existing pension rights in different ways. For example, for employees in the private sector (eligible for a pension from IKA) who entered the labour market before 1993, the new reform package made almost no change with regard to retirement ages, years of service, and replacement ratios. The only new measure for this category of employees was the provision for a full pension after 37 years of service irrespective of age. For private sector employees who entered the labour marker after 1993 there were significant gains: (a) the right to a full pension after 37 years of service irrespective of age (no such provision existed in the 1993 law), (b) an increase of the replacement ratio for primary pensions from 60% to 70%, (c) the granting of up to 4.5 pensionable years of service to women with children, and (d) a significant increase in the level of the minimum pension granted at 65 (for both men and women) after 15 years of service (4500 days).[22]

Reppas's reform hit employees in the public sector, state-controlled companies, and the banking sector harder. Here the new package mostly 'penalized' employees who entered the labour market between 1982 and 1993 in there ways: (a) an increase of two years of service (from 35 to 37) before qualification for a full pension, irrespective of age. However, the possibility remained for a reduced pension for both men and women at 58 after 30 years of service (the previous regime was 60 years for men), (b) a gradual (over nine years starting from 2008) reduction of the replacement ratio for primary pensions from 80% to 70%, and (c) the calculation (from 2007) of the exit salary on the basis of the average earning of the past five years of employment (as opposed to the last salary under the previous regime).[23] However, in a significant concession to those who entered the labour market after 1993, the replacement ratio of the primary pension was raised from 60% to 70%.

With regard to the organizational restructuring of the pension system, the success of the Reppas reform was considerable. The Law 3029/2002 contributed to the significant 'tidying-up' of the system with provisions for

- the compulsory incorporation, by 1 January 2008, of all primary pension funds of salaried employees into IKA, which would be renamed Joint Pension Fund for the Salaried (Ενιαίο Ταμείο Ασφάλισης Μισθωτών, IKA-ETAM);[24]
- the creation of a Joint Fund of Auxiliary Pensions for the Salaried (Ενιαίο Ταμείο Επικουρικής Ασφάλισης Μισθωτών), which incorporate (initially voluntarily, later on a compulsory basis) the myriad of funds which provided auxiliary pensions to different groups of salaried employees. The two measures above were considered a major step in dealing with the fragmentation of the Greek pension system;

- the creation of a National Actuarial Authority (Εθνική Αναλογιστική Αρχή), operating as an independent administrative authority, with the responsibility of regulating the operation of the pension funds and conducting regular studies regarding their financial position;
- the organizational and functional separation of the primary and auxiliary funds, allowing for a more transparent evaluation of their management and finances;
- the legal framework for the creation of 'fully funded' auxiliary funds, along occupational lines (with contributions from employees and employers), operating independently from the state and placed under the regulatory oversight of the National Actuarial Authority (*To Vima*, 9 June 2002).

The most difficult and protracted negotiations between the unions and the government focused on the issue of the tripartite financing of the pension system. One of the GSEE's main demands during both Giannitsis's and Reppas's reform initiatives was that the government should extend its commitment to finance 3/9 of pension expenditure for all employees (and not only for those who entered the labour market after 1993). The government, however, was reluctant to accept this, fearing that the costs involved could derail macroeconomic stability and throw into disarray its EMU commitment to lower its budget deficit. Reppas himself had been ambiguous over the amount of new resources that he was prepared to commit to the system, linking this issue with the overall package of reform under negotiation with social partners. Faced with very stiff opposition from GSEE, the government was eventually pressured to pay handsomely for GSEE's consent on the other aspects of the proposed reform.

The final agreement on financing made staggering reading. It included

- the writing off of €5 billion of IKA's debts to the Greek state
- the granting of €3.8 billion to IKA from the budget over a two-year period starting in 2002
- the settling of €1.5 billion of IKA's debts to other welfare organizations within five years
- an agreement that the Greek government would channel 1% of GDP to IKA's finances over the next 30 years. Also an additional clause was introduced whereby the government would guarantee (with additional funding if necessary) that IKA's finances will always be in surplus for the same period.

- an understanding that the government would provide further funding to IKA if its finances were to be adversely affected by the incorporation of debt-ridden pension funds into its structures as foreseen by the new reform package (*in.gr*, 23 May 2002).

The agreement between the government and GSEE on all three aspects of the reform package (pension entitlements, organization restructuring, and financing) was announced on 30 June 2002, allowing the government to submit the pension reform bill to Parliament the following week. The announcement of the agreement unleashed much acrimony within the union movement. GSEE's President, Christos Polyzogopoulos, was accused by rival fractions within GSEE (controlled by ND, Synaspismos, and KKE) of cosying up to government and betraying his comrades. ADEDY too opposed the reform and, together with GSEE's opposition fractions, called for a general strike on 18 June (*in.gr*, 31 May 2002 & 6 June 2002). The unions of the banking sector (OTOE) and those of the state-controlled companies also opposed the reform and called for industrial action (*in.gr*, 14 June 2002). Earlier Polyzogopoulos has launched a scathing attack to his critics arguing that half of the two million employees in the private sector would secure better retirement conditions under the proposed package and that only 15,000–20,000 employees in the state-controlled companies and the banking sector would be worse off (*in.gr*, 4 April 2006).

For their part the employers associations (SEV and ESEE) kept a relatively low profile through the social dialogue, confining themselves to general declarations about the need for an 'economically viable and socially just pension system . . . as a precondition for economic and social progress' (*in.gr*, 5 March 2002). In the aftermath of GSEE's deal with the government in June, the President of SEV, Odysseas Kyriakopoulos, declared the agreement as 'a major step forward', although at a later stage expressed reservations about the overall cost of the reform package causing a stinging rebuke by the President of GSEE who accused SEV of lacking a credible alternative proposal (*in.gr*, 23 May 2002; 24 May 2002; and 29 May 2002).

In the party-political arena Reppas's reform attracted criticism from all sides of the political spectrum. During the discussion of the pension reform bill in Parliament, all parties on the left (Synaspismos and KKE) voted against the government, condemning the bill as a neoliberal monstrosity which was the result of '. . . pre-determined government policies and not that of social dialogue' (*in.gr*, 13 June 2006). On the right, the main thrust of criticism focused on the projected financial

cost of Reppas's reform and on the dangers attached to the incorporation of nearly bankrupt pension funds into IKA. The harshest criticisms
came from the usual suspects: former Prime Minister Constantinos
Mitsotakis and former Minister of National Economy Stefanos Manos
(by now an independent MP), who argued that the new law would further exacerbate the actuarial deficit of the Greek pension system which
stood at 300% of GDP – the worst such record in Europe (*in.gr*, 13 June
2002).

The official response of ND was also critical, but somewhat more
restrained. Its key political strategist, George Souflias (a former Minister
of National Economy), accused the government of swiping the pension
problem under the carpet, while the Secretary of the Central Committee
of the party, Vaggelis Meimarakis, argued that the reform did not secure
the viability of the pension system but instead undermined its future
(*in.gr*, 10 June 2002). During the discussion of the pension bill in
Parliament, ND pointed to the fact that the Minister of Labour had
refused to disclose the study of Government Actuaries (that Reppas himself had commissioned at the beginning of the social dialogue) which
would give an objective assessment of the true cost of his reform.
Similar criticisms were directed to the Minister of National Economy,
Nikos Christodoulakis, who projected the pension deficit over the next
30 years somewhere between 3.5%–7% of the GDP, an estimate that was
well below the 11.1% that Tasos Giannitsis had acknowledged the year
before. Yet for all its criticism of the government's timidity, the leader of
ND, Costas Karamanlis, was careful not to endanger his party's carefully
crafted move to centre politics. When challenged by PM Simitis in
Parliament, Karamanlis refused to commit that his party would repeal
Reppas's law or that it would pursue a new round of pension reform if
elected in office (*in.gr*, 18 June 2002).

The new pension reform Law (3029/2002) was adopted by Parliament
on 20 June 2002. Reppas had managed to deliver a reform package that
introduced some important improvements to the organizational structures of the pension system and to introduce some elements of consistency in pension entitlements. More importantly he had done so by
engaging in a reasonably consensual social dialogue with the unions
(particularly GSEE). This stood in sharp contrast with the Giannitsis's
ambitious, but ultimately doomed, reform initiative the year before. Yet
Reppas's reform had come at a very high cost and, critics argued, had
done little to alleviate the long-term financial sustainability of the Greek
pension system. Some of the most glaring discrepancies of pension entitlement remained (e.g. 'pre-' and 'post'-1993 employees), whereas other

'black holes' of the system (e.g. disability benefits) were untouched. If this was a reform at all, it was certainly its first instalment, not its endpoint. Within the next 18 months both Dimitris Reppas and his boss, Costas Simitis, would be out of their jobs.

4.8 Let's wait for a while: ND at the helm (2004–7)

The arrival of ND in power following its victory in the March 2004 election brought a considerable slowdown in the urgency to pursue pension reform. The new Prime Minister, Costas Karamanlis, was sensitive to the fate of the last ND Premier, Costas Mitsotakis (1990–3) who, during his brief term in office, had attempted to open simultaneously many reform agendas with ultimately very little success. Karamanlis had also witnessed his immediate predecessor, Costas Simitis, paying a considerable political cost (with dubious results) for his attempts to restructure the Greek pension system. Thus, the issue of pensions was put on the backburner, with a conspicuous absence from ND's election manifesto of a commitment to legislate on this matter during the course of the next Parliament.

Under these circumstances the task of the new Minister of Labour, Panos Panagiotiopulos, and his successors, Savvas Tsitouridis (February 2006–April 2007) and Vasilis Magginas (April 2007–September 2007),[25] was largely confined to the full implementation of Reppas's pension law. This was by no means a politically neutral exercise. Law 3029/2002 had foreseen the incorporation of all primary pension funds for the salaried into IKA-ETAM (Single Social Security Fund for the Salaried / ETAM: Ενιαίο Ταμείο Ασφάλισης Μισθωτών) by 2008. This would have to involve delicate negotiations with the unions of the banking sector and state-controlled companies who guarded the independence of their pension funds (and the privileges they provided) jealously. It would also have to involve the major restructuring of many auxiliary pension funds and their incorporation into ETEAM (Single Auxiliary Social Security Fund for the Salaried / ETEAM: Ενιαίο Ταμείο Επικουρικής Ασφάλισης Μισθωτών) where future entitlements were considerably lower. Reppas's law also provided for the re-examination of the list of 'arduous and unhealthy occupations' by the end of 2004, a potentially explosive issue which could bring the government in conflict with some of the most militant, blue-collar unions in the country.

The government got a taste of the problems involved with the full implementation of Law 3029/2002 when, during the course of 2005–6, it pursued the incorporation of the primary and auxiliary pension funds of the banking sector into IKA-ETAM and ETEAM respectively (*in.gr*, 17 June 2005; 16 December 2005; 29 March 2006). The move was largely dictated by the implementation of new international accounting standards which required banks to incorporate the liabilities of their pension funds into their balance sheets. This development would have created serious knock-on effects on the appeal to international investors of many state-controlled (but also private) Greek banks whose pension funds were heavily indebted. It would have also most certainly derailed the process of privatization of the Emboriki Bank which was a top priority for the government. The 'compulsory' incorporation of the banking pension funds into IKA-ETAM (and ETEAM), reportedly at a cost of €0.5 billion per year to IKA's finances (*in.gr*, 28 June 2005), caused a storm in the government's relations with OTOE (the banking sector union). The latter responded with a series of strikes and legal challenges that disrupted the government's agenda for months (*Imerisia*, 16 December 2005). The transfer process was thrown into further disarray by administrative weaknesses within IKA-ETAM to cope with the 18,000 new entrants into the system as well as by suggestions that the government's solution to the 'pension problem of the banking sector' could be challenged by the European Commission as illegal state aid to Greek banks.

In the aftermath of the confrontation with the unions over banking sector pensions, the government declared its intention to launch a new round of social dialogue over the long-term future of the Greek pension system. To this end, in June 2006, the Minister of National Economy, George Alogoskoufis, and the Minister of Labour, Savvas Tsitouridis, issued a 'road map' for the government's pension strategy until the end of its term in office that included, among others,

- the continuing implementation of Law 3029/2002
- the better management of the assets of pension funds
- setting up of a committee to re-examine the list of 'arduous and unhealthy occupations' (in line with Reppas's Law)
- the improvement of IKA administrative structures (*in.gr*, 14 June 2006).

The announcement of the road map as such provided few fresh ideas. The initiative to launch a new round of social dialogue, however, said to be in preparation of a new round of pension reform in the next parliament (2008–12), served a twinfold purpose: on the one hand, it allowed plenty of time for the new government and the social partners to build trust and agree on the main parameters of the 'pension problem' and its possible solutions and, on the other, it provided the government with considerable breathing space in order to consider its next steps on this issue.

To support the process of public consultation, a new committee of 'wise men' was established in August 2006 headed by the vastly experienced Nikos Analytis, a former long-serving SEV official and the current President of the Economic and Social Committee (OKE). The committee's task was to produce, within a year, a 'technical' report on the future prospects of the system. Its membership was open to a wide range of policy experts and representatives of the social partners as a gesture for its inclusive character. Yet both GSEE and ADEDY refused to send representatives accusing the government of lacking a clear reform agenda. Unions were further alienated by the decision of the Minister of National Economy, with the agreement of the committee of 'wise men', to 'outsource' the parts of their anticipated report to international consultants (*in.gr*, 6 October 2006). This decision was a clear indication that the government had little faith on existing actuarial studies prepared by GSEE's Institute of Labour or, indeed, on the ability of the newly established National Actuarial Authority to prepare one. Trust between the government and the social partners received another major blow following the controversy (the so-called structured bond scandal) regarding the mismanagement of pension reserves by government-appointed pension fund managers, an issue that dominated the news agenda for weeks and eventually claimed the head of the Minister of Labour, Savvas Tsitouridis, in April 2007.

By the end of ND's term in office (March 2004–September 2007), the record of the Karamanlis government on pensions displayed limited ambition and inconclusive results. The government had attempted no new major reform initiative, focusing instead on carrying out a difficult resolution of the pension problems in the banking sector. Yet almost five years since its adoption, the implementation of the Reppas Law (which ND had dismissed as too timid) remained incomplete, with many pension funds of state-controlled companies still in limbo and no resolution on other important the issues such as the re-examination of the list of 'arduous and unhealthy' occupations. The new round of social dialogue inaugurated by the government in 2006, while still in its infancy, displayed little evidence of consensus between the social partners. Against a background of financial uncertainty, increasing EU pressure for reform, and domestic contestation over 'acceptable solutions', the scene is set for yet another chapter in bloody politics of solving the Greek pension puzzle.

4.9   Conclusion

The pension system has proved to be an extreme case of low reform capacity in Greece. Reform initiatives have faced a quagmire of informal veto points: repeatedly, they have been scaled back or shelved. Reform has been gradual and incremental, as more radical attempts have evaporated. Governments have had their 'fingers burnt' politically, and their reform credibility has seriously undermined.

Government strategies have varied, but each has failed to break out of this cycle. Intragovernment tensions have arisen from differences of reform commitment and of the perceived political costs. Key Ministers have had dysfunctional relationships; the support of the Prime Minister has been unclear. Union opposition has been vociferous, with numerous strikes and action. Fears of reform have been enlarged: the fiscal issues and actuarial projections have been almost lost from view amidst public anxieties over future security. SEV, the main employers' organization, by contrast has generally maintained a low profile. Its initial response to the Reppas package in June 2002 was positive, then ambiguous because of the costs. Opposition parties have sought political advantage: Karamanlis, for example, 'sat on the fence' when the Reppas package was debated in Parliament. Andreas Papandreou had been no more helpful to the Mitsotakis Government. Pension reform has been too hot to handle politically. Attempts at social dialogue have elicited little substantive agreement. Moreover, the purpose and agenda of the dialogue has been disputed. Government commitment to the dialogue process has been questioned. Mistrust has run deep, opinions have diverged, and leadership all too timid.

The key actors have not fully shared the diagnosis of the problem. Governments have repeatedly used outside experts to report on the issues and options for reform. This has been a clear signal of the need for external legitimization and the scepticism of internal analyses. The external reports have had many themes in common. Yet the official forecasts of financial ruin have varied. Moreover, GSEE's own INE Report in 2001 failed to stimulate a common understanding. The condition remains 'critical', however, as the Greek pension system faces one of the largest deficits in Europe and current provision fails to meet contemporary needs and aspirations.

The pension system also testifies to the embedded political and social commitment to statism in Greece. In the face of financial crisis, successive governments have picked up the bill to sustain the system. The Reppas package of 2001 – the most recent reform – settled for modest adjustments of provision but at a huge cost to the State. Even this package was strongly attacked. The Government had attempted to build trust, but it had to pay dearly for it. Moreover, the knowledge that governments have in the past bailed out the system creates strong disincentives to compromise among current stakeholders today. Credibility and ambition are scaled down.

The EU has entered this quagmire with the strong stick of the EMU criteria and the soft instruments of the Lisbon process. The hard commitment device of the EMU entry offered scope for exceptional external empowerment, as Greece's fiscal position had to be rectified to achieve this major national goal. It could have restructured the domestic debate and facilitated meaningful reform. In the event, the opportunity was lost. Thereafter, the OMC process offers little constraint though it has helped to shape policy ideas. Learning and isomorphism have been facilitated, as policy specialists look further afield. Yet the domestic bottleneck to agreement and implementation has not been broken.

Preferences and interests in reform have been determined in the context of current provision. The willingness to compromise on the part of current beneficiaries has been undermined by the shortcomings of the contemporary welfare regime and by their employment position. Public sector employees, for example, suffer relatively low pay but can expect more generous pensions. Isolated reform on pensions threatens this model without other compensation. The centrality of the pension system in Greek welfare is actually part of the problem. Further, the constituency blocking reform is much stronger than that advocating it. The benefits of reform are often long-term – to future generations – while the costs are borne by the currently privileged. Those excluded at present lack voice.

Moreover, the reform agenda on pensions cannot be divorced from that in other areas. Changes to labour market regulation threaten other parts of the current Greek 'model'. The rational voter prioritizes security, and reforms in these sectors and others – if not linked – increases anxiety and resistance. It is here that the notion of complementarities developed in the 'varieties of capitalism' literature is made relevant. Interests are endemic to the system, including its various parts. The politics of pension reform has frequently shown a mutual sensitivity to that on labour law. Moreover, both cases show how self-interest is asserted in a manner that neglects those who are currently excluded from provision or protection. In both cases, the voice of the 'insider' has been strong and restrictive, maintaining the distortions of the prevailing regime. Internationally, the discourse in Greece is thus caught between an underdeveloped 'welfare state' and new politics of 'post-industrial' adjustment (Pierson, 1998). As such, it reflects wider contradictions of Greece's development.

Table 4.1   Pension reform in Greece, 1990–2006

Apr. 1990:	ND, under the leadership of Konstantinos Mitsotakis, wins general election
Sep. 1990:	Souflias's pension reform law (1902/90) passes through Parliament. Main provisions: • The gradual increase in social security contributions by 3% (from 27% to 30%) • Increases in the retirement age for men and women to 60 and 58, respectively • The indexation of pensions to the salaries of public sector employees • Tightening of the rules governing the granting of incapacity pensions
Sep. 1992:	Sioufas pension reform law (2084/92) passes through Parliament. Main provisions: • An increase of retirement age to 65 for both men and women (employed after 1 January 1993) • Increase in social security contributions by 3.65% (from 30% to 33.65%) • A reduction of the 'ceiling' of the primary pension/exit salary ratio from 80% to 60%
Sep. 1996:	PASOK, under the leadership of Kostas Simitis, wins general election
Oct. 1996:	The 'Spraos Committee' of experts is set up to report on a long-term economic policy'
Oct. 1997:	The 'Spraos' report on pensions is published. No specific proposals made. Government distances itself
Apr. 2000:	PASOK, under the leadership of Kostas Simitis, wins general election
May 2000:	Government commissions long-term pension study to UK-based Government Actuaries
Apr. 2001:	After months of speculation, Giannitsis unveils government plans on pension reform. Main proposals: • Introduction of a uniform retirement age of 65 applicable to all employees • The capping of replacement ratio for primary pension to 60% of the exit salary • Full pension entitlements after 40 years of employment irrespective of age • The calculation of the exit salary based on the average earnings during the last 15 years of employment • The abolition of all 'pension benefits' for working mothers. Instead pension subsidies (in years of service) per child

	• Re-evaluation of the occupations termed 'arduous and unhealthy' • Organizational restructuring of the pension system • A substantial, but means-tested, increase in the minimum pension • The extension of 'tripartite financing' to the entire pension system (under certain conditions)
May 2001:	The government is forced into a retreat and pledges dialogue with the unions 'without preconditions'
Oct. 2001:	Government reshuffle. Giannitsis is replaced by Dimitris Reppas
Mar. 2002:	Government launches new social dialogue on pension reform. Unions agree to engage.
Jun. 2002:	Reppas's pension reform law (3029/2002) passes through Parliament. Main provisions:
	• Establishment of a common retirement age of 65 for a full pension • Full pension after 37 years of service irrespective of age • Ceiling in the replacement ratio of primary and auxiliary pensions set at 90% (combined) • The granting of up to 4.5 years of pensionable service for women with children (after 1 January 2003) • The re-examination, by the end of 2004, of the list of 'ardours and unhealthy occupations • Compulsory incorporation of all primary pension funds of salaried employees into IKA (in due course) • Creation of a Joint Fund of Auxiliary Pensions for the Salaried • New legal framework for the creation of 'fully funded' auxiliary funds along occupational lines • Extension of 'tripartite financing', including agreement that 1% of GDP would be channelled to IKA finances over the next 30 years & government guarantee that IKA's finances will always be in surplus
Mar. 2003:	ND wins general election. No plan for pension reform in this term in office
Dec. 2005:	Government pushes through the compulsory incorporation of the Emporiki Bank pension fund into IKA. Process extends to other banking sector pension funds
Aug. 2006:	A 'wise men' committee is set up by the government to prepare the ground for a new round of pension reform during the course of the next Parliament.

5
The Puzzle of Jobless Growth: The Challenge of Reforming the Greek Labour Market

5.1 Introduction

The EU's aspiration of creating an open, flexible market among its member states confronts head-on the twin dilemmas of the limitations of its own policy instruments and the in-built resistance to liberal reform found at the domestic level. The single European market created new sets of competitive pressure at the national level, but left governments to choose their own reform paths. With the EMU, the concerns about adaptability and asymmetries increased and the EU sought to broaden its economic policy coordination. But it was the Lisbon 2000 agenda that focussed the attention on a prescribed model of structural reform. The EU had the aspiration, but it was equipped only with exhortation, reporting, and peer pressure as instruments for policy implementation.

At the same time, the domestic economies of the EU had built up entrenched structural differences. Those of southern Europe were more marked by the extensive reach of the state, clientelism, and the power of producer interests. Each diverged from the model of liberalized, flexible labour markets. The reform of employment practices and privileges faced embedded cultural constraints, conflicting political interests, and well-organized veto points. The message of globalization was seen as adapt or die, but the EU was giving itself few means by which to stimulate domestic reform. The EU offered little empowerment to governments and the latter were left to steer their own way through the opposition.

In Greece, the challenge was among the greatest: relatively high recent economic growth had created few extra jobs, a sign of entrenched labour market rigidities. Its economy was seen as falling well behind the EU average and its domestic politics seemed to eschew consensus over means and objectives. Governments faced great difficulties in shifting the terms of the debate and in employing an effective strategy. The task would challenge their unity of purpose, their consistency, and their guile. The agenda highlighted the economic challenge for Greece in remaining at the EU's core in a period in which the new member states from central and eastern Europe showed greater capacity for radical reform and, perhaps, for growth.

5.2   The EU stimulus to domestic reform

As elsewhere in Europe, the domestic initiatives on labour market reform in Greece have been linked to the developments occurring at the EU level. For Greece, this linkage – more implicit, than explicit – has existed in both ideational and strategic terms. The definition of policy objectives and the content of reforms has come to owe much to the developing EU agenda in this area, as, again, Greece has been a 'policy receiver' rather than a 'policy initiator'. Moreover, the overriding political priority in this period has been to keep Greece within the EU's core, thus sustaining a wider strategic interest in linking the domestic agenda to that of her partners.

The EU stimulus has affected both the direction and pace of domestic reform. The EU's agenda has been a broad one, with different strands, and it developed apace after the signing of the Maastricht Treaty. Since the launch of the Single Europe Market programme in 1985, much public debate has centred on the need for Europe to become more competitive, by shifting away from state regulation and relatively high levels of taxation and welfare provision. The search for new ways of reforming the European economy and enhancing its international competitiveness received renewed impetus in the aftermath of Maastricht with a number of high-profile initiatives introduced in this direction, including the Delors White Paper on 'Competitiveness, Growth and Employment' in 1993 and the creation of the advisory group on competitiveness chaired by Carlo Azelio Ciampi in 1995.

The Amsterdam Treaty (1997) brought the issue of employment to the heart of the EU's agenda with the inclusion of an Employment Title into the body of the Treaty. While reaffirming that employment policies remained under the competence of national governments, the Amsterdam Treaty prioritized job creation and declared employment as an issue of 'common concern' (art. 126). Within this context member states were encouraged to develop national employment strategies on the basis of European priorities and to introduce mechanisms of national surveillance and the sharing of best practice (art. 128). On the basis of the provisions set out in the Amsterdam Treaty, the Luxembourg Job Summit (November 1997) introduced the EES. As a part of this new policy instrument, annual 'European Employment Guidelines' were developed, grouped under four priorities:

- Employability
- Entrepreneurship
- Adaptability
- Equal opportunities

These priorities formed the basis for the production of 'National Action Plans' (NAPs) which were to be assessed by a joint Report by the Commission and the Council, assisted by a new Employment Committee which became the institutional 'hub' of the EES.

The EES acquired new importance within the context of the Lisbon Programme (2000) which promised to transform the European economy to ' . . . the most competitive and dynamic knowledge-based economy in the world' (European Council, 2000a). 'Softer' mechanisms of policy coordination, peer pressure, and sharing of best practice, first introduced within the context of the EES, had clearly informed the 'design' of the Lisbon process, structured around the OMC. On employment, the targets set by Lisbon were, indeed, ambitious: the achievement of 70% employment rates (60% for women) across the EU by 2010. A mid-term review of the EES in the same year also recommended greater emphasis to be placed on the 'adaptability' pillar, an implicit acknowledgement that the slow pace of job creation in the EU necessitated the 'loosening-up' of labour market regulation. This approach was also reflected in the assessment of the Greek National Action Plan for 2000, in which the Employment Committee pointed to the country's 'double' low employment/ high unemployment problem and urged the Greek government to 'strengthen a partnership approach and promote concrete commitments by the social partners at all appropriate levels on the modernisation of work organisation, with the aim of making undertakings more productive and competitive while achieving the required balance between flexibility and security' (European Commission/Council, 2001).

In the aftermath of the first five years of the EES in 2002, a series of reforms were introduced with the aim of streamlining its objectives, increasing its visibility, and better coordinating it with other instruments within the Lisbon process, most notably the Broad Economic

Policy Guidelines. In this context a new set of objectives were introduced focusing on the themes of

- full employment
- quality and productivity at work
- cohesion and an inclusive labour market (European Commission, 2002b).

In view of the EU's disappointing record on job creation, however, a new European Employment Task force was set up in 2003 under the chairmanship of Wim Kok in order to provide new thinking on the way forward for the EES. The Kok report, produced later that year under the evocative title *Jobs, Jobs, Jobs: Creating More Employment in Europe*, issued a stark warning that 'unless the member states step up their efforts, it is looking increasingly unlikely that the overarching [Lisbon] goal of 2010, and the employment objectives, will be attainable' (Employment Taskforce, 2003: 2). The report also recommended the intensification of efforts to reform the EU's labour markets along four main axes:

- Increasing adaptability of workers and enterprises
- Attracting more people to the labour market and making work a real option for all
- Investing more and more effectively in human capital
- Ensuring effective implementation of reforms through better governance

In its assessment of the Greece's employment record, the Kok report reiterated the need to boost employment and reduce unemployment (a demand that featured in all previous reports of the Employment Committee) and made a series of recommendations, including the need to foster ' . . . a more employment friendly business environment' (Employment Taskforce, 2003: 65).

In the years that followed the publication of the Kok report, the EU has embarked on a wholesale review of the EES which since 2005, in the context of the mid-term review of the Lisbon Programme, has become an integral part of the *Growth and Jobs* initiative launched by the Commission President Jose-Manuel Barroso. Under the 'revamped' Lisbon Programme the guidelines on the EES have been significantly reduced and merged with those of the BEPGs into a single set of Guidelines for Growth and Jobs to be implemented within a three-year cycle (2005–8) (European Commission, 2005b).

The overall trajectory of the EES and the Lisbon Programme over the past decade has elevated the issue of job creation to the top of the EU's agenda. Within this context the issue of labour market reform has moved from an implicit policy recommendation to an explicit priority for safeguarding the long-term competitiveness of the European economy. With 'jobs' now a dominant feature of the European discourse, no member state can claim immunity from the strong adaptational pressures emanating from the EU on this matter. Yet, in practical terms, the implementation of labour market reform on the ground remains very much a prerogative of national governments as the EU lacks both a clear blueprint for reform and the 'hard' instruments to enforce it. This ambiguity over policy objectives and the cost of non-compliance makes the process of domestic translation and interpretation extremely important. The ongoing tensions between the European and domestic levels develop in a political space at home where discourses, political leadership, and coalition building are essential components of the Europeanization process. These will be explored in detail in subsequent parts of this chapter.

5.3   'Greece isn't working': The weaknesses of the Greek labour market in perspective

Much of the Greek 'labour market problem' since the second half of the 1990s has been understood within the context of a rapidly growing economy that has been unable to generate high rates of job creation. During the period 1995–2001 the Greek economy grew on average by 3.3% per year as opposed to 2.4% for the EU (Eurostat, 2004). Over the same period, however, the average yearly employment growth in Greece stood at less than a quarter of that of the EU (0.3% and 1.2% respectively). Throughout the 1990s the rate of unemployment rose steadily from 6.4% in 1990 to 9.2% in 1995, reaching its peak in 1999 at 11.6% (10.2% in 2001). During the same period the number of long-term unemployed grew by over 60%, accounting for 52.90% of total unemployment in 2001 (EU=44.5%). For the same years unemployment for the under-25s stood at an astonishing 28.1% (EU=14.9%), whereas the figure for young women was even higher at 35.8% (EU=16.0%). In 2001 the employment rate in Greece stood at 55.4%, the third lowest in the EU (ahead only of that of Italy and Spain) and 8.5% lower than the EU average (63.9%) (European Commission, 2002a).

Throughout the 1990s labour costs in Greece remained the second lowest in the EU (only Portugal registered cheaper labour costs – see

Table 3.13). In terms of their structure, these costs have not been too dissimilar to those of Greece's EU counterparts. Despite popular conceptions, for example, in 2000 the ratio of total taxes on employed labour[1] in Greece was marginally lower than the EU average (37.0% and 37.4% respectively) (European Commission, 2003b). The competitive advantages associated with low labour costs, however, have been consistently undermined by Greece's poor productivity record. In 2001, for instance, labour productivity per hour worked stood at a disappointing 69.2% of the EU average (ahead only of Portugal) (Eurostat, 2004). Chronic public underinvestment in education (3.7% of GDP in 1999, the lowest share in the EU) as well as disappointing indicators of life-long learning and R&D (the worst in the EU) has been regarded as a major contributor to the country's persistent productivity problem.

In 2001 43.3% of the Greek workforce was self-employed. This was the largest share among all EU member states and almost three times larger than the EU average (14.8%). In the same year, part-time employment accounted for only 4.0% of total employment, registering the smallest such share among the EU member states (EU=17.9%) (European Commission, 2002a). In terms of temporary employment (fixed-term contracts) the Greek figure of 12.6% was only marginally smaller than the EU average of 13.4% (European Commission, 2002a). Yet flexible employment in Greece seemed to have more frequently been borne out of necessity rather than choice. In 1999 the Greek average for involuntary part-time employment (43.8%) was almost two and half times higher than the EU average (16.8%). The same is also true for employment based on involuntary fixed-term contacts where the Greek average is almost twice as high the EU one (Sabethai, 2000).

The legislative framework regulating the Greek labour market has traditionally remained incomplete and slow to react to new employment trends (both within Greece and internationally).[2] Overall it is widely recognized that working conditions in the public sector are far more 'employee friendly' than that of the private sector. The labour market regime in the private sector (which forms the main focus of this Chapter), has traditionally displayed a strong bias towards the protection of existing 'conventional' full-time employment. This has been mainly achieved through higher levels of severance pay than the EU average (29 weekly wages in Greece as compared with 17 in the EU)[3] as well as through tight limits on collective redundancies (significantly tighter than those stipulated by the EEC directive 75/129).[4] Additionally employers pursuing collective redundancies have been required by law to engage in consultations with the unions as well as to secure approval from the Ministry of Labour, the latter often being a lengthy and extremely bureaucratic process.[5]

The considerable levels of protection for 'conventional' forms of employment, however, did not extend to those employed under more flexible working arrangements. Employees working on a part-time, seasonal, or fixed-term basis often found themselves short-changed by the existing legislation. Discrimination against these employees has often included lesser forms of protection with regard to their working hours, holiday entitlements, and severance pay as well as their pension and social security rights. The big discrepancies between the legal obligations associated with full-time employment, on the one hand, and part-time/temporary, on the other, may also explain why the latter (particularly fixed-term contacts and contract work) has been used extensively by employers over the last few years. Further elements of flexibility in the Greek labour market have been provided through the measures of 'temporary suspension' (διαθεσιμότητα) and 'compulsory overtime' (υπερεργασία). The former relates to the managerial prerogative (i.e. without union consent) to suspend employment for a part (or the totality) of the workforce for a period of up to three months per year, during which the employees receive a fraction of their normal pay.[6] 'Compulsory overtime' relates to a unique characteristic of the Greek labour market legislation that provides employers with easy and relatively cheap access to overtime employment. This measure has been utilized widely since its introduction in 1975. It has allowed employers to introduce overtime employment of up to eight hours a week (on the basis of individual, rather than union, consent) with the relatively moderate pay increase of 25%.[7]

Yet an analysis of the Greek 'labour market problem' based exclusively on the content of the existing legislation may depict a rather misleading picture. Many of the peculiarities of the Greek case lay not so much in what the legislation actually stipulates, but rather on the range of labour relations it manages to regulate as well as on whether the legal framework can be effectively enforced. In this sense issues of coverage and implementation are of crucial importance. In 2001 the extent of the black economy in Greece stood at 28.5% of GDP, the highest figure among all the OECD members (Dell'Anno and Schneider, 2003: 25). The vast majority of jobs (perhaps in their hundreds of thousands) that fuel this illegal economic activity remain unprotected by the labour market legislation. The widespread existence of the black economy is not new; it has been a feature of Greek economic and social life for many decades. Over the last decade, however, the problem has taken an altogether different turn with the arrival of unprecedented numbers of illegal economic migrants in the country. In the absence of reliable official statistics, estimates about their numbers have varied significantly, with the most conservative of them converging around the 650,000 figure (Sabethai, 2000; Petronoti and Triandafyllidou, 2003). Astonishingly for most of the 1990s the Greek state made no effort to register the existence of these people and incorporate them into the labour market. As a result the vast majority of them remained outside the protection of the labour market (or indeed any other) laws, and have often been subjected to terrible living and working conditions. In 1998 the government's initiatives to introduce 'green cards' saw the legalization of approximately 250,000 illegal economic immigrants, but still an unknown number of foreign workers continue to be employed in the black economy.[8]

The problems associated with the legalization process of foreign workers and the control of undeclared employment (both by foreign and Greek workers) reflect wider regulatory weaknesses of the Greek state (Pagoulatos, 2003). Many of these stem from the well-documented (Sotiropoulos, 1993) inadequacies of the Greek public administration that, with regard to the labour market, have only been exacerbated by considerable delays in modernizing the respective legislation (see above).[9] On a different level, many of the problems of regulating the Greek labour market are associated with the very structure of the Greek economy. The very high levels of self-employment and, more importantly, the very small size of the average Greek business (99% of businesses employ less than 20 staff accounting for more than 60% of total employment) (Kouzis, 2000) make the Greek labour market a notoriously difficult sector to police. In the highly personalized, non-unionized, environment of the typical Greek business the violation of labour market legislation is far more difficult to resist or discover. Indeed it is the archipelago of small enterprises, rather than the large companies, that the hand of the law finds it harder to reach. It is there that Greek labour market meets much of its de facto flexibility.

5.4   We really mean dialogue, honest! The road to the 1997 Confidence Pact

The reform of the Greek labour market has been a key feature of the social dialogue on 'development, competitiveness and employment' initiated by the Simitis Government in March 1997 (for a full chronology of the labour market reform in Greece look at Table 5.1). Fresh from the September 1996 electoral victory, many within PASOK urged the Prime Minister to seek the maximum social consensus for his reform agenda, aimed at securing Greece's qualification for the third stage of the EMU by 2001. Interestingly, however, neither the title of the social dialogue nor the invitations to the social partners made reference to the EMU. The reasons behind this omission are not entirely clear. A plausible explanation is that the government wanted to avoid the austerity connotations associated with EMU qualification and, at this early stage, was keen to get the fiercely eurosceptic communist wing of GSEE involved in the process (something that in the end did not prove possible).

The government's strategy of reaching out for the consensus of the social partners on such a wide range of issues carried with it not only valuable opportunities but also significant risks. In many ways the whole experiment entered politically into unchartered territories. If successful, the process could legitimize the government's reform agenda and create an environment of social calm upon which the success of the government's plans (and profile) depended. On the other hand, processes of social consultation had not been a part of Greek political culture. In the past their use had been sporadic and limited to a very narrow agenda, whereas their outcome had always been insignificant (e.g. the Fakiolas Committee in the 1992 pension reform). Within the context of the tight timetables of Greece's revised convergence plan, the social dialogue cost the government precious time. By inviting the social partners into a public dialogue over its reform plans, the government also risked damaging displays of conflict which could provide useful ammunition to the opposition. If unsuccessful, the social dialogue also threatened to cause long-term damage to the government's relations with the social partners (particularly the unions) and endanger the successful conclusion of its reform agenda.

In its official invitation to the social partners of 14 April 1997, the government clarified its position regarding the scope, structure, and membership of the social dialogue. In terms of the dialogue's agenda, the government took a rather maximalist position proposing a total of 19 subject areas[10] grouped around three main themes:

- Structural policies for development
- Policies for boosting competitiveness and employment
- The regulation of employment and social protection towards the year 2000

For all its considerable width, however, the dialogue's agenda included some noticeable omissions. Despite union demands for the opposite, neither pension nor education policies were placed on the negotiating table. The government's refusal to do so was largely determined by political considerations. Recent attempts to reform both policies had been met with massive opposition from the unions and large sections of the Greek society. Revisiting these issues in the context of the social dialogue was likely to refuel tensions and undermine the government's efforts of securing consensus. As a result, a 'mini package' of pension reform[11] was to be subjected to a separate process of consultation in the early 1998, following the conclusion of the current social dialogue. Education was altogether excluded from any 'formal' consultation process.

In terms of its composition, the social dialogue remained essentially tripartite in nature. The driving force behind the whole process was a nine-member Political Secretariat consisting of three members nominated by the government,[12] three representatives from the private sector union (GSEE),[13] and one representative each from the three main employers associations: SEV representing large industries, ESEE representing commerce, and GSEVEE (General Confederation of Professionals, Medium and Small Businesses and Traders/ΓΣEBEE: Γενική Συνομοσπονδία Επαγγελματιών Βιοτεχνών Εμπόρων Ελλάδος) representing small- and medium-size businesses and self-employed professionals. A further 22 organizations were also loosely associated with the process through the infrequent meetings of the social dialogue's plenary session, but without providing any significant input into it. A notable absentee from the process was the newly established Economic and Social Committee (OKE). Moreover, no independent research institutes or non-governmental organizations participated in the social dialogue. For the 19 policy areas included in the agenda, small groups of experts were established where government representatives presented specific proposals and invited delegates from the two sides of industry to comment. Each group of experts then presented its findings to the Political Secretariat which set itself a deadline for the end of 1997 before the final document-outcome of the social dialogue was signed.

Discussions over labour market reform, which came to dominate the proceedings of the social dialogue, formed part of its third theme entitled 'regulation of employment and social protection towards the year 2000'. In its opening proposals to the social partners the government focused its attention on six main issues, including

- the calculation of working time on a six-, nine-, or twelve-month basis (rather than the existing weekly basis) and the introduction of measures to discourage overtime (particularly in its 'compulsory' form)[14]

- the introduction of part-time work to the public sector and measures to ensure the better regulation of part-time employment
- measures to better regulate new forms of employment (e.g. telesales, working from home, etc.) and ensure that employees in these sectors are better linked to the pension, healthcare, and social insurance systems
- the introduction of territorial employment pacts (TEPs) where pay could be set below the national minimum wages agreed by the National General Collective Agreement (ESSE/ΕΣΣΕ: Εθνική Συλλογική Σύμβαση Εργασίας) in order to boost employment in areas suffering industrial decline
- measures to discourage the participation of pensioners in the labour market
- measures to protect young and long-term unemployed as well as those who have been victims of collective redundancies.

The re-calculation of working time, the introduction of part-time employment in the public sector, and the promotion of TEPs proved to be the most controversial of all the government's proposals. In their submission to the social dialogue, the unions (both GSEE and ADEDY) opposed the annualized calculation of working time and repeated their long-standing proposal for the introduction of a 35-hour week without corresponding pay cuts. In addition they encouraged the government to restrict both compulsory and voluntary overtime. The public sector union, ADEDY, made it clear that the government's proposals on part-time employment in the public sector was a non-starter, whereas the private sector union, GSEE, argued that TEP's should not undermine the pay deals agreed within the context of the National General Collective Agreement (ESSE).

On the employers' side, the National Confederation of Greek Commerce (ESEE) urged the government to introduce much more radical measures for promoting part-time employment (including for those in retirement) in the private sector and asked for lower levels of redundancy pay and national insurance contributions for employers. ESEE strongly opposed GSEE's proposal for a 35-hour week and expressed serious reservations regarding the TEPs. The League of Greek Industries (SEV), on the other hand, pressed the government for more flexibility on collective redundancies (both in terms of the limits imposed on the number of employees subjected to collective redundancies and of the amount of money that those losing their jobs were entitled to) and strongly supported the annualized calculation of overtime. In addition SEV insisted that the TEPs should be able to set wages below those agreed by ESSE and asked the government to introduce legislation allowing the creation of private employment agencies. The position of GSEVEE stood somewhere in between those of ESEE and SEV. On the issue of working time, for instance, GSEVEE's position was similar to that of ESEE, accepting the unions' calls for a 35-hour a week, only if the corresponding pay cut was introduced (SEV rejected the proposal for a 35-hour week altogether). As far as part-time employment in the private sector was concerned, GSEVEE sided with SEV in suggesting the introduction of incentives for those companies employing and training part-time employees.

Throughout the course of the six months, the search for a common ground between the positions of the social partners proved elusive. Within the context of the social dialogue two distinct logics emerged. On one hand, the employers regarded high unit costs and the inflexibilities of the Greek labour market as a brake on the competitiveness of Greek businesses and ultimately as important contributors to the inability of the Greek economy to create employment at a faster pace. The unions, on the other hand, argued that the cost of employment in Greece was among the lowest in the EU and that the competitiveness of the Greek economy would be better served through increased productivity, not the deregulation of Greek labour market, which they already regarded as being very flexible and badly policed. On its part, the government struggled to find a compromise between these logics, but its own proposals fell short of achieving the consensus on which the successful conclusion of the social dialogue so depended. Similar difficulties were also evident in the other two themes of the social dialogue where too agreement became impossible to find.

As the social dialogue ran into serious trouble during the autumn of 1997,[15] keeping the unions engaged with the process became a pressing priority for the government. Having invested so much political capital in this process, a union walkout at this stage would be nothing short of a catastrophe. Within GSEE, PASOK controlled just 22 out of the 45 votes of the union's governing body (Presidency). As all other factions demanded GSEE's disassociation from the process, the union's President, Christos Polyzogopoulos (a member of PASOK's Central Committee and one of the architects of the social dialogue), struggled to keep even his own PASOK-controlled fraction (PASKE: Fighting Union Movement of Greek Employees / ΠΑΣΚΕ: Πανελλήνια Αγωνιστική Συνδικαλιστική Κίνηση Εργαζομένων) on board. In the end, it was only when the GSEE's President utilized his double vote (provided for by GSEE's constitution) that the necessary majority was achieved. This allowed GSEE to sign, on 10 November 1997, the concluding document of the social dialogue entitled 'Confidence Pact between the Government and the Social Partners towards the Year 2000'. The document was also signed by SEV and ESEE, but not by GSEVEE, probably on orders of the Greek Communist Party (KKE) which controlled its leadership. The Confidence Pact was also denounced by all opposition parties in Parliament, including centre-right ND, the Greek Communist Party, and the populist DIKKI.

In the process of securing consensus, however, the government had paid a heavy price. The signed document remained vague and confined largely to some general targets. The Pact provided for above-inflation pay increases in the private sector for 1998–9 and made rather vague references to the need for 'structural changes in the labour market' in order to adapt to new forms of employment as well as to new measures to promote the integration of young and long-term unemployed into the labour market. In addition the Pact referred to the 'voluntary' introduction of part-time work in the (state-controlled) public utilities and the 'experimental' introduction of this measure to some regional authorities (but not in the central ministerial bureaucracies). As far as the TEPs were concerned, no mention was made to the possibility of wages been set below the nationally agreed minimum wages. More astonishingly, the Pact did not include any reference to the recalculation of working-time and overtimes (despite these issues dominating the agenda of the social dialogue), in an apparent move to appease the PASOK-wing of GSEE. Putting a brave face on it, the government argued that the Confidence Pact was always meant to produce a basic political agreement, not to agree on the specific content of reform. However, the government's initial strategy of a clearly defined agenda and the creation of expert groups to deal with its items had revealed rather different objectives. That said, the signing of the Confidence Pact gave the government the opportunity to claim that an agreement of this kind signified a real breakthrough in its relations with the social partners. Yet the disagreements over the specific direction of reform remained as wide as ever. Many of these would return with a vengeance when the government brought forward its legislative proposals for the reform of the Greek labour market.

5.5   What confidence? The 1998 labour market law

Soon after the conclusion of the Confidence Pact in November 1997, the government's relations with the unions took a sharp turn for the worse. In the early January 1998, the Minister of National Economy, Giannos Papandoniou, introduced a legislative amendment (to a draft law on taxation) whereby the management of public utilities could alter the labour regimes in these companies unilaterally, without prior agreement of the unions. Papandoniou's bold move was meant to send a clear signal to the markets that the government was serious about the reform of public utilities, particularly of the much-troubled Olympic Airways. In retrospect the amendment might have also been linked with the (secret) negotiations with the Commission regarding Greece's entry into the ERM. Regardless of the motivation, Papandoniou's move surprised and infuriated the unions which accused the government of betraying the spirit of the social dialogue (where such a measure had not been discussed), let alone agreed upon. With GSEE's elections only two months away (March 1998), the government's move came as a particular blow to GSEE's President, Christos Polyzogopoulos, who, under very difficult circumstances, had invested his own personal credibility on the signing of the Confidence Pact. Papandoniou's determination to see the amendment through also caused difficulties to many of his cabinet colleagues, particularly to the more consensual Minister of Labour, Miltiadis Papaioannou, who had been waiting for the end of GSEE's elections before introducing the government's proposals on labour market reform.

Indeed, within a week of GSEE's election, in which Christos Polyzogopoulos was marginally re-elected as president, the government's strategy of labour market reform was put in motion. In typical style (Featherstone et al., 2001), the government's intentions became gradually clear through a series of leaks to the press, before Miltiadis Papaioannou officially presented them to journalists on 24 June 1998. The proposals were a compromise between the Cabinet's 'maximalist' camp led by the Minister of National Economy and its more 'consensual' wing led by the Minister of Labour. They included

- the calculation of working time on a three- and six-month basis according to the company's size with the possibility of extending the working day for up to two hours (again, depending on the company's size and provided that total hours worked in a year averaged the 40-hour week rule)
- for any changes on the calculation of working time, union consent was required. This went against the employers' demand (supported by the Minister of National Economy) for a management prerogative on this issue. In addition, the government ignored SEV's proposal for a substantial increase in the limits for collective redundancies (which was also supported by Papandoniou).

- the introduction of TEPs where wages could be set below those agreed by the ESSE. The opposition of GSEE to this measure was, thus, ignored.
- no limit was set on the number of part-time workers that could be employed in a company. GSEE's demand for a 20% upper limit on this issue was not taken on board by the government.
- the introduction of part-time employment in state-controlled companies
- the creation of private employment agencies
- measures for the better policing of the labour market (by bringing the Labour Inspectorate under the control of the Ministry of Labour) and the improvement of the legislative framework regulating 'atypical' and part-time employment
- provision for the Social Security Foundation (IKA) to provide medical and pharmaceutical cover for the young (under 29 years) and long-term unemployed.

With some very minor changes, all of the government's June proposals formed a part of the Labour Market law (2639/98) which passed through Parliament on 7 August 1998 amidst a climate of social tension and mutual recrimination. During the parliamentary debate the government faced strong criticism by all opposition parties. ND accused the government that its indecisiveness and collusion with the unions had produced an incomplete reform that lacked a clear sense of direction. For the smaller left-wing parties the 2639/98 law reconfirmed PASOK's move to the right and its strategy to deregulate the Greek labour market on orders from the EU and big industrial interests. To this end the leader of DIKKI, Dimitris Tsovolas, accused the government of being 'subservient to big employers and big capital', while KKE made reference to an "immoral bill" suitable for 'a funeral oration on social democracy' (*Ta Nea*, 5 June 1998 and 6 August 1998).

The passage of the labour market law through Parliament was also met with scepticism from the social partners. GSEE, for instance, was resentful of the fact that the new legislation included provisions for which the social dialogue had produced no agreement (i.e. TEPs) or were altogether absent from the text of the Confidence Pact (i.e. working time). Many in the unions' leadership felt that the government had betrayed their trust and, in the end, presented them with unacceptable dilemmas: i.e. either to agree on the 'consensual' (with union agreement) recalculation of working time or allow 'unilateral' management prerogative on this issue (Kouzis, 2000: 165). The way in which the

'Papandoniou amendment' (allowing for unilateral, management-driven changes in the labour regimes of public utilities) was engineered earlier had already raised serious union suspicions about the government's sincerity and trustworthiness. The timing of the 1998 reform did little to alleviate the unions' fears. Following more than a year of deliberations between the social partners, the 2639/98 law was finally brought for debate in the Parliament's summer session, as the government hoped to capitalize from the feel-good factor and desertion caused by the mid-summer holiday.

For their part, the employers remained rather unimpressed by the new law. For them the laborious process of the social dialogue had resulted in a 'soup', not the far-reaching reform they had hoped for. For a start their demands for reducing the burden (administrative and financial) on collective redundancies were largely ignored by the 2639/98 law. On working time, their proposals over unilateral management prerogative were also disappointed. Even their second line of defence – changes of working time on the basis of agreement between management and individuals – had to be abandoned in favour of full union consent. For the employers, the labour market reform was hardly a reform at all; it was a reflection of the government's interventionist logic which delivered even more unwanted regulation and ran against European and international trends. As for the government, the huge political capital invested in the 1997 Confidence Pact had produced a mixed return. The process of social dialogue had arguably sown the first seeds of a more consensual, 'grown up', policymaking style. Yet the government had often found itself unable to lend the process the credibility and trust it so needed. Against this background the full fruits of its 'corporatist experiment' were yet to be harvested. As for the outcome of the 1998 labour market reform, the government was soon to grow as unconvinced as its critics. Within a couple of years a new labour market law would be placed on the negotiating table.

5.6   This time is for real . . . or is it? Enter the 2000 labour market reform

Despite its very tight result, the April 2000 election gave PASOK the opportunity to go into its third successive term in office with a relatively comfortable parliamentary majority. Having secured Greece's entry into the eurozone and won his second successive election, the position of Prime Minister Simitis within his party was significantly strengthened. With most of his internal opposition disunited and silenced many thought that Simitis, for the first time during his premiership, would be able to form a truly 'Simitite' Cabinet in his own likeness in order to pursue an agenda of radical reform. Throughout the electoral campaign, Simitis had made it clear that his new government would focus its attention on rectifying some of the more structural problems of the Greek economy, which would allow Greece to compete successfully with other eurozone members (*To Vima*, 5 March 2000). In the Prime Minister's strategic planning, two of the thorniest problems of his previous term in office – labour market and pension reform – would be tackled within the first 18 months of his new term, allowing enough time for his government to recover its strength before the next election.

In order to pursue this ambitious reform agenda, Simitis appointed one of his closest and most trusted allies, Tasos Giannitsis, to the Ministry of Labour. Giannitsis was a man of many contradictions. A German-educated economist (Ph.D.), he had served as the chief economic adviser to the Prime Minister under both Andreas Papandreou (1994–5) and Simitis (1995–2000). During this time he acquired a reputation of being a hard-working, low-profile operator whose background in economics had provided a vital input to the design of the government's economic strategy leading to Greece's qualification for the third stage of the EMU. Yet Giannitsis was not a politician by trade. He was not a Member of Parliament and had openly declared that his political ambitions did not extend beyond the lifetime of this government. In this sense, his appointment as Minister of Labour was a gamble. On the one hand, his standing as an extraparliamentarian Minister gave him a considerable degree of freedom from the re-election worries facing career politicians. On the other hand, unlike his predecessor, Miltiadis Papaioannou, Giannitsis's knowledge of day-to-day politics was limited and, crucially, he lacked close links with the party's machinery and the unions. These were qualities that his Deputy Minister, Christos Protopapas[16] (who had also served under Papaioannou), had in plenty. Giannitsis's ideological profile was strongly influenced by his educational background and his close association with Professor Aggelos Aggelopoulos.[17] In many ways he was an archetypical 'German Social Democrat', a strong believer in the state's regulating role over the economy whose profile contrasted sharply with that of Giannos Papandoniou, the Cambridge-educated Minister of National Economy who had long been pressing for an economic reform agenda modelled on the Anglo-Saxon tradition.

The relationship between the two Ministers got off to a bad start when, on 11 July 2000, Papandoniou leaked to the press that the government's plans for labour market reform would be 'a strong shock' for the unions (*Kathimerini*, 11 July 2000). Papandoniou's remarks, which came just two days before the government's official announcement on this issue, angered Giannitsis who felt his credibility in the eyes of the unions was unnecessarily undermined. When the Minister of Labour eventually presented his reform proposals, he revealed the government's determination to revisit some of the 'unfinished business' of the 1998 reform. Stating PASOK's pre-election commitment to reduce unemployment by 40% in four years (by creating 300,000 new jobs), Giannitsis announced his intentions to

- establish further flexibility on working time (based upon managerial prerogative)
- radically restrict overtime
- reduce employers' national insurance contributions for newly recruited staff
- relax limits on mass redundancies (*EIRO*, 27 July 2000).

Giannitsis also revealed that the process of consultation with the social partners was to be radically different from that which had led to the signing of the Confidence Pact in 1997. For a start, the allocated time was considerably shorter. The government planned to begin consultations with the social partners at the end of August with a view to concluding the process by early October. The dialogue's agenda was structured around nine items[18] which would be negotiated in parallel, with no disagreement in one item being allowed to stall progress on other items. Unlike 1997, the government would negotiate with the social partners on a bilateral basis, not through the establishment of tripartite groups of experts, while plenary sessions were to be fewer. Publicly the government also appeared to encourage bilateral contacts between the unions and the employers with a view to encourage them in making joint submissions to the dialogue (*EIRO*, 27 July 2000).

Despite their fierce condemnation of the government's agenda, both the union of the private sector, the General Confederation of Greek Workers (GSEE), and the union of public sector employees (ADEDY) did not turn down Giannitsis's invitation. The big three employers associations, the League of Greek Industries (SEV, Συνομοσπονδία Ελληνικών Βιομηχανιών), the National Confederation of Greek Commerce (ESEE), and General Confederation of Professionals, Medium and Small Business and Traders (GSEVEE) also decided to participate in the process. In the first meeting of the social dialogue on 24 August 1998 new tensions emerged as GSEE decided to temporarily walkout of the process accusing the government of submitting a paper to the social dialogue that was far too general and was not backed by any statistical data. GSEE also warned the government that it would not give its consent to any reforms that involved unilateral managerial prerogative on working time, the reduction of limits on collective redundancies, and any strategy that would encourage the extension of part-time employment in the private and public sector. For its part, the government continued its consultations with the employers' side and promised the unions that a detailed document with the government reform proposals would be presented to the social partners by early September.

Indeed, on 4 September 2000 the Minister of Labour, Tasos Giannitsis, published a document entitled 'Policies for Combating Unemployment' in which the government's proposals for reforming the Greek labour market were explicitly spelt out (Ministry of Labour 2000). The content of the proposals were interpreted as a conciliatory gesture towards the unions (*To Vima*, 3 September 2000). They included

- The annualized calculation of working time, based on union consent. Thus, the idea of managerial prerogative on this issue was dropped. In addition, the annualized calculation of working time was linked to the reduction of the working week from 40 to 38 hours. This was designed to please the unions' leadership, which had long argued for the introduction of a 35-hour week.
- On mass redundancies, the existing limits on large businesses (with over 250 staff) remained unchanged and the changes introduced for medium-sized businesses (20–250 staff) were not dramatic (four redundancies per month). Both stood well below what the EEC directive 75/129 stipulated. Certainly the government had not taken on board a maximalist agenda that argued for a complete abolition of such limits.
- The government's proposals on the reduction of overtime were more radical. The eight-hour a week 'compulsory' (under management prerogative) overtime (41–48 hours) was to be cut down to three hours per week (41–43 hours). Pay for 'compulsory' overtime would increase from 125% of normal wages to 150%. For 'normal' overtime (on the basis of management–union consent) between 44–48 hours per-week pay would increase to 175% of normal wages (from 125% previously).

For overtime over and above eight hours per week (i.e. over 48 hours) pay was set at 250% of normal wages (up from 200%).

- On the reduction of employers' national insurance contributions for newly recruited staff, the government hinted that the proposed cuts would be in the region of 20–30%, but the precise figure was left open for the social partners to agree upon.
- Finally, on the issue of part-time employment, the government pushed for a 7.5% wage increase (above the minimum wage, proportionally) for those employed for less than four hours a day who would also qualify for one-third of unemployment benefit during their first year of employment (Ministry of Labour, 2000).

Despite their conciliatory tone (compared with earlier announcements by the government), Giannitsis's proposals met very strong opposition by the unions. For GSEE even the slightest increase in the limits of redundancies was a *casus belli*, while the whole thrust of the proposals was seen as yet another indication of the government giving in to employers' demands and promoting the further deregulation of the Greek labour market (*in.gr*, 5 September 2000; *To Vima*, 5 November 2000). If Giannitsis had managed to alienate the unions, however, he had certainly failed to impress the employers. According to SEV, the government's proposals were bound to increase labour costs by up to 8% (*in.gr*, 16 November 2000) while the reduction of redundancy limits were deemed far too moderate to have a real impact. Moreover, SEV remained disappointed that the government did not accept its proposal for managerial prerogative on working time. ESEE and GSEVEE also resented the increase in the cost of part-time employment which is much more widespread among commerce and small businesses than in large industries (Sabethai, 2000).

Above all what united all three employers' associations in their opposition to Giannitsis's plans was the almost complete abolition of 'compulsory' overtime. For years, this peculiar arrangement had been a built-in feature of flexibility for the Greek labour market (Sabethai, 2000; Kouzis, 2001). Taking into consideration that the Greek labour market had been heavily biased towards protecting existing employment (through strict redundancy limits and costly severance pay), most employers preferred to utilize their workforce more intensively (through compulsory overtime) rather than resorting to new recruitment. This option offered many employers the best of both worlds: access to relatively cheap additional employment from existing employees as well as protection from the strict legislative framework associated with the recruiting (or potential dismissal) of new staff. Interestingly, Giannitsis's position on this issue did not even get the unqualified support of the unions which recognized that overtime provided many of their poorly paid members a means of supplementing their income. Against a background of entrenched positions and serious misgivings about the government's proposals, the process of social consultation made little headway during September and October 2000.[19]

As consensus with the unions became all the more difficult to find, internal disagreements within the Cabinet and PASOK began to grow. While Giannitsis's proposals enjoyed the almost unconditional support of the Prime Minister, both the content of the proposed reform and the government's strategy behind it were openly questioned by some of the Cabinet's heavyweights, including Defence Minister, Akis Tsochatzopoulos, and Minister of Culture, Theodoros Pagalos (*Eleftherotypia*, 3 November 2000; *Ethnos*, 20 November 2000). The latter was eventually removed from the Cabinet in November 2000 following a highly damaging public row with the Prime Minister (*Eleftherotypia*, 20 November 2000). The sacking of one of Simitis's former key 'modernizing allies' was seen as a clear indication of the Prime Minister's determination to see through the new labour market reform without making any significant alterations to Giannitsis's 'compromise' proposals in September. Indeed, following a period of intensive consultation within PASOK, the government was able to create the necessary consensus for its troubled reform initiative.[20] When submitted to Parliament for discussion (on 24 November 2000), the draft bill on labour market reform differed little from the proposals that Giannitsis had presented back in September. With most internal disagreements within PASOK ironed-out over the previous weeks, the discussion of the draft bill in Parliament provided no further surprises for the government other than the expected condemnation by all opposition parties and a one-day strike announced by GSEE for 7 December 2000 (Hellenic Parliament, 2000; *Eleftherotypia*, 23 November 2000 and 7 December 2000; *To Vima*, 26 November 2000). On the same day, the 2874/00 law on 'Promoting of Employment' was adopted by the Greek Parliament.

The passage of 2874/00 law through Parliament was a Pyrrhic victory for the government. The tensions and recriminations that dogged the 2000 labour market reform bore little resemblance to the consensual profile that the government had tried to build with the 1997 Confidence Pact. In the process of promoting its reform agenda, the government had failed to broker consensus and alienated itself from both the unions and the employers (Economic and Social Committee, 2001). Along the way, Giannitsis stood accused of picking the wrong fight, of delivering a reform that was both politically costly to the government and unable to achieve its primary objective: that of radically reducing unemployment. Many of the government's problems were, indeed, self-inflicted. Early in the summer of 2000, SEV and GSEE had been close to concluding a bilateral deal on labour reform. Both social partners urged the government to wait for their agreement before it launched its own reform initiative. However, Giannitsis did not trust the imminent deal, fearing that the government would eventually be asked to pick up the cost of what was agreed by the social partners. Instead, the Minister of Labour decided to keep close control over the reform agenda counting on his own political instinct and policy expertise. As it turned out, the gamble failed to produce its anticipated results: the 2000 labour market reform was neither radical nor was it consensual. A few months later, its acrimonious legacy would cost the government dearly when it attempted to reform the troubled Greek pension system. With most of the unions' goodwill exhausted, the reactions to the pension reform proposals brought the government to its knees, eventually forcing it into an embarrassing retreat during the summer of 2001 (see chapter 4). Three months later, in September 2001, Tasos Giannitsis was removed from the Ministry of Labour.

Short-term strategic mistakes aside, the difficulties experienced by successive PASOK governments in shifting the labour market status quo and creating a more conducive environment for job creation highlighted longer-term issues of trust and consensus-building between the government and the social partners. In both its 1998 and 2000 reform initiatives, for example, the government had shown major inconsistencies over the purpose and importance it attached to the process of social dialogue. The length, structure, and membership of each consultation exercise had varied significantly depending on the political expediencies of the day. These inconsistencies reflected wider disagreements within the cabinet over the pace and extent of the required labour market reform as well as different policymaking styles of key Ministers. Miltiadis Papaioannou, for example, was much more consensual than his successor to the Ministry of Labour, Tasos Giannitsis, while both were far less aggressive than the all-powerful Minister of Economy, Giannos Papandoniou. For his part Prime Minister Simitis, for all his good intentions to provide cover for his battered Labour Ministers (particularly Giannitsis), failed to ensure that his government spoke with one voice to the social partners. Confused and undecided over its reform strategy, the government was consequently unable to persuade all players involved that processes of social dialogue were not simply used as pretexts to justify reforms for which the government had already made up its mind.

Suspicion over the government's commitment to the social dialogue is symptomatic of wider confusion with regard to the outlook and functioning of Greek capitalism and the role of the social partners in it (see Chapter 3). Despite the proliferation of institutions with a distinctly corporatist outlook in recent years (for example, the Economic and Social Committee/Οικονομική και Κοινωνική Επιτροπή and the Organization for Mediation and Arbitration/Οργανισμός Μεσολάβησης και Διαιτησίας), there has been little common understanding on the purpose of social consultation. The unions, for example, had long argued that the government should feel bound to legislate upon any agreement (with no direct financial implications) reached between the two sides of industry on lines similar to those followed in the case of collective wage bargaining in the private sector. The government for its part had taken a much more cautious approach stressing instead that these processes perform mainly a consultative function that do not substitute the government's responsibility to govern. Giannitsis's decision in 2000 to reject the joint proposal by unions and employers on the reform of the Greek labour market was the clearest manifestation of this thinking. Without clearly defined 'rules of engagement', however, the 'corporatist experiment' of the 1990s was all too often been reminiscent of a Potemkin village, pleasing to the eye but ultimately disposable when faced with the harsh political pragmatism associated with the pursuit (and opposition) of structural reform in Greece.

Neither can the shortcomings of PASOK's corporatist experiment be fully understood without reference to the problems of legitimacy and representation affecting social partners in Greece on both sides of the divide (trade unions and employers' association). These were elaborated in detail in chapter 3. In this context, like the government itself, many of the key players in the reform of the Greek labour market were fragile coalitions with a need to appeal to diverse constituencies, not all of which necessarily shared the same stakes in reducing unemployment. The 'collective escape' from the weaknesses of the Greek labour market required a delicate package deal that could appeal to these diverse agendas and at the same time retain enough radicalism to deal with complex and difficult problems. In his determination to ensure the latter, Giannitsis underestimated the former. In the process he failed on both.

5.7 'You cannot make an omelette without breaking eggs': ND in power, 2004–7

The arrival of ND in power following the 2004 general election prom-ised to reinvigorate efforts for job creation in the Greek economy. The improvement of the country's competitiveness was a central theme of ND's election manifesto. The manifesto made no explicit reference to the need for labour market reform, but set ambitious targets for the reduction, by 2008, of unemployment by 2.5–3% and the increase of employment rates to over 60% (from 56.7% in 2003). ND also promised a radically improved business environment which involved, among others, 'the reduction of labour costs through greater productivity' (New Democracy, 2004). This was interpreted as an implicit commitment that, once in power, the Karamanlis government would pursue a shake-up of the Greek labour market.

A year into its term in office and faced with criticism over its timidity to upset the status quo in the Greek economy, the government announced its intention to see through a series of structural reforms in 2005, including revisiting Giannitsis's 2000 labour market law, extending the opening hours of shops, and reducing the labour market discrepan-cies between employees in the public and private sectors. In the words of the influential Secretary of ND's Central Committee, Vaggelis Meimarakis, the time had come for the government 'to break eggs' (*in.gr*, 27 May 2005). The Minister of National Economy, George Alogoskoufis, was also adamant that 'there is a need for imminent changes in the labour market . . . some of which will take place in the summer' (*in.gr*, 27 May 2005).

Timing was indeed a key element of the government's reform strategy. The well-choreographed announcements made by two of Karamanlis's most trusted allies revealed the government's plan to group together the revision of Giannitsis's 2001 law with the issue of opening hours for shops. Both items would be pursued in parallel with a view to new leg-islation been passed through Parliament during the summer months. This would allow the Prime Minister to silence his critics and appear in the September Thessaloniki Trade Fair (an important centre stage for publishing the government's economic policy) with his reformist profile boosted.

The responsibility for the revision of Giannitsis's 2000 labour market law was assigned to the Minister of Labour, Panos Panagiotopoulos. Panagiotopoulos was a man of many contradictions. A former TV jour-nalist who made a seamless transition into politics, he soon established himself as a prominent figure within ND with good links both with the party's leadership and its rank and file. A self-proclaimed 'man of the people', Panagiotopoulos had earned the nickname 'Red Panos', a profile that was well suited to his ministerial portfolio. Panagiotopoulos's deputy, Gerasimos Giakoumatos, was also a prominent champion of ND's populist wing, the so-called popular right (λαϊκή δεξιά).

The relations between the Ministry of Labour and the unions came under severe strain in early July 2005 when Panagiotopoulos announced that the government was ready to bring a new labour market law in Parliament by the end of the month and called for consultation with the social partners to start within 24 hours. According to newspaper reports the government's proposals focused on two main issues:

- The reduction of the cost of overtime which had been substantially increased by 2874/00 law
- The introduction of the principle of management prerogative for the calculation of working time (a measure that Giannitsis had tried and failed to introduce in 2000) (*To Vima*, 7 July 2005)

As predicted, the government's proposals received a positive welcome from the employers associations (SEV, ESEE, and GSEVEE), all of whom had been very critical of the high cost of overtime brought by the 2000 labour market law and the lengthy (and cumbersome) process of acquiring union consent for the adoption flexible working time (*in.gr*, 7 July 2005). GSEE, on the other hand, accused the government of bullying tactics and refused to take part in what it termed as 'smokescreen dialogue' (*Ta Nea*, 13 July 2005). GSEE also warned the government not to legislate on issues that should be the subject of bilateral negotiations between the unions and the employers associations. In a somewhat unusual show of unity, the leader of the ND-affiliated fraction of GSEE, Costas Poupakis, joined the rest of GSEE's leadership in condemning the government proposals, focusing in particular on the issue of managerial prerogative. Similar discontent against the Minister of Labour was also expressed by leading ND trade unionists, including the party's trade union Secretary, Costas Kollias, and MP Giannis Manolis (himself a former GSEE official).

Under pressure from the unions and faced with mounting internal opposition, the government was soon forced to reconsider some of its initial ideas. Following a meeting with the Prime Minister and the Minister of National Economy, Panagiotopoulos faced the media and declared that the government 'had never argued in favour of managerial prerogative and had no intention of introducing such a measure' (*in.gr*, 13 July 2005). According to the Minister, the government's legislation was necessitated by the fact that the social partners had failed to find a common ground between the unions' refusal to negotiate any shift from the status quo and the position of the employers' associations who demanded the radical reduction of cost of overtime and full managerial prerogative on the calculation of working hours (*in.gr*, 15 July 2005). On 15 July 2005 the government brought to Parliament a draft bill with its 'compromise' proposals. These included

- 'Compulsory' overtime (υπερεργασία) would increase from three to five hours per week (41–45) and pay would be reduced from 150% to 125% of normal wages.[21]
- 'Normal' overtime up to 120 hours, calculated on an annual basis, would be remunerated at 150% of normal wages (down from 175%).
- 'Normal' overtime over 120 hours, calculated on an annual basis, would be remunerated at 200% of normal wages (down from 250%).
- The calculation of working time on a four-month basis (down from 12 months), with the exception of seasonal businesses where the annual calculation of working time was retained. Within these periods daily working hours could be set up to ten hours without extra pay, on proviso that employees would not work, on average, over 40 hours per week during the reference period.
- The principle of union consent for the adoption of flexible working hours remained. However, in non-unionized businesses or in cases where the unions would not consent, employers could resort to 'compulsory mediation', where the application of flexible working hours could be approved by a five-member committee at the prefecture level (*Ta Nea*, 19 July 2005).[22]

During the discussion of the labour market bill in Parliament, the Minister of Labour defended his proposals by arguing that the Giannitsis law had been tested and failed and that the government simply reintroduced the labour market regime that exited prior to the law 2874/00 (which itself had been in operation for decades). The opposition, on the other hand, accused the government of revealing its 'right-wing DNA' that, in the words of PASOK's Parliamentary rapporteur, had returned the Greek labour market 'back to 1896' (*in.gr*, 20 July 2005). On the other side of the political spectrum, SEV was also not impressed by the government's proposed reform that had taken little notice of the employers' demands for managerial prerogative, opting instead for the ambiguous scheme of 'compulsory mediation' scheme. For the representatives of commerce (ESEE) and small businesses (GSEVEE) there was definitely better news both from the reduction of overtime costs and a last minute amendment introduced by the Minister of Labour that allowed small business (with less than 21 employees, where first-level union representation is not possible) to make 'individual agreements' with employees on flexible working hours.[23] The new labour market law (3385/2005) was approved by Parliament on 2 August 2005.

The last-minute changes incorporated into the new law were widely seen as a conciliatory gesture to representatives of medium and small businesses with whom the government had had a bruising row over the extension of working hours for shops. This was the second item of the government's reform agenda that ran in parallel with the revision of Giannitsis's law during the summer months of 2005. The regulation of the retail sector came under the brief of the Minister of Development, Dimitris Sioufas, an experienced politician and a close ally of the Prime Minister Karamanlis. As a part of the government's commitment to boost entrepreneurship and create a more business-friendly environment for the Greek economy, Sioufas pledged to reform the legal framework regarding the opening hours of shops. The pre-existing regime provided for a 'ceiling' of 20.00[24] on the closing time of shops between Monday to Friday and 18.00 on Saturday. The precise length of opening hours, however, was determined at the level of prefectures following agreements between local commercial associations and trade unions. The need for local consensus in setting opening hours had acted as a safeguard clause in favour of small businesses which could veto the demands of larger retailers for the full utilization of the opening hours permitted by the law. Hence, the typical opening hours of shops in urban areas, for example, were as follows:[25]

- Mondays, Wednesdays, and Saturdays (9.00 to 15.00)
- Tuesdays, Thursdays, and Fridays (9.00 to 14.30 and 17.30 to 20.30)
- Sundays: closed

In late June 2005, having engaged in little consultation with the social partners, the government announced its intention to bring a new bill to Parliament aimed at introducing a nationally set framework for the opening hours of shops. This was set at 21.00 (Monday to Friday) and 20.00 (Saturdays), with Sunday as a public holiday where all shops would remain closed. By abolishing the requirement for local agreements on the setting of opening hours, the government had effectively ended the veto powers held by small shops against the desires of larger retailers. According to the government the new regime provided consumers with better choice, encouraged competition and would lead to the creation of more jobs. This was not a view shared by the opposition who accused the Minister of Development of giving in to the demands of big multinational retail chains and squeezing out of the market the medium- and small-size businesses that formed the backbone of the Greek economy. PASOK's 'development spokesperson' and former European Commissioner of Social Affairs, Anna Diamantopoulou, also argued that the European experience had shown that such liberalizing measures had been damaging to the world of labour (*in.gr*, 23 June 2005).

The reactions of the social partners to the new proposals were more diverse. The greatest opposition was registered by GSEVEE, the small- and medium-size businesses association, which accused the government of unilateralism and announced a series of protests across Greece, including the blockade of key junctions of the motorway system (*To Vima*, 5 July 2005). GSEE too issued a statement of condemnation of the government's agenda, but fell short of declaring a general strike as it had done, for example, in the case with the revision of Giannitsis's law. Instead GSEE urged its support for the one-day strike declared by two of its constituent parts, the Greek Federation of Private Employees (OIYE/ OIYE: Ομοσπονδία Ιδιωτικών Υπάλληλων Ελλάδας) and the Athens Labour Centre (ALC). The reaction of ESEE, the association of Greek commerce, was one of muted disapproval. The official position of the association stressed that the existing framework regarding opening hours offered a good balance between convenience and choice and hence the government's proposals for extended hours of operation served no useful purpose. ESEE, however, refused to join GSEVEE in an all-out confrontation with the government (*in.gr*, 6 July 2005). This ambivalent position by ESEE reflected growing tensions within its ranks between representatives of small, family-run commercial businesses who felt under threat from the new measures and the largest retail outlets who offered an enthusiastic reception to the government's plans.[26]

Having faced a rather fragmented opposition by the social partners the government was able to push the new law on opening hours (3377/2005) through Parliament on 26 July 2005. Although not strictly a labour market reform, Sioufas's law affected a very large section of the Greek labour force, namely the myriad of small retail outlets sustained by the self-employed or by family-run businesses. By grouping the two items of labour market reform together (laws 3377/2005 and 3385/2005 went through Parliament within a week of each other), the government was able to neutralize some of the opposition by 'giving something to everybody': i.e. lower cost of overtime for small business, extended opening hours for the large retail outlets, a half-baked managerial prerogative on working time for SEV, and a repeal of Giannitsis's law for the unions who had opposed it in 2000. While not a radical departure from the status quo, the labour market package of July/August 2005 was a victory of sorts for the Karamanlis Government. In strategic terms, the decision to bring swift legislation to Parliament without a lengthy process of social consultation had arguably paid off for the government by confining the negative publicity attached to the process within the space of a month (during the summer period). This was a very different story to the experience of PASOK in previous years, where longer processes of social dialogue had had a protracted 'chipping-off' effect on the popularity of Simitis's government without ever producing their desired outcome: a consensual path to domestic reform.

Having seen through its 'twin' labour market reform during the summer months, the Karamanlis Government set out to implement the third 'instalment' of its labour market strategy before the end of 2005: the review of labour practices in state-controlled enterprises. The leading drive behind this reform initiative was the Minister of National Economy, George Alogoskoufis, a London School of Economics-educated economist and former academic, seen by many as the key architect of ND's economic programme. Alogoskoufis had earned a reputation as hard-nosed free market enthusiast who fitted somewhat awkwardly in Karamanlis's carefully crafted centrist profile. Despite his relative political inexperience, however (he was first elected in parliament in 1996), Alogoskoufis was not afraid to take risks. Indicative of this was his controversial decision to challenge the accuracy of the figures (presented by PASOK's government) that brought Greece into the Eurozone.

The decision of the government to review labour practices in state-controlled enterprises carried with it significant risks considering that they were among the most heavily unionized and least productive of the Greek economy. Collectively known as 'DEKO' (Public Utilities/ ΔΕΚΟ – Δημόσιες Επιχειρήσεις Κοινής Ωφέλειας), these enterprises consisted mainly (but not exclusively) of public utilities where the state had retained either full ownership or a controlling stake in their shareholding structure. The management procedures and employment practices within these enterprises had been shaped by a long history of state paternalism, built on political expediency and clientelism, which had resulted in very weak mechanisms of social (or any other form of) accountability. The hybrid legal status of these enterprises had allowed them to occupy a privileged position between the private and public sectors where financial losses were too easily justified in the name of 'public service' and accumulated privileges were seen as a legitimate outcome of the 'market'. Hence, the employees of DEKO enjoyed lifelong job security similar to that of civil servants, but, like their counterparts in the private sector, they engaged in 'free' collective bargaining with the management of these enterprises who were, nevertheless, appointed by the government and also included two union members (out of a total of nine) in their ranks. The net result of this set-up was a strong disposition towards 'non-management' (on this, see chapter on Olympic Airways), where union collusion with the management of these enterprises (and the political leadership of supervising ministries) encouraged the development of highly preferential working conditions and a much higher pay (and pension entitlements) than in the private sector.

The revision of working practices within DEKO formed part of a wider government plan for their restructuring which included the implementation of international standards on corporate governance and accounting practices. The prospective reform served a twinfold purpose for the government: on one level, the driving down of operating costs in DEKO (many of whom suffered huge financial losses) and, on the other, the 'grooming' of these enterprises for their eventual sell-off to private investors (either though flotation in the stock market or one-off buy-outs). A first blueprint of the government's plans for DEKO came in May 2005 when the President/CEO of OTE, Panagis Vourloumis (himself a government appointee), reached a breakthrough agreement with the unions regarding the ending of lifelong job security for the newly appointed staff in the organization in exchange of a hugely generous early retirement scheme for existing employees aimed at reducing overall staffing levels.

The 'OTE solution', which had generated a wave of internal recriminations in the union movement, informed many of the government proposals presented by Alogoskoufis in November 2005. These included, among others,

- the ending of lifelong security for all new employees whose contracts would be brought much closer to those offered in the private sector. Open-ended contracts would be offered after a seven-year probation period.

- for loss-making enterprises (the vast majority of DEKO), an obligation on behalf of the management and the unions to renegotiate, within 4 months, a new employment code (κανονισμός προσωπικού). In the event of disagreement, these employment codes would be imposed by law.
- the requirement for all DEKO to adopt, within nine months, new operational procedures (εσωτερικός κανονισμός λειτουργίας) compatible with international standards on corporate governance.
- for enterprises where the government held a minority stake, recruitment would not be subjected to the stringent (but time-consuming) procedures applicable in the public sector (regulated by ASEP: Higher Council for the Selection of Personnel/ΑΣΕΠ: Ανώτατο Συμβούλιο Επιλογής Προσωπικού) (*in.gr*, 29 November 2005).

Alogoskoufis's announcement was followed by a fierce reaction by GSEE (including all its ND-affiliated members) which accused the government of undermining (though the compulsory renegotiation of employment codes in loss-making DEKO) collective bargaining which formed the cornerstone of industrial relations in the country (*in.gr*, 30 November 2005). Similar reservations were also expressed by OKE as well as by SEV which, nevertheless, was generally supportive of the government's plans (*in.gr*, 7 December 2005). During the debate on the DEKO bill in Parliament, PASOK warned that the distinction between 'new' and 'old' employees in state-controlled enterprises was unconstitutional and accused the government of trying to sell them off on the 'cheap' (*in.gr*, 14 December 2005). Similar attacks were also launched by KKE and SYN. None of these, however, seemed to deter the government which, making use of its comfortable parliamentary majority, was able to see the bill through Parliament on 20 December 2005.

The record of ND in the field of labour market reform stands in sharp contrast to its timidity in the area of pensions and its foot-dragging in the case of Olympic Airways (see Chapters 4 and 6). In the case of its 'twin' labour market reform of July/August 2005 the Karamanlis Government was able to deliver a modest reform agenda by crafting a package deal that divided the opposition and delivered some side payments to most players on the negotiating table. The ambition on DEKO reform was certainly greater. Here the government was able to take on and defeat the powerful unions of the state-controlled enterprises, even if that risked alienating some of the party's own trade unionists. This was an important difference from PASOK, whose power base was much more reluctant to upset the status quo in the 'wider' public sector.

Yet ND's 'victory' in DEKO was not unqualified, having to rest on an uncomfortable (as well as morally and legally questionable) distinction between the working practices of the 'old' and the 'new' employees.

More to the point, three years into its term in office, the record of the ND government in reducing unemployment was hardly a cause for much celebration. By the end of 2006 Greece's unemployment rate stood at 8.7%, having fallen by less than 1% since 2003 (against a self-proclaimed target of 2.5%–3%). This was the worst rate of unemployment among all members of the Eurozone and the third-worst rate among all 25 members of the EU (Eurostat, 2007). During the same period the Greek economy had grown at a yearly average of 3.8% as opposed to 1.4% for the EU 15 (Eurostat, 2007). This remained a poignant reminder that, like its predecessors, the Karamanlis Government had not been able to break the puzzle of Greece's jobless growth.

5.8 Conclusion

This has been a case study of political leaderships across governments largely sharing a belief in the need for Greece to adapt to a changing external economic climate: one requiring greater labour market flexibility. Their task was one of 'how?' not 'why?'. The systemic constraints were again immense. The achievements of reform have been modest.

Some contrast over time is evident. The Simitis Government had started with good intentions. It chose a strategy of social dialogue: a major break with the past. A pressing reform need was to be tackled by consensus – this, in turn, would legitimate the otherwise difficult agenda. The successful implantation of a stable and even limitedly successful social dialogue would have been a significant innovation in the Greek system. Yet the government itself fell victim to the pressures of the system: it lacked unity of purpose and was inconsistent in its strategy, alienating its intended partners and exacerbating issues of commitment and trust. The government had undermined its own solution and the outcomes were limited. Indeed, its actions had the effect of reviving the political fortunes of the unions. Thus, the record of protracted failure had bequeathed a difficult legacy for the incoming Karamanlis Government. However, in this area the latter appeared to show more strength of conviction and more strategic guile than in other sectors. It neutralized opposition by bringing forward package deals with mixed incentives and it proved willing to face down opposition from its own allies. It enjoyed some initial success with two reform packages: reform from 'within' was achieved, despite the past and without firm EU levers.

A struggle for attrition has occurred, with the policy ground being prepared over the Simitis and Karamanlis Governments. Given the strength of the systemic constraints on reform, it would be shallow and naive to assume that a change of personnel can easily overcome them. The structural impediments are deeply rooted. The challenge of sustaining the momentum is evident – with further tactical ingenuity required – and the issue of reform capacity remains very much to the fore. The ideological distance between the various business and union organizations is considerable and they retain sharply different notions of their strategic interest. Moreover, public attitudes on matters of such reform remain fluid and unreliable.

The case study testifies to the relative impotence of EU instruments to lever structural economic reform across different systems. 'Europeanization' had offered an agenda, one radically different from the Greek tradition and this served to focus and legitimize a domestic debate. The EU agenda had highlighted the degree of 'misfit' with Greek conditions, but the distance between the domestic actors with veto potential had stymied reform. EU commitments provided no direct empowerment: there was little constraint to apply or resist. Instead, the two early reform packages of the Karamanlis Government came from more effective strategic calculation and strength of purpose on the part of the Athens leadership. The relevant reform Ministers had not been left politically isolated to fight alone. Strategy showed a keen sensitivity to what public opinion might accept. This was change at the level of leadership direction.

The timing of the domestic reform owed little to the EU momentum. But neither did it appear to presage a substantive restructuring of the sector in terms of power or of ideology. The relevant actors were still far apart in the calculation of their strategic interests and the form of their interaction had not been reshaped. The rules of the game had not been disturbed. The system appeared resilient and largely uncompromising. The outlook for future liberal reform remained daunting.

Table 5.1 Reforming the Greek labour market, 1997–2005

Sep. 1996:	PASOK, under the leadership of Kostas Simitis, wins general election
Apr. 1997:	Government launches social dialogue 'on Development, Competitiveness and Employment'
Nov. 1997:	The government and the social partners sign the 'Confidence Pact towards the Year 2000'
Jan. 1998:	The 'Papandoniou avengement' passes through Parliament allowing the management of loss-making state-controlled enterprises to change their code of employment without prior consent from the unions
Aug. 1998:	Papaioannou's labour market law (2639/98) passes through Parliament. Main provisions: • Calculation of working time on a three- and six-month basis based upon union consent • Introduction of TEPs • Improvements in the regulation of 'atypical' and part-time employment • Introduction of part-time employment in state-controlled enterprises • Creation of private employment agencies • Medical and pharmaceutical cover for the young (under 29) and long-term unemployed
Apr. 2000:	PASOK wins general election. Promise for a 40% reduction in unemployment (300,000 new jobs)
July 2000:	Papandoniou calls for a new labour market reform that would be 'a strong shock' for the unions
July 2000:	Giannitsis announces consultation with social partners on a new labour market law to be concluded within two months
Sep. 2000:	Giannitsis unveils government plans on labour market reform. Fierce opposition from within PASOK
Nov. 2000:	Minister of Culture, Theodore Pagalos, is sacked after criticizing the government's handling of the reform process
Dec. 2000:	Giannitsis's labour market law (2874/00) passes through Parliament. Main provisions: • Annualized calculation of working time, based on union consent and linked to a 38-hour week • Substantial increases in the cost of overtime

	• Small reduction of limits on collective redundancies for medium-sized businesses • Reduction of employers' national insurance contributions for newly recruited staff • Small increase for the wages of part-time employees (working under four hours a day)
Mar. 2003:	ND wins general election. Promise for a 30% drop in unemployment (60% employment)
Mar. 2005:	Secretary of ND's Central Committee, Vaggelis Meimarakis, announces government is ready 'to break Eggs' in its pursuit of a three-stage labour market reform
Jul. 2005:	Panagiotopoulos calls for consultation with social partners to begin 'within twenty-four-hours' for the revision of Giannitsis's 2000 labour market law. Unions refuse to attend
Jul. 2005:	Sioufas's 'opening hours' law (3377/05) passes through Parliament. Main provisions: • Nationally set framework of opening hours (replacing local agreements) introduced • Opening hours: daily up to 21:00 and Saturdays up to 20:00 (Sunday: closed)
Aug. 2005:	Panagiotopoulos's labour market law (3385/05) passes through Parliament. Main provisions: • Cost of overtime to revert (nearly) to its pre-2000 levels • The calculation of working time on a four-month basis (with exceptions) based on 40-hour week • Flexibility on working time based on a system of 'compulsory mediation' (half way house between union consent and managerial prerogative) • Last-minute amendment allowing small businesses to negotiate 'individual agreements' with employees
Dec. 2005:	Alogoskoufis's 'DEKO' law (3429/05) passes through Parliament. Main provisions: • Ending of lifelong security for all new employees (contracts similar to those of the private sector) • New employment codes (within four months) for all loss-making DEKOs (by law, if necessary) • New operational procedures, compatible with international standards on corporate governance • Recruitment for DEKOs floated in the stock exchange no longer subject to ASEP

6
Destination Nowhere: Restructuring Olympic Airways/Airlines

6.1 Introduction

The domestic impact of the EU entails a mix of policy instruments emanating from 'Brussels'. Some are 'hard' laws, such as EU directives or policy rules set by treaties. Others involve policy coordination with 'soft' instruments of sharing best practice and/or the Commission urging preferred solutions. Domestic actors must distinguish between these instruments to determine their constraints. They must also judge how 'hard' law instruments might be used by the Commission to promote domestic reforms drawn from 'soft' agendas. To politicians and the public, what 'Europe' expects in terms of domestic policy and practice can be a matter of some confusion.

'Privatization' – the selling-off by governments of state-owned enterprises – can be placed in this context. The EU law provides no obligation on member states to privatize any such enterprise. The Commission may exhort, but it has no competence to require or impose such a policy. The EU competition policy, however, does provide the Commission with powerful instruments by which to prohibit governments offering unfair subsidies and aids to either public or private firms. Thus, enterprises must be open to fair competition – state monopolies are not allowed in an increasing number of sectors – but their ownership structure is not a matter for the EU.

The air passenger transport sector is a case in point. European and domestic markets must be open to competition and aids to state enterprises must be approved by the Commission. The Commission has strong powers to act in order to prevent such subsidies. But, while Commissioners for Transport may urge the selling-off of ailing national carriers, there is no obligation to follow such notions.

Over the last 15 years, the aviation industry in Europe has undergone revolutionary change, as well as unprecedented growth. According to data provided by the European Commission between 1992 and 2003 the number of intra-Community routes and EU-based airlines had increased by 40% and 25% respectively. Between 1990 and 2002 productivity also rose by 87%. In 2005 with a network of 450 airports, 130 airlines, and 60 service providers the aviation sector was said to employ 3 million workers contributing almost 1.5% to the European GDP.[1] Despite the overall vibrancy of the aviation sector, however, a number of national carriers have faced serious financial difficulties in the context of the increased competition. Belgian carrier, Sabena, filed for bankruptcy in November 2001 after the collapse of its strategic partner, Swissair. Another state enterprise, Alitalia, has also struggled to survive, and the left-of-centre government of Romano Prodi announced in December 2006 that it would seek to sell-off 50% of the company. Several strategic partners have been touted: Air France-KLM and Lufthansa, most notably. The former was reported to have insisted on complete privatization as a preliminary condition. The Spanish government successfully privatized Iberia in 2001, with British Airways (BA) and American Airlines taking a small stake. In each of these cases, the EU Commission was a central player in regulating state funding and monitoring restructuring plans.

National governments were placed in a difficult position, strategically. Ailing state airlines were a drain on public funding and faced uncertain futures in the newly liberalized European market. The cost of a government allowing a national airline to collapse, however, was high in terms of the job losses, labour relations, reputation, and public opinion. EU legislation did not mandate state sell-offs. On the other hand, the scope for state investment to help restructure the airlines was severely curtailed by the EU's competition rules. Governments were obliged to negotiate with the Commission to work out 'rescue packages' and the bargaining led to reciprocal obligations and understandings over time. The relationship with the Commission was marked by a mix of law, informal understandings, and bargaining perceptions. Governments had to test the scope of the strictures set by the Commission, be inventive in creating new options, and build up credibility and trust with Brussels. There was much room here for misunderstandings and miscalculation. At the same time, governments had to manage their domestic political constraints and these would affect their negotiations in Brussels.

The case of Olympic Airways in Greece amply illustrates the difficulties faced by government's intent on reform. Domestically, a range of restructuring options were pursued over an extended period. The approval and support of the Commission was sought repeatedly. Politically, governments faced severe constraints at home. Greek Ministers made their calculations crossing both bargaining arenas: the EU and the domestic. Latterly, crucial miscalculations were made as to the support forthcoming from the Commission. Whether this was due to genuine misunderstandings or wilful political challenge remains unclear. In the highly charged negotiations, calculations and perceptions of what the Commission wanted and what it might accept would have been central. What is certain is that an agenda that began with 'Europeanization' concluded with the Commission being the major opponent of the attempted domestic reform.

This case of Olympic Airways displays the problems of EU governance when confronting domestic adaptation to the single European market. The Commission had an agenda of market liberalization and it had a clear preference for the option of privatization. Yet the instruments at its disposal had an asymmetry: a mix of tough anti-state-aid rules and 'soft' policy exhortation. Domestically, the government was desperate for reform, trying various options, but ultimately it could not reconcile the pressures of the Commission and of the company. As one option failed and another attempted, credibility was lost. Olympic was left as a 'basket case' – perceived as a lost cause. At the same time, the case poses important questions about the capacity of the Commission to manage a programme of economic reform. It is a case of failure, for both the Commission and the national government proved unable to realize their core preferences. The Commission had sought restructuring sufficient to ensure viability and had signalled that the most likely means to achieve this was through privatization. The Greek government had sought to cut the cost on the state's budget and to maintain a national carrier. Over time it had moved towards privatization as the solution. The outcome was a contested restructuring package and no privatization, with the airline continuing to struggle to survive.

The chapter begins by explaining the Commission's competence to act and its apparent strategy. It then examines the national attempts at reform, with reference to the stimuli and constraints set by the Commission. The domestic political process is outlined in terms of the actors involved, their interests, and their structural power to affect reform initiatives. The outcomes for the company are elaborated. The story concludes with the backlash of the Commission – referring the national restructuring package to the European Court of Justice (ECJ).

6.2   The EU stimulus to domestic reform

With its unique juxtaposition of roles and complex variety of competences, the Commission is both a referee and a player in the process of
market liberalization. The Commission's competence to act in this field
derives from several sources: the treaty provisions on transport, its powers to intervene on market-distorting 'state aids', and the application of
internal market rules to the aviation industry. Air transport in the EU
was liberalized in three successive stages. The first package of measures
adopted in December 1987 relaxed pre-existing government controls
over pricing and allowed the sharing of seating capacity between member states. The second package was adopted in June 1990 and provided
for greater flexibility over fares and capacity sharing. In addition it
extended the right to the fifth freedom[2] and opened up the third[3] and
fourth[4] freedoms to all Community carriers.[5]

The third, and more substantive, package was adopted in 1992 and
applied from January 1993. The 'third package' gradually introduced
the freedom to provide services within the EU and led in April 1997 to
the freedom to provide cabotage, i.e. the right for an airline of one
member state to operate a route within another member state. It com-
prised common rules on the licensing of air carriers, rules on access for
Community air carriers to intra-Community air routes, rules on fares
and rates for intra-Community air services, and the full application of
the competition rules of the Treaty to the liberalized air transport
market.[6]

In the general area of competition policy, the Commission's role is an
exception from the wider norm: it has supranational authority to act
and the objects of regulation are the national governments themselves
(Cini & McGowan, 1998: 136). Within this regulatory framework, however, a key element is the Commission's bargaining, on a bilateral basis,
with national governments in relation to industry restructuring. The
bargaining process requires the Commission to elaborate its priorities,
strategies, and tactics, providing scope for interpretation and adjustment. The latter is, inevitably, affected by changing political agendas
and leadership personalities. By the 1990s, the stress was undoubtedly
on deregulation and the abandonment of state aids distorting competition. Loyola De Palacio, the Transport Commissioner from September
1999 to November 2004, pursued her strategy with vigour, at times
heightening the sense of confrontation with member governments.[7]

The Commission acknowledged implicitly the sensitivities that would
arise if it were to call directly for privatization in the sector, but its

repeated assertion of the need for a fully liberalized European market and its insistence that state intervention (in the form of aid, subsidies, and patronage) should end showed a clear stimulus to national carriers being run on fully commercial lines. The Commission went as far as it could to structure the reform path: indeed, in 1994 it had granted aid to various European companies, 'which would allow . . . their possible privatisation' (European Parliament, 1999). Loyola De Palacio, as the relevant Commissioner, was clearly frustrated by the lack of reform and the lack of transparency in accounting in the case of Olympic Airways.

De Palacio outlined the Commission's approach on a number of occasions:

> *Our objective has been to devise a vision of what the air transport* market *should look like and to focus on how to ensure air services are provided in the most efficient and competitive way possible . . . Europe's airline industry and economy was not strengthened by unquestioning national support for inefficient national flag carriers and the building of national champions – on the contrary, it was actually weakened. We have seen how difficult Olympic Airways and TAP have found it to develop a successful long-term strategy in spite of state aid and restructuring plans . . . Ten years after liberalisation [the establishment of an internal market for transport services in 1992], the true benefits of a clear focus on a liberalised European* market *– and* not *on specific airlines – are becoming clear for European consumers. . . . Our initial objective is to maintain and improve the liberalised European marketplace* [emphases in original].
> (de Palacio, 2002)

A more general outline of her policy perspective was given in a speech in Spain:

> Air transport within the European Economic Area is now governed by common rules on licensing, market access and pricing freedom. After eleven years of implementation it can be said that thanks to these measures there has been an unprecedented expansion of air transport in Europe. Old monopolies have been swept away. . . . European aviation has moved from a highly regulated market to a highly competitive single market . . . In the area of State aid we are still faced with the problem of restructuring of some still heavily indebted flag carriers and the attendant issue of state aid and competition that this implies. The Commission has pursued a very strict policy to avoid distortions. For the first time in Europe even flag-carriers have gone

bankrupt. This policy must continue in the future in order to be more competitive and efficient.

(de Palacio, 2004)

The preferences of the Commission can be inferred from such public statements: the will to act was clear. The Commission's stress was on efficiency, competition, the abandonment of state aids – broadly defined – and a vibrant European marketplace.

This is a case, therefore, that begins with the Commission taking action over the use of state aids. Indeed, it remains the central basis of the Commission's competence to act as the case develops. However, over time, the Commission also gave important signals of its preferences in relation to domestic privatization. No national government could have failed to recognize the existence of the latter or to have understood that they would serve to define, in part, the range of acceptable policy solutions when flexibility on state aid rules was being sought.

Yet criticisms of the Commission's performance in this area could also create some doubt as to its future intentions. Some suggest that liberalization in this sector has been 'one of the Commission's success stories' (Cini and McGowan, 1998:174). However, while considerable progress has been made in removing the internal market barriers within the sector (Button, 2001), a greater coherence in the system of regulation has been called for (Sebastiani, 2002; Pelkmans, 2001). More generally, well-publicized disputes over the Commission's decisions on company mergers, under EU competition policy, have provoked 'increasing public criticism about the quality of analysis underpinning some . . . decisions' (Morgan and McGuire, 2004: 45). This has been sharpened by ECJ rulings overturning Commission vetoes on mergers. These factors would give member governments additional reason – over and above their domestic constraints – to carefully review the signals emanating from the Commission and to its decisions.

The EU pressure was felt by the Greek government on several fronts. Firstly, there were the three directives on market liberalization in the air transport sector launched in the early 1990s. Secondly, there was the increasingly rigorous attack on state aids. Finally, there were also the demands of the convergence criteria for entry into the single European currency, creating an additional lever with its stringency on the fiscal stability of national governments. The EMU was itself a major pressure across the Greek political landscape (Featherstone, 2003). The relevance of these three sets of EU pressure to the case of Olympic fluctuated over the course of the 1990s, though each involved 'hard' rules. The difficulty faced by the Commission was to craft an effective strategy likely to attain Greek compliance.

The crafting of such strategy, however, was subject to the Commission's own interpretation of state aid and competition rules against the backdrop of continuing bargaining with the Greek government. Inevitably, the 'negotiated application' of these rules meant some variation over time in the signals, tactics, and strategy of the Commission, creating some uncertainty for the Greek government to factor into its own calculations. The response of the Greek government to the actions of the Commission cannot be fully understood without reference to this unpredictability. At the same time, the uncertainty created the opportunity for Athens to seek to manipulate the bargaining relationship to its own advantage.

But what 'advantage'? The strategy of the Simitis Government was determined by its interaction in two arenas: the EU and the domestic. The constraints of the latter impelled it to seek 'slack' from the Commission – allowing some manipulation of the EU rules – in order to satisfy its narrow domestic 'win-set'. Indeed, the domestic constraints provided the Greek government with inducements to manipulate, evade, and contest.

6.3 Olympic Airways: The politics of non-management

Olympic Airways was founded in 1957 following the acquisition of the tiny Greek state-owned airline TAE (Technical Aviation Undertakings/ ΤΑΕ: Τεχνικαί Αεροπορικαί Εκμεταλεύσεις Τεχνικαί Αεροπορικαί Εκμεταλεύσεις) by Greek magnate Aristotle Onassis. During Onassis's reign Olympic was closely associated with its founder's glamour, developing a reputation for excellent service and an extensive network which made it arguably the first Greek company with a truly global reach. The company's logo based on the five Olympic circles and its motto as 'the airline of the five continents' became a source of national pride for many Greeks who, over the years, developed a very high regard for Olympic and its employees. Behind the glossy exterior, however, the finances of OA under Onassis's stewardship were never entirely transparent. While the company remained overall in a healthy financial position, management priorities and accounting practices were always closely intertwined with a complex web of companies upon which Onassis built his massive business empire. A series of special arrangements for OA negotiated directly between Onassis and the Greek state in the 1950s (including a generous tax regime for the airline) had also contributed to company's success. Many of these deals were reflective of the highly paternalistic nature of state-business relations in post-war Greece which are already well documented in the literature (Mavrogordatos, 1988; Lavdas, 1997).

By the early 1970s Onassis's love affair with Olympic began to wane as a result of changing business priorities and personal tragedy. High fuel prices and the subsequent worldwide recession caused by the 1973 oil crisis hit the airline industry hard. Onassis's persistent requests for the Greek government to provide assistance to OA met the refusal of Greece's (then) military rulers. In the same year the Greek tycoon had to deal with a major personal blow due to the death of his only son, Alexandros – himself a keen OA pilot – in a plane crash near Athens. This incident added new urgency to Onassis's determination to offload Olympic Airways. By then he had allegedly come to the conclusion that OA was a 'bucket of swage' which once it was about to overflow he would 'flog' it to the Greek state. A year later a new democratic government was formed under Constantinos Karamanlis following the collapse of the military dictatorship in early 1974. The new government soon came under pressure from Onassis to buy OA, but then Minister of Co-ordination (Finance), Panagis Papaligouras, resisted this prospect. Papaligouras's objections, however, were eventually overruled in Cabinet which finally gave the green light to the deal in late 1974. As a result Olympic Airways came under the ownership of the Greek state on 26 June 1975 (Law 96/75) (for a full chronology of the Olympic Airways privatization attempts look at Table 6.1).

The transformation of Olympic Airways from a privately run airline to a public utility (DEKO/ΔΕΚΟ) opened a new chapter for the company's history during which its relentless exposure to the clientelistic practices of the Greek party-state has become the defining feature of its operations. Political parties, the state bureaucracy, and a myriad of sectoral interests both in Greece and abroad have all, under the pretext of the OA's 'national mission', sought to use Olympic as a tool for political expediency and easy moneymaking. The company, for example, was for years forced to operate loss-making routes to remote Greek islands and transport state officials for free without ever being compensated by the Greek state. Political parties too developed a destructively close relationship with OA. In addition to their excessive interference over appointments and personnel matters within the company, all major political parties received significant travel benefits from OA. The most astonishing of these was the obligation by OA to transport party supporters during national, European, and local elections at well-below-cost prices. Political patronage has also allowed a number of private business interests to exert undue influence on the business plan of OA. Under pressure from the powerful Greek diaspora, for example, Olympic had agreed to pay extortionate commission to Greek travel agents in the US and Australia, whereas influential press barons in Greece had also managed to negotiate special deals with Olympic for the transportation of their press outlets at only a fraction of international prices (Doganis, 2001: 189).

The OA's position as a public utility made it almost impossible to monitor its financial position with some accuracy. While by the mid 1980s it was already clear that OA was suffering heavy losses (see below), the full extent of these losses was not fully appreciated as the company was not required to produce detailed accounts. The picture of the OA's finances was further blurred by the fact that the Greek state chose not to pursue the company's huge tax and national insurance arrears, whereas Olympic was not required to pay airport taxes and handling charges. The difficulties in assessing the scale of OA's financial problems reflected wider weaknesses of the Greek state to regulate effectively its own public utility monopolies. While the sole shareholder of OA was the Ministry of National Economy, the supervision of the airline industry came under the remit of the Ministry of Transport. The latter, however, has always been a small and relative weak ministry which lacked the expertise and human capital to perform its regulatory role adequately.

This role has almost entirely been delegated to the Hellenic Civil Aviation Authority (YPA/ΥΠΑ: Υπηρεσία Πολιτικής Αεροπορίας), a powerful and well-consolidated quasi-independent authority (reporting to the Ministry of Transport), whose extensive competences included, among others, safety, air-traffic control, the running of Greece's airports (all state-owned), and the production of statistics on flight and passenger numbers. While successful in retaining an excellent safety record, YPA's ability to act as truly independent regulator of an increasingly diverse market has been questioned. Many of the OA's competitors have argued that during the years of the OA's virtual monopoly of the Greek civil aviation market, the boundaries between the regulators (YPA) and the regulated (OA) have all but disappeared leading the two to develop essentially from the same 'statist material', thus creating an entrenched bias against newcomers to the Greek airline industry.

Nowhere else have the disruptive effects of clientelistic statism been more vividly manifested themselves than in the management of

Olympic Airways. In the 30 years under government control, the chairmanship of Olympic Airways has changed 32 times, often filled with candidates that had little or no experience in the industry. The company's top management scheme has also remained fluid, reverting – according to political expediencies of the day – from a 'dual leadership' (i.e. distinct roles for the Chairman and Chief Executive Officer–CEO) to a 'single authority' (i.e. a combined Chairman and CEO role) and backwards. Over the same period, the changes in the membership of the OA's Board of Directors have been ever more frequent, reflecting an almost endless appetite of successive governments to use the well-paid management positions in OA in order to reward their political friends. At no stage during the past 30 years had the Chairman or the CEO of Olympic been able to work with a Board that was not directly or indirectly controlled by the government.

The relation between Olympic's management and their political masters in the Ministry of Transport has been one of convenience and subservience. While the OA's management was expected to run the day-to-day business of the company, Ministers were heavily involved in all major decisions affecting the future of Olympic, often with blatant disregard about the management's authority and judgement. The government's increasing reliance on external consultants to perform even the most routine management tasks within the OA group has been indicative of this disregard.[8] In the very few cases where the airline's management sought to assert its authority against the government, the latter was always quick to restore order by sacking those with a more independent disposition. Recruitment and procurement policies have been two of the areas where excessive political interference with the management of Olympic has had its most devastating effects. During the 1970s and, particularly, the 1980s staffing levels in OA rocketed as a result of party-political electioneering. By the early 1990s the Greek flag carrier had accumulated a workforce in excess of 11,500, more than double of its size in the early 1970s and well over the staffing levels of similar-size airlines across the world. Procurement strategy was also affected by the need of different governments (at different times) to appease powerful international allies. As a result, in the early 1990s Olympic's 55-strong fleet[9] contained seven different types of aircraft, thus contributing to substantially increased maintenance costs (Lavdas, 1997: 195).

The weakness of the OA's management vis-à-vis the government of the day had an almost paralysing effect on its ability to deal effectively with the company's workforce. Like many of Europe's flag carriers, OA has been heavily unionized. A total of 17 sectoral unions operated within the OA group reflecting the very diverse range of activities (aviation, technical, handling, and administrative) performed by its numerous subsidiaries. All 17 sectoral unions formed part of the Federation of Civil Aviation Unions (OSPA/ΟΣΠΑ: Ομοσπονδία Σωματείων Πολιτικής Αεροπορίας), the umbrella union for the entire workforce of the OA group. Owning to its diverse and fragmented membership, OSPA has always been a rather board church. Traditionally, internal union politics were dominated by the divide between ground staff, on the one hand, and pilots and cabin crew, on the other. Due to their numerical strength within the OA group, the unions of manual and administrative staff were able to control the leadership of OSPA, which often looked with suspicion towards its two most powerful members: the pilots (EXPA: Union of Civil Aviation Pilots/ΕΧΠΑ: 'Ενωση Χειριστών Πολιτικής Αεροπορίας 'Ενωση Χειριστών Πολιτικής Αεροπορίας) and flying attendants (EISF: Union of Flying Attendants/ΕΙΣΦ: 'Ενωση Ιπταμένων Συνοδών και Φροντιστών) unions. Party political loyalties also affected the shape of unionism within OA. The Pan-Hellenic Socialist Party (PASOK), for example, has always been very influential in OSPA, whereas centre-right ND has traditionally controlled the pilots union (EXPA). The partisan affiliation of the flight attendants union (EISF), on the other hand, has been more volatile shifting from PASOK to ND and backwards according to the political expediencies of the day.

Yet despite their internal quarrels, the OA's unions have been remarkably united in the fierce defence of their employment conditions (which are widely regarded to be more privileged than those enjoyed by Olympic's international and domestic competitors) and militantly opposed to the prospect of the Greek flag carrier slimming down its operations or losing its state-owned character. The unions of OA have also taken a rather narrow view over their membership and objectives, despite the fact that their names are, with no exception, defined in national or industry-wide terms. As a result their leadership has not yet allowed employees from private competitors or other foreign flag carriers operating in Greece to enrol in their membership. While the failure to open up their membership is officially blamed on administrative oversights and practical obstacles, many senior union leaders within OA remain openly hostile to this prospect, fearful that an enlarged membership would dilute their opposition to the importation of 'dark age' working conditions from the private sector into Olympic.

The unions' close involvement with the management of Olympic has been a persistent feature of the company's history dating back to the days of Onassis when employees (particularly the pilots) were encouraged to develop a strong sense of co-ownership of the airline's fate. In the absence of a strong management in the post-Onassis period, however, the unions' influence in the running of Olympic grew out of all proportions. During the 1980s their strength became all the more evident, as the influential mistress and later wife of PM Andreas Papandreou, Dimitra, herself a leading figure in the flying attendants union (EISF), encouraged a more maximalist union agenda and rewarded her former colleagues with a number of extra privileges (through the so-called Dimitra-laws). Over the same period the credibility of the airline's management in the eyes of its employees diminished further with many union leaders expressing open contempt for their bosses or bypassing them altogether, opting instead to lobby directly government Ministers and party bosses with whom they enjoyed open channels of communication through their party-political affiliations.

By the end of the 1980s the unbalanced and poorly demarcated responsibilities between the three corners of Olympic's 'ruling triangle' (government, management, unions) had rendered the Greek flag carrier virtually ungovernable. It is estimated (European Commission, 1994) that in 1992 Olympic Airways had accumulated a debt of ECU1.6 billion and the company was confronted with new costs for the modernization of its ageing fleet. Despite its relative low unit costs, OA's medium- and long-term prospects for survival were fatally undermined by low productivity, an irrational flying schedule and an anachronistic employment regime underpinned by a huge network of ad hoc agreements negotiated between the management and the unions without reference to a viable business plan. Yet despite the fact that the financial cost of keeping Olympic afloat became increasingly hard for the Greek government to bear, any suggestion that disturbed the status quo was defeated by a constellation of power that has effectively produced a deadlock.

Underlining this deadlock was wider confusion on behalf of the country's political elites over the role and outlook that Olympic ought to develop. Should the losses of the Greek flag carrier be tolerated in the name of its 'national' mission and its service to vulnerable communities within Greece and abroad; or should Olympic be forced to develop as a private airline subjected to the laws of the open market? Much of this confusion was also reflected in the attitudes of the Greek public who, despite having grown increasingly impatient with OA's losses and poor service, still remained attached to the symbols and grandeur of Olympic's golden past and its perceived social mission. In the face of weak domestic impetus for reform, the EU-driven agenda for eliminating state subsidies and opening up the European civil aviation market acted as a catalyst for the future of Olympic Airways. In the turbulent and traumatic decade that followed, the Greek flag carrier would come under increased scrutiny and tremendous pressure to change. The manner in which Olympic Airways responded to this pressure is explored in the next section of this chapter.

6.4   No cure available: Attempts to reform Olympic Airways 1994–2000

As the Commission's drive for opening up the EU's civil aviation market gathered momentum during the early 1990s, the financial position of Olympic Airways continued to worsen. In July 1993 the Greek centre-right (ND) government, by reference to the 'serious economic disturbance' clause provided in Article 93 of the EEC Treaty, notified the Commission of its intention to implement a rescue plan for Olympic involving financial aid of ECU1.1 billion (in the form of debt write offs, conversion of debt to equity, and capital injections) and the extension of state guarantees over the next five years for the modernization of Olympic's fleet to the tune of some ECU246 million. To supplement these measures the government also announced a plan for returning the airline to profitability by 1997 structured around a freeze on staff recruitment and a remodelling of the OA's route network, with more emphasis on European services. The proposals of the Greek government, however, met with strong opposition by the Commission, which challenged both the credibility of the proposed rescue plan and the data upon which it was based. The Greek government was also accused of stalling the implementation of the third package of air transport measures agreed by the EU and continuing to distort competition by maintaining Olympic's privileged relationship with the Greek state (European Commission, 1994).

By the time the Commission had decided, in March 1994, to initiate an investigation into the illegal state aid to Olympic by the Greek government (the first step towards referral to the ECJ), PASOK had returned to power. Anxious to find a compromise with Brussels and tackle Olympic's mounting financial crisis, the new government moved fast to submit a revised rescue plan for the beleaguered airline. In a new set of data sent to the Commission in May 1994, the full scale of Olympic's financial troubles was revealed. The Greek government by now had accepted that the total amount of recapitalization needed for Olympic was in excess of ECU1.7 billion and proposed (a) the write off of ECU1.4 billion of accumulated debt, (b) the conversion of ECU209 million of debt into equity, (c) a capital injection of ECU177 million in three yearly instalments between 1995 and 1997, and (d) the extension of ECU300 million of state guarantees to Olympic until the end of 1997. Following intensive negotiations between the Commission and the Greek government over the summer months, the proposed bailout (the second largest in the EU behind Air France's) was finally approved in October 1994 (Doganis, 2001 Chapter 8; European Commission, 1994).

The Commission's approval, however, had come at a heavy price for the Greek government. As part of the Olympic's restructuring programme, a commitment was undertaken to implement a string of 21 measures which included, among others, a 30% reduction in labour costs by 1995 through a mixture of staff cuts, pay freezes, and changes in employment conditions; the discontinuation of OA's services to Tokyo and all US destinations other than New York; an immediate end to government interference with the management of Olympic; an end to state guarantees for the OA's borrowing requirements after 1997; and the full implementation of the EU's third air transport package by the end of 1994 (European Commission, 1994). Against the backdrop of persistent wildcat strikes and fierce union opposition, the law on the restructuring of Olympic passed through Parliament in November 1994 (Law 2271/94). It included provisions for the voluntary exit of 10% of Olympic's 10,500-strong workforce in 1994 and a further 5% staff reduction for 1995. In addition a pay freeze was introduced for two years, estimated to cost (due to inflation) OA employees a 20% drop of their real wages (Doganis, 2001: 207–9). The promised revision of employment conditions was, by comparison, far more moderate affecting only some marginal benefits enjoyed by the staff of OA. The failure to address this key issue more forcefully (seen by many as the core of OA's problems) was yet another indication of the powerful veto points that resisted far-reaching reform in the Greek flag carrier (Lavdas, 1997: 199–200).

Yet despite its shortcomings the new law, combined with the state aid package agreed by the Commission, offered a lifeline for Olympic. In early 1995, the Minister of Transport, Thanassis Tsouras, appointed Rigas Doganis, a well-respected Professor of Transport at Cranfield University in the UK, to the post of Chairman and CEO of Olympic Airways with the task of implementing the agreed rescue plan. Indeed under Doganis's stewardship the airline began to show the first signs of revival. In 1995 the Commission agreed to the release of the first instalment of the capital injection (ECU62.7 million) provided for by the

1994 deal and, following a series of cost-cutting measures, Olympic was able to post a profit of ECU29.7 million by the end of the year, the first time it had been able to do so since 1978 (Doganis, 2001: 208). Yet, in January 1996, the arrival of a new Transport Minister, Charis Kastanidis (the fifth since 1993), brought Doganis onto a trajectory of conflict with the government. Frustrated by what he perceived as constant government interference in his work, Doganis visited Brussels in February 1996 and asked the Commission to apply pressure on the Greek government to allow him greater independence over strategy, recruitment, and the appointment of members in the OA's Board of Directors (*Eleftherotypia*, 17 February 1996). Unaware of Doganis's visit to Brussels, Kastanidis felt undermined by the actions of the OA boss. Less than a month later, Rigas Doganis was informed of his dismissal through the Reuters news agency.

Doganis's departure plunged Olympic into a new crisis and seriously undermined the credibility of the Greek government's commitment to the restructuring process. Two months later, the Commission refused to authorize the release of the second instalment of the government's planned capital injection to Olympic worth ECU75 million (*Eleftherotypia*, 30 April 1996). In its decision, the Commission listed a series of defaults from the rescue plan agreed in 1994 and concentrated its criticism on the continued political interference with the management of Olympic as well as the government's decision to retain the OA's preferential tax regime and finance the airline's programme of voluntary redundancies in 1994–5 to the tune of ECU36 million. This, the Commission argued, constituted unauthorized state aid to the Greek flag carrier (European Commission, 1996). The Commission's decision reignited fears over the imminent collapse of Olympic's finances as the airline's credibility took a further blow by protracted industrial unrest during the peak summer months. In a desperate attempt to restore order, the OA's management (with the blessing of Minister Kastanidis) caved in to unions' demands for a 20% pay increase. This move effectively killed the 1994 restructuring plan. With OA's profits for 1996 having evaporated and with a predicted deficit in the region of ECU48 million for 1997,[10] Kastanidis's position became untenable, leading to his replacement by Tasos Mantelis in September 1997.

The timing of Mantelis's arrival in the Ministry of Transport was crucial as the Greek government struggled to convince its EU counterparts about the merits of its accession into the ERM II, the first step towards the country's entry into the Eurozone.[11] During these discussions the government's commitment to fiscal discipline and particularly its ability to control spending in its public utilities came under close scrutiny. Mantelis, a close political friend of Prime Minister Costas Simitis, entered the government on a promise to pursue painful reforms in the public utilities under the control of his Ministry.

For Olympic, Mantelis's plans included a 'double' strategy: in the first instance, the lifting of the Commission's objections on the second cash injection to OA (blocked since 1996) through the launching of a new rescue plan and, consequently, the pursuit of a strategic alliance with a major international airline which could, in the future, buy a stake in Olympic and take over its management. The latter was a significant departure from the strategy of previous years which had focused exclusively on the task of restructuring Olympic under the ownership and management of the Greek state.

The pursuit of a new rescue plan for Olympic began in earnest in February 1998 when a high level cabinet meeting chaired by PM Simitis announced the government's intention to legislate on the future of OA within two months (*Eleftherotypia*, 11 February 1998). Leaked reports to the press suggested that the government did not intend to proceed with involuntary redundancies, but it would be pursuing a radical shake up of the airline's employment code with a view to slashing labour costs and increasing productivity. Days later the management of Olympic also declared its commitment to implement a report prepared by external consultants McKinsey with a list of recommendations for a new employment code (particularly for cabin crew) that could save the airline between ECU73-150 million a year (*Eleftherotypia*, 13 February 1998). The plans for reforming the airline's employment code were met with fierce opposition by OA unions. Even the PASOK-controlled wing of the flight attendants union (EISF-PASKE) warned the government that '. . . the battle for OA will be similar to the miners' struggle in Britain' and declared that their union 'remained faithful to the socialist vision of Andreas Papandreou' (*Eleftherotypia*, 12 February 1998).

In the months that followed, industrial unrest in the airline reached unprecedented heights as communication between the government, the OA management, and the unions broke down. The government threatened that unless the OA management and the unions reached a compromise on a new employment code, it (the government) would do so unilaterally by incorporating a new blueprint for labour relations in the draft bill introduced in Parliament (which also dealt with a number of other issues relating to the operation of Olympic). The government proposals included, among others, a substantial increase of flying hours for cabin crew, more flexible working hours, reduction of rest time after transatlantic flights, fewer numbers of cabin crew per flight as well as significant cutbacks on pilots' per-mile compensation, and the abolition of food allowance for cabin crew (*Eleftherotypia*, 19 March 1998). Following weeks of acrimonious negotiations (often marked by violent clashes between the police and the unions) and under the threat of unilateral government action in case of failure, the OA management and the unions finally struck a compromise deal in early April 1998. This deal was later incorporated into 'OA restructuring law' (the second since 1994) which passed through Parliament on 9 April 1998 (Law 2602/98).

While the changes of the OA employment code enshrined in Law 2602/98 were seen by many as a watered-down version of the government's original proposals in March 1998, they did little to improve the breakdown of industrial relations in Olympic. Soon after the law was adopted, Minister of Transport, Mantelis, put a brave face on the government's decision to accept a compromise deal, thought to have reduced the anticipated savings for OA from ECU51.2 million to ECU36.6 million per year, by arguing that he was happy to achieve 85% of his objectives through consensus than 100% through conflict (*EIRO*, April 1998). Yet on the ground there was little evidence of consensus to be found. During the Easter vacations and the summer months of 1998, a continuous series of wildcat strikes by OA pilots, technicians, and flight attendants caused widespread disruption to Olympic's schedule causing an estimated loss of 600,000 passengers (*Ta Nea*, 29 April 1998; *Eleftherotypia*, 20 July 1998).

Despite the turmoil within Olympic, however, the new restructuring plan equipped the Greek government with sufficient credibility to request from the Commission the release of the two remaining instalments of capital injection for OA that had been blocked since 1996. In the negotiations that followed, the government accepted the Commission's claim that the financing of the OA's early retirement scheme and the airline's preferential tax treatment beyond 1994 constituted illegal state aid and agreed that a total of ECU38.6 million should be deducted from the subsequent two instalments of capital injection to the airline. The Commission, on the other hand, agreed to the immediate release of a second instalment of ECU41 million and authorized state loan guarantees of $378 million to be provided to OA by the end of 1997 for the purchase of new aircraft. The release of the third and final instalment (worth ECU22.8 million) in June 1999, though, was made conditional on the successful implementation of the government's restructuring plan (European Commission, 1998).

Having secured the Commission's agreement for his plan, Mantelis was now free to turn his attention to the search for a strategic partner for Olympic Airways. In June 1999, the Greek government announced a deal with British Airways which through its consultancy subsidiary, Speedwing, would take over the management of OA until the end of 2001 for an estimated fee of £7 million. Rod Lynch, a former BA director, was appointed Chief Executive of OA and his management team was allocated two seats in the OA's 13-strong Board of Directors, with a promise by the Greek government that its representatives in the Board would back Speedwing's main strategic choices. Crucially the deal also included a clause allowing British Airways to purchase a 20% stake in Olympic once the operations of Olympic were streamlined by the new management (*The Independent*, 22 June 1999).

By the time the new management was installed in its position, the situation in Olympic had once again become untenable. Many of the provisions of the 1998 restructuring plan had effectively been cancelled by subsequent agreements between OA's former management and the unions which managed to regain many of the privileges they had agreed to give up the year before, thus pushing staff costs to over 40% of the OA's total operating costs for 1999. Following months of industrial unrest, passenger numbers and punctuality declined rapidly and financial projections for 1999 revealed losses in excess of €75 million instead of the government's promise to the Commission of a €61.4 million profit (*Eleftherotipia*, 24 December 1999). Against this background the Commission, in May 1999, refused to authorize the release of the third instalment of the capital injection planned for OA under the 1994 rescue deal. In addition to the pressure from Brussels, the arrival of the British management was also met with suspicion by OA unions, who 'welcomed' the new deal with a series of strikes during the summer months of 1999 (*The Observer*, 5 July 1999). Union sentiments were best reflected in the words of OSPA's president, Nasos Stavridis, who made reference to Speedwing as '. . . the wolf who came to look after the lambs' and hinted that his union might take the Minister of Transport to court over the deal with the BA managers (*Eleftherotypia*, 24 June 1999).

The blueprint of the BA managers for the future of Olympic was published in October 1999, the third restructuring plan since 1994. Central to the vision of the new management was the drive to win back passenger numbers who had abandoned Olympic during the 1990s. Rather than placing all its attention on cutting costs and shrinking the airline's activities, the plan provided for the expansion and modernization of

Olympic's fleet, a 1000-strong increase of its workforce[12] and an aggressive restructuring of its network aiming to make Athens a major transit route to the Balkans, the Middle East, and Africa. The airline's routes to the US, Canada, Australia, and South Africa would be retained. To finance this expansion Speedwing planned a mixture of borrowing and asset selling, including Olympic's real estate portfolio in London and New York as well as the sell-off of minority stakes in its subsidiaries Olympic Catering and the Galileo booking system.

The emphasis on expansion (rather than cost cutting) afforded the OA's new boss, Rod Lynch, a precarious truce with the powerful pilots (EXPA) and flight attendants (EISF) unions (but not OSPA) and the full support of the Minister of Transport, Tasos Mantelis. Yet Speedwing's plans for expansion were met with scepticism by the Commission, which regarded them as a departure from the 1998 restructuring plan. The Commission's advisers also expressed concern that the forecast increases of the OA's revenues were 'too optimistic' and could not ensure the viability of the airline in the long run (European Commission, 2002c). With a general election scheduled less than six months away, Lynch had little time to prove whether his gamble would pay off. As a new political leadership arrived in the Ministry of Transport in April 2004, relations between the Greek government and the BA managers were to be tested to breaking point.

6.5 Now you see it, now you don't! The birth of Olympic Airlines

PASOK's marginal election victory in 2000 brought to Simitis's new cabinet a number of fresh faces, including the new Minister of Transport and Telecommunications, Christos Verelis. Verelis was among the 'new breed' of PASOK politicians who had made much of his political fortune as manager of public utilities during the 1990s, where he had acquired a reputation for efficiency and good partnership with the unions. A loyal supporter of Premier Simitis, Verelis was keen to prove his modernizing credentials to his new boss and relished his extended responsibilities which included the preparation of some of the country's key infrastructure in view of the 2004 Olympic Games, the opening up of Greece's closed network industries (particularly in the telecommunications, electricity, and gas sectors) in line with EU requirements and, of course, the search for a remedy for the long-suffering Greek flag carrier. This was an agenda, which, if pursued successfully, could propel the ambitious Verelis within the higher echelons of PASOK.

Within weeks of his arrival in the Ministry, Verelis announced the government's intention to sell off a stake in Olympic Airways to the private sector and offered BA a 45-day deadline to exercise its option, under the 1999 deal, to buy a 20% share in the airline (*Ta Nea*, 19 May 2000). The Minister's relationship with the British managers, however, was already showing signs of discord. Leaks to the press suggested that Verelis was critical of Speedwing and that he doubted the sincerity of BA in acquiring a stake in Olympic, particularly in the aftermath of Rod Eddington's appointment as BA's CEO in May 2000 (*Ta Nea*, 3 May 2000). Thus, BA's announcement, on 2 June 2000, that it was no longer pursuing the deal with Olympic came as no surprise. Less than a year after his arrival in Athens, Rod Lynch's Olympic adventure was over as Speedwing's managers were given two months to vacate their offices and leave the Greek airline (*Eleftherotypia*, 5 June 2000).

The departure of the BA management marked a major new development in the saga of Olympic Airways that generated a great deal of controversy in Athens. For the Minister of Transport, the termination of the BA deal was a natural conclusion of what he regarded as inept management and a lack of commitment on behalf of BA to put their money where the mouth was in order to buy a stake in Olympic. For his opponents, however, Verelis has made a huge miscalculation. Many blamed the Minister of Transport for being too easily convinced by the unions' complaints of Speedwing's management and too ready to pass judgement on its performance in less than a year, without having waited for the financial results of the summer months which normally boost Olympic's revenues. Even if the Minister was dissatisfied with Lynch's management style, the 1999 agreement gave the Greek government the right to ask for his replacement (by BA), an option that was never used. Above all, Verelis stood accused of torpedoing the deal with BA without having secured a viable alternative for Olympic. In the early 1990s, the Greek flag carrier had repelled the possibility of an alliance with Lufthansa, one of Europe's largest airlines. A decade later the Greek government seemed to have lost a second opportunity of linking Olympic's destiny with a major European player, a mistake that, many argued, would be fatal for its long-term survival.

In response to new situation, Verelis moved quickly to announce the sell-off of a majority stake (up to 65%) of the whole Olympic Airways group (including subsidiaries) to a private investor who would also be solely responsible for the management of the airline. In an attempt to entice potential investors, Verelis also floated the idea that the government might be willing to assume all of Olympic's debts (*Eleftherotypia*,

7 July 2000; *Ta Nea*, 7 August 2000). In the meantime, Verelis announced that an independent consultant (Price Waterhouse Coopers) would undertake a financial audit of Olympic so as to offer transparency prior to the international tender for the sale of OA scheduled for late 2000. The new rescue plan for Olympic was received with dismay by the unions which feared that the government was planning further job cuts and accused Verelis of trying to sell off the airline 'on the cheap' (*Eleftherotypia*, 9 August 2000).

As Verelis battled with the OA's unions at home, the reaction to his rescue plan in Brussels was mixed. The Commission had criticized the Greek government over its compensation to Olympic for the move to the new Athens airport (scheduled for 1 March 2000) and continued to withhold the third instalment of capital injection forseen in 1994 restructuring plan. However, in the aftermath of Verelis's meeting with Commissioner for Transport, Loyola De Palacio, in October 2000 the Greek Minister appeared confident that the Commission would be willing to accept the write-off of OA's debts – a perception that would prove critical later – provided that such a move would lead to transfer of the Greek flag carrier to private hands (*Eleftherotypia*, 8 September 2000). Encouraged by what he perceived as the Commission's silent consent to his plan, Verelis pushed ahead with the publication of an international tender for the sale of the OA group in December 2000. The tender made reference to the sale of a majority stake in OA on condition that Olympic would (a) continue to operate as an airline, (b) be based in Athens, and (c) keep the same name and logo. In exchange the Greek government undertook to cover all past debts of the airline and, crucially, to absorb any 'excessive OA staff' by re-employing it in other services in the wider public sector (*Ta Nea*, 7 December 2000). Athens was making a big pitch for a sell-off.

Faced with a disappointing response to the international tender and confronted by mounting industrial unrest, the government, in July 2001, announced its decision to start negotiations with its preferred bidder Axon Airlines, a small private Greek airline owned by Thomas Liakounakos (*Ta Nea*, 6 July 2001). The government's hopes for a quick sale of Olympic Airways were soon to be dashed by the events of 9/11 and the subsequent global crisis that engulfed the airline industry. By February 2002 negotiations had ended in failure, leaving the Greek government in limbo. During the same period, pressure by the Commission also began to mount. Following a series of complaints by Olympic's competitors, the Commission announced its intention to launch a new investigation into the state aid to Olympic and threatened that the

Greek flag carrier might have to return to the government all state aid authorized since the 1994 restructuring plan, worth in excess of €1.5 billion (*Financial Times*, 19 February 2002 and 6 March 2002). Amidst a period of high uncertainty for the international aviation industry, the Commission appeared to have lost faith with the Greek government and delivered a serious blow to Olympic Airways. This was the beginning of a tense relationship between the Greek Transport Minister and the Transport Commissioner.

As relations with the Commission continued to deteriorate, the government announced in February 2002 yet another plan for the rescue of Olympic. Acknowledging that the potential suitors of Olympic Airways were 'too small' to buy the entire OA group (including all its subsidiaries), Verelis was now ready to accept a 'salami slicing' strategy for the privatization of Olympic. According to the plan the most profitable non-aviation subsidiaries of the OA group such as Olympic Catering, the Galileo booking system, Olympic Fuel, and, in time, the OA's technical base and handling services would be sold separately to private investors. At the same time, all aviation services performed by Olympic Airways and its subsidiaries would be merged under one company and sold off. In order to entice potential investors, the government also promised to terminate OA's loss making route to Australia and absorb any staff that would not be needed by the airline's new owners (*Eleftherotypia*, 22 February 2002).

Under the threat of a new Commission investigation and the possibility of being forced to return huge amounts of illegal state aid to the Greek government, the interest of potential investors in the purchase of Olympic was predictably limited and confined predominantly to a small group of Greek businessmen. In December 2002, Golden aviation, a consortium led by Greek shipping tycoon Stamatis Restis, was announced as the government's preferred candidate to buy Olympic (*Ta Nea*, 7 December 2002). The initial optimism, however, that a deal could be finalized within two months was shattered following the publication, in December 2002, of the Commission's decision on state aid to Olympic. In there, the Commission produced a damning report of the handling of Olympic's 'restructuring' since 1994 and focused, in particular, on fresh allegations of state aid since 1998. The Commission's decision concluded that the Greek government should recover from Olympic an estimated €119 million that the airline received as aid (in the form of non-payment of social security contributions, VAT on fuel, airport charges to Greek airports, and a special airport tax known as Spatosimo) over the period 1998 – 2002 as well as €41 million that

Olympic received in the summer of 1998 as part of the second instalment of the 1994 rescue plan (European Commission, 2002c).

The Greek Minister of Transport responded angrily to the Commission's decision and accused De Palacio of trying to shut down Olympic at a time when the Greek government was negotiating its sale (*Ta Nea*, 12 December 2002). In an attempt to keep the process of privatizing Olympic alive, Verelis insisted that the Greek government would resist the Commission's decision all the way to the ECJ and that the new owners of the airline would not be burdened with €160 million that the Commission had asked OA to return to the Greek state. In the meantime, the airline would continue to operate as normal (*The Times*, 12 December 2002; *Financial Times*, 9 December 2002). Despite Verelis's protestations, however, the cloud that the new Commission decision cast over the future of OA had fatally undermined the negotiations between the Greek government and Golden Aviation which, in February 2003, announced it was no longer interested in buying Olympic (*Eleftherotypia*, 5 February 2003).

With the OA privatization process in tatters and his relations with the Commission suffering a complete breakdown, Verelis announced that the Greek government would now seek to implement a Swissair-like solution for Olympic. For this purpose, the Minister proposed the creation of a new company, called Olympic Airlines, which would take over all aviation activities of Olympic Airways. The new airline would service the entire network of the 'old' Olympic, but it would be much smaller than its predecessor. It would employ a total of 1850 staff (out of the 5000 employed in the aviation side of the 'old' Olympic), all of which would have to sign new revised collective agreements with the new airline. These agreements would provide for salary cuts and a much tighter employment regime in the new airline and they were designed to replace the incredibly complex (and generous) network of 240 sectoral and ad hoc agreements signed between the union and the management of the 'old' Olympic. Crucially, Olympic Airlines would be free from all debts of the 'old' Olympic which, by the end of 2001, had reached €500 million. These debts, together with the staff that would not join the new airline, would remain in the 'old' Olympic (renamed Olympic Airways-Services) which would oversee an early retirement (or redeployment) scheme for excess personnel before eventually been closed down. The new plan also provided for the privatization of all subsidiaries of the Olympic Airways group which, it was hoped, would generate enough proceeds in order to finance the OA's early retirement scheme as well as the return of €160 million of illegal state aid from the 'old' Olympic to the Greek government (if the Commission's 2002 decision was upheld) (*Eleftherotypia*, 9 February 2003; *To Vima*, 9 February 2003).

In the aftermath of Verelis's announcements, the government came under a barrage of criticism from the OA unions. Despite the fact that the new plan made no reference to compulsory redundancies, the proposed salary cuts and job loses met huge opposition particularly from the pilots (EXPA) and the flight attendants (EISF) unions. The mathematics of the exercise was indeed challenging. The 'old' Olympic had a total of 649 pilots and 1100 fight attendants whereas the new plan provided for 420 and 600 vacancies respectively. For their part, the unions were confronted with the dilemma of whether to accept the proposed job loses and encourage their members to opt for the early retirement scheme on offer or to resist the changes to the bitter end. The Minister of Transport, on the other hand, was forced to choose his friends carefully. Having secured the agreement of the ground staff unions to join the new airline, Verelis knew full well that his experiment was doomed to failure if the pilots did not get on board. The cost of achieving this consent was an early retirement package worth €200,000 for each of the 140 pilots who opted to join the scheme.[13] In addition, EXPA was promised that pilots would be given a share of the 'new' Olympic once the airline was privatized (*Eleftherotypia*, 5 July 2003; *To Vima*, 20 July 2003).

Verelis was far less generous to the flight attendants union. EISF had taken a rejectionist line, arguing that flight attendants had already accepted significant sacrifices during the 1990s and that they were entitled to a similar deal to that of the pilots. Verelis refused and EISF engaged in a 66-day-long strike. Under Verelis's instructions, the management of OA moved quickly to recruit fixed-term contract staff to replace EISF's striking members and keep Olympic operational. As the new law on Olympic Airlines passed through Parliament in September 2003, the momentum of EISF's strike began to dwindle (*Eleftherotypia*, 19 December 2003). By the time the new Olympic Airlines officially replaced Olympic Airways on 12 December 2003, the majority of EISF's members had agreed to transfer to the new airline while 256 of them had opted for early retirement.

The birth of Olympic Airlines was greeted with enthusiasm by the Minister of Transport who argued that the complex handover had gone smoothly. He insisted that the outcome of the 2003 reform was the best possible outcome under the circumstances. Faced with an exceptionally difficult period for international aviation and confronted with what he regarded as the disruptive influence of the Commission in the process of privatizing Olympic, the Minister defended his legacy with rigour. The new Olympic Airlines, he argued, was a slimmer, more competitive, and debt-free airline that would be more attractive to international investors. By separating Olympic Airlines from the 'old' Olympic, the liabilities of the Greek state and future investors were now clear and transparent. For his opponents, however, Verelis's strategy had achieved little. Four years into his ministerial post, Olympic was still an entirely state-owned airline that continued to lose huge mounts of taxpayers' money. Having failed to 'offload' Olympic from the Greek state, Verelis's preoccupation during his last 18 months in the Ministry had been how to avoid the airline collapsing and thus damaging his political career.

In any event, Verelis's EU nemesis did not take long to arrive. In October 2003 the Commission referred Greece to the ECJ arguing that the Greek government had failed to meet the February 2003 deadline for the recovery of €160 million of illegal state aid referred to in the Commission's decision in December 2002. When the ECJ published its judgement on the case in May 2005, the Commission's claims were upheld almost in their entirety. While the Court did not rule on the issue of legality of the Commission's 2002 decision,[14] it argued that the creation of Olympic Airlines '. . . created an obstacle to the effective implementation of the [Commission's] Decision 2003/372 and to the recovery of the aid . . . The purpose of that decision, which aims to restore undistorted competition in the civil aviation sector, was thus seriously compromised' (ECJ, 2005). In practical terms the ECJ's ruling meant that the financial consequences of the recovery of the illegal state aid would have to be borne by the company which was effectively responsible for the activities which benefited from the aid (i.e. Olympic Airlines). Verelis's attempt to rid Olympic Airlines from the debts of its predecessor (Olympic Airways) was effectively dead.

6.6 Pantheon what? ND in power, 2004–7

In the meantime, the centre-right ND won the March 2004 Greek elections and a new government was formed under the premiership of Costas Karamanlis. The hot potato of Olympic landed in the hands of the incoming Minister of Transport, Michalis Liapis (a cousin of the new PM), who was anxious to re-establish cooperation with the Commission in order to facilitate the government's stated ambition to sell the newly formed Olympic Airlines to a private investor. The government's commitment to this end was echoed by Olympic's new Chairman, Petros Papageorgiou, who declared his intention sell the airline for just 'one euro', if necessary (*To Vima*, 17 July 2005). In a clear good will gesture towards Brussels, the new leadership of the Ministry of Transport also announced that it would not pursue Verelis's case in the Court of First Instance against the legality of the Commission's 2002 decision.

By the time the ECJ's ruling was published in May 2005, the government's attempt to privatize Olympic Airlines was already under way. Despite news that during the first year of its operation, Olympic Airlines had accumulated loses in excess of €87 million (*To Vima*, 17 July 2005), the government was able to sign, on 6 August 2005, a 'memorandum of basic positions' for the sale of the airline with a group of investors (York Capital/Olympic Investors) headed by Costas Alexakis (*Athens News Agency*, 6 August 2005). The privatization attempt, however, was thrown into disarray when, in September 2005, the Commission announced the outcome of its investigation (which started in March 2004) into allegations of illegal state aid to Olympic since December 2002. According to the Commission's decision the Greek government was found to have provided over €540 million of illegal aid to both Olympic Airlines and Olympic Airways-Services broken down as follows:

- €40 million for the cost of leasing aircrafts for Olympic Airlines
- €90 million for the compensation of Olympic Airways for the loss of its assets when Olympic Airlines was set up in December 2003
- €350 million for the non-payment of tax and social security contributions by Olympic Airways for the period 2002–4
- the assumption by the Greek state of Olympic Airways' financial liabilities to the tune of €60 million (European Commission, 2005c)

As expected, the publication of the Commission's decision effectively killed any hopes for the privatization of Olympic Airlines which was now liable for the return of €700 million to the Greek state (on the basis of the Commission's 2002 and 2005 investigations). In the aftermath of the decision, former Minister of Transport Christos Verelis was quick to accuse the government that its new cooperative attitude towards the Commission – as part of which the government had dropped its legal case over the legality of Commission's 2002 decision – had produced no benefits for the beleaguered airline. Verelis also argued that the management of the company (appointed by the new government) had given in to union pressure and revised the airline's employment code to the cost €50 million per year. The finances of the airline were further harmed, according to Verelis, by the management's decision to resort to expensive 'wet leases'[15] for the execution of the airline's summer schedule (*To Vima*, 14 July 2005).

The bad news from Brussels, coupled with the collapse of the privatization attempt at home, forced the Greek government to seek new solutions to the problems of Olympic. Prime Minister Karamanlis, during his annual keynote speech at the Salonika International Trade Fair, acknowledged that Olympic 'can no longer continue its operations in the present form' (*To Vima*, 11 September 2005). Yet within the government, the future of Olympic became a source of serious disagreements between the Minister of Transport, Michalis Liapis, on the one hand, and the Minister of Economy and Finance, George Alogoskoufis (and his deputy Petros Doukas), on the other. Liapis, a figure of a more statist persuasion, was adamant that Olympic should continue its operations in its present form and that more time was needed in order for the government to find a new investor for the airline. This was also a view shared by the Chairman of OA, Petros Papageorgiou, who, in a newspaper article, lambasted those who undermined the credibility of the airline by calling for its immediate collapse (*Kathimerini*, 7 September 2005). The powerful Minister of Economy and Finance, however, had different ideas. Anxious to limit the drain caused by the continuing operation of Olympic to the budget, Alogoskoufis jockeyed for a Sabena-like solution for the Greek flag carrier: the immediate liquidation of both Olympic Airlines and Olympic Airways-Services and the creation of an entirely new airline where the state would only hold a minority stake (or no stake at all). This was also the view of the European Commission as expressed by Commissioner of Energy and Transport, Jacques Barrot,[16] in an interview with a Greek TV channel (*in.gr*, 6 October 2005).

Following a series of top government meetings in which Prime Minister Karamanlis tried to reconcile the differences between his Ministers, the government's strategy for the future of Olympic was announced in November 2005. It involved action along three main axes:

- The swift creation of a new legal framework for setting up an entirely new airline with a 'mixed' stakeholding base, involving both the Greek state and private investors. Initially the Greek state would be the majority shareholder, but its shake will eventually drop as more private investors came into the new scheme. The government hoped that, by April 2006, the process of attracting new investors would be completed. The new airline would serve a smaller network of destinations than Olympic, incorporate its own handling services and technical base and operate on the basis of a viable business plan. For this purpose the independent civil aviation consultants Sabre were asked to prepare a new business plan by January 2006.

- Both Olympic Airlines and Olympic Airways would be liquidated and all income form the sale of their assets would be returned to Greek state as recovery of the state aid channelled to the two companies since 1994. No assets of the Olympic group would be directly transferred to the new airline so that the latter would not be considered a successor of Olympic Airlines or Olympic Airways-Services (and hence be liable for their debts). Hence, the landing slots of Olympic Airlines would be exchanged for new ones and its fleet of aircraft would be sold off. The new airline would be given the opportunity to purchase the name 'Olympic' and the 'Olympic circles' logo, both of which were considered valuable assets of the Olympic group.
- The government guaranteed that there would be no compulsory redundancies in the Olympic group. Instead, Ministers would negotiate with the unions a new code of employment for the staff that would be transferred to the new airline as well as measures for encouraging the early retirement of surplus staff or their transfer to other posts in the public sector. A key concern in this regard was the unions' consent for not pursuing compensation claims for the staff that would be made redundant from Olympic and consequently be rehired by the new airline (*Kathimerini*, 16 November 2005).

When the government's draft bill on the new airline was presented in Parliament on 18 November 2005, the compromise between Liapis and Alogoskoufis was plain for all to see. The proposals acknowledged that the Olympic group had reached the end of the road. However, no firm date for its liquidation was announced. The new airline would be open to private investors (once they were found), but the state remained the majority (and, possibly, the only) shareholder for the foreseeable future. In the meantime the government would continue to foot the bill for Olympic's losses. Crucially the government offered no plan B; what would the future be of the new airline (and of Olympic) if private investors kept well clear from the new endeavour? The draft bill was a long way off Alogoskoufis's call for a swift and 'clean' solution for Olympic. Liapis's caution had compromised the agenda of the Minister of Economy and Finance. The reaction to the government's plans from opposition parties was mixed. In a somewhat surprising move, PASOK's spokesperson on social affairs (a portfolio that also included transport), Evaggelos Venizelos, agreed to meet with Minister Liapis to discuss the future of Olympic and announced that his party would '. . . support every positive effort that has potential and is coherent . . .' (*in.gr*, 15 November 2005; *Eleftherotipia*, 18 November 2005). Such conciliatory gestures must certainly have infuriated PASOK's former Minister of Transport Christos Verelis. The leader of Synaspismos, Alekos Alavanos, mocked the government's draft bill as a legal monstrosity and argued that the new airline should be given the name 'Frankenstein Airways' (*Kathimerini*, 19 November 2005).

In January 2006 the government published the main recommendations, prepared on its behalf by Sabre, regarding the business plan of the new airline. According to this the new airline would have a reduced fleet of 30 leased aircraft and serve a more limited network of destinations with the loss of all long-haul flights (with the exception of New York). The staff employed in the new airline would not exceed 4500. The remaining 2500 staff employed in the Olympic group would be offered either early retirement or alternative employment in the public sector (*Ta Nea*, 16 January 2006). In the weeks that followed the government faced delicate negotiations on two fronts: on the one hand, convincing investors that the new airline, called Pantheon, was a plausible proposition and, on the other, persuading the Commission to drop its demands for the return by Olympic of the €700 million of state aid to the Greek state. The latter was of crucial importance. As the liabilities of the Greek flag carrier outweighed its assets by 5:1, the return of state aid by Olympic would effectively cause its immediate collapse, with the loss of its market share and its valuable name and logo. Without an 'orderly transition', however, investors in Pantheon would not be able to purchase Olympic's business brand and build on its market share, while the Greek government would face a huge bill for redundancy payouts to Olympic's 7000 staff. Timing, here, was of essence. For the plans of the Greek government to materialize, cooperation from Brussels was essential.

Yet, under pressure from Olympic's competitors such as BA and Lufthansa, the Commission appeared to be sceptical towards the plan (*in.gr*, 18 Match 2006). Against the backdrop of persistent rumours that the Greek government had agreed the sale of 65% of Pantheon to a group of investors led by Greek shipping tycoons Panagiotis Tsakos and Stamatis Restis, the Commission, on 4 April 2006, sent a reasoned opinion to the Greek authorities for their failure to comply with the ECJ ruling of May 2005 according to which Olympic should have returned €160 million[17] of illegal state aid to the Greek state for the period 1998–2002 (European Commission, 2006e). This was seen as the first step towards a new referral to the ECJ where, if found guilty, the Greek government would be forced to pay substantial damages for every day of non-compliance with the ECJ's ruling. In a separate development a few days later, the Commission also referred the Greek government to the ECJ for its failure to recover from Olympic Airlines and Olympic Airways-Services state aid worth €540 million granted to the two airlines since December 2002 (European Commission, 2006f). The Commission and the Greek government seemed, once again, locked in a trajectory of conflict.

The threat of fresh legal challenges against the Olympic group ignited a new round of speculation over the airline's future. These were compounded by the dismissal of the Chairpersons of both Olympic Airlines and Olympic Airways-Services by the Minister of Transport, Michalis Liapis (*in.gr*, 20 April 2006). In an attempt to calm down fears that Olympic's summer schedule would be disrupted, the Minister of National Economy, Alogoskoufis, reassured that the airline will continue its operation until at least September–October 2006 (*in.gr*, 26 April 2006). In response to its new referral to the ECJ, the Greek government submitted a new proposal to the Commission suggesting an out-of-court settlement for Olympic. According to the plan the amount of state aid repayable by Olympic would have to be recalculated, taking into account 'hidden' debts of the Greek state to the national carrier. Subsequently the Greek government would present the Commission with a detailed plan for the recovery of the state aid channelled to Olympic. The airline would then be privatized and the Greek state would retain a small minority stake in it. For this purpose the deputy Ministry of Economy and Finance, Petros Doukas, sent to the Commission a detailed list of investors (comprising Greek shipping tycoons, private equity funds, and groups from the United Arab Emirates) committed to buy the airline once the issue of its debts had been resolved (*in.gr*, 27 April 2006). The Greek government was making a desperate plea to the Commission for Olympic to be sold while still in operation.

The European Commission, however, would have none of it. Brussels remained firm in its demands that Olympic should be closed down and the new airline (Pantheon) should be created 'from scratch'. Speaking from Stockholm in June 2006 the Commissioner for Transport, Jacques Barrot, argued that '. . . so far we have seen no progress. Hence we are obliged to refer Greece to the ECJ for non-compliance with Community rules . . . We have to ensure respect for European rules. It is not possible to for us to allow Olympic Airlines to continue to receive state aid. It is not possible!' (*in.gr*, 2 June 2006).

Faced with the Commission's intransigence, the Greek government was fast running out of options. In this context the Greek state's alleged 'hidden debts' to Olympic became a new line of defence for the government. For this purpose Olympic had launched a series of legal challenges against the government in the Greek Supreme Court demanding compensation of over €1 billion for (a) the non-payment of state subsidies (since 1992) to the airline for operating loss-making routes to remote Greek islands and (b) lost assets when Olympic was forced to move out from the old Athens airport. With regard to the first case (non-payment of state subsidies), the Greek courts, in December 2006, awarded Olympic €563 million whereas the ruling on the second case (financial losses incurred by the move to the new Eleftherios Venizelos airport) was still pending in September 2007 (*in.gr*, 20 December 2006; *To Vima*, 23 September 2007).

In a separate development the Greek government also decided to 'resurrect' the case against the legality of the Commission's 2002 decision (initially launched during the ministerial watch of Christos Verelis in 2003), which had remained dormant since the arrival of Michalis Liapis in the Ministry of Transport in the name of good cooperation with the Commission. Through that case, the Greek government had hoped to prove that the Commission had acted unlawfully and, hence, Olympic should not be held responsible for the return of €160 million of illegal state aid (according to the Commission's 2002 decision). In September 2007, the European Court of First Instance ruled against the main thrust of the argumentation put forward by the Greek government, upholding the Commission's demands for the recovery of illegal state aid from Olympic, albeit to the reduced tune of €130 million (Court of Justice of the European Communities, 2007).

By the end of ND's first term in office (September 2007), the relations between the Commission and the Greek government had deteriorated to a level reminiscent to that of the Verelis–Palacio saga. Speaking to the Greek Parliament in September 2006 the Minister of Transport, Michalis Liapis, made clear that the government was committed to keep Olympic alive until the next general election (*To Vima*, 12 August 2006). A couple of weeks later, despite protestations by the Commission, the government legislated in Parliament to extend Olympic's protection from its creditors until October 2007 (*in.gr*, 29 September 2006). All of these seemed a long way off the government's early promises of a swift solution to the problem of Olympic or the Prime Minister's statement of September 2005 that the Greek flag carrier had reached the end of the road.

Like its predecessors, the Karamanlis Government had tried and failed to tackle the puzzle of Olympic with its innumerable legal, financial, and political complexities. Squeezed between the demands of its domestic audience and the intransigence of the European and unable to develop a consistent and credible exit strategy in order to attract private investment for the airline, the government failed to produce a win-set capable of appealing to all interested parties. In the meantime Olympic continued its flight to nowhere, an airline that refuses to live or die.

6.7   Conclusion

This has been a case study in which the EU largely shaped the agenda for domestic reform, but where domestic pressures determined solutions that proved to be failures. The three directives on market liberalization for the air transport sector, the increasingly ferocious attack by the Commission on state aids to national carriers, and the EMU discipline on the fiscal position of national governments – each of these developments created strong pressures for domestic compliance. Olympic Airways was already in a vulnerable position given its dependence on subsidies, the encroachment of clientelistic politics in its internal management, and the emerging international market trends in the aviation sector. But it was the occurrence of the EU-level pressures that made the reform of Olympic a pressing and unavoidable issue for government. It is in this sense that the case study is one of 'Europeanization'.

Yet the EU pressures need to be differentiated. The critical actor was the Commission, but the instruments at its disposal were limited. It possessed executive authority on state aids, but this was a negative power of blunt form in relation to determining domestic policy solutions. The strategic change was the more robust leadership of Loyola De Palacio, adopting an uncompromising stance on state subsidies but at the same time urging radical restructuring solutions of privatization. She overreached her authority, though she acted consistently with the broader agenda on liberalization of the Commission as a whole. It was difficult to play this hand. Inevitably, it rested on calculations, signals, and perceptions, as well as hard law. Effective communication and the building up of credibility and trust were crucial. The strategy was vulnerable to misinterpretation, innocent or wilful, and to domestic blockages.

Over time, the Commission had become increasingly frustrated by the failure of successive Greek governments to pursue consistent and effective reform in relation to Olympic Airways. Athens was seen as untrustworthy and lacking credibility. It did not deliver what had been expected. Ultimately, it came up with a cunning plan that failed to resolve the underlying problem of large state aids. Realities were being masked, not tackled. But the Greek government fell foul of the power of the Commission to determine acceptable solutions and its recourse to legal judgement in the ECJ. An effective strategy is more likely to involve a mix of cooperation and coercion (Tallagreg, 2002), but the Commission's frustration led it to shift from one to the other.

The Simitis Government had in fact displayed a rational set of preferences on the future of Olympic. The essential interest was one of divestment of OA from the state and this was consistent with a range (and sequence) of solutions.[18] Several factors interceded to prevent the Greek government from sharing the Commission's stance. Its will to comply was limited by its electoral interests (the potential loss of jobs and the ambiguity of public attitudes on the company's future) and by internal disagreements between Ministers over the risks involved. Its ability to comply was dissipated by the strength and complex structure of the domestic veto players. The tactical guile of the Verelis law of 2003 was to gain the acquiescence of the ground staff and the pilots and isolating the flight attendants in a manner that prevented them blocking the reform. The domestic constraints faced by Greek Ministers provided strong incentives for them to seek solutions that tested the limits of what the Commission would accept.

Moreover, the case is not one of stable positions and a simple test of compliance: both the Commission and the Greek government shifted their bargaining positions, to some degree, and the latter was not simply evading the prior instructions of the former. The agenda shifted, as solutions were tried and failed. Ministers in Athens showed themselves to be involved in a learning process: the options seen as feasible changed over time. Moreover, what the domestic obligations were, in the context of what the Commission would find acceptable, was not always clear to Ministers.

The case testifies to the limits of 'Europeanization'. The existence of strong EU pressures for reform belied the narrowness of the Commission's powers to attain acceptable solutions. The national government expressed a willingness to pursue reform, but what was feasible domestically proved unacceptable to the Commission's rules. It was impossible to reconcile the constraints of the EU and domestic levels. Moreover, preferences shifted, communication may have been faulty, and the credibility of solutions melted away. The case suggests the relevance of two linked agendas of governance: the ability of the Commission to steer an EU-wide agenda of economic reform, given its current policy instruments, and the capacity of a government like that of Greece to deliver on EU level commitments.

Table 6.1   Olympic Airways: A troubled history

Jan. 1975:	The Greek state takes over the ownership of Olympic Airways (OA) from Aristotle Onassis (Law 96/1976)
Mar. 1994:	The Commission announces investigation on illegal state aid to Olympic Airways
Oct. 1994:	The Commission authorizes over ECU 2 billion of state aid to Olympic Airways (in three instalments), conditional on restructuring the airline and the opening up of competition in the field of air transport
Nov. 1994:	The Greek government passes law (2271/94) on the restructuring of Olympic Airways
May 1995:	The first instalment of the aid package to OA is released
Apr. 1996:	The Commission refuses to authorize the release of the second instalment of aid to OA and launches investigation into illegal state aid by the Greek government since 1994
Apr. 1998:	The Greek government passes law (Law 2602/98) on the restructuring of Olympic Airways
Jul. 1998:	The Commission authorizes the release of the second instalment of the aid package to OA and drops the investigation into illegal state aid by the Greek government
Jun. 1999:	The Greek government announces deal with British Airways for the management of Olympic Airways
Oct. 1999:	The management of OA announces a new restructuring plan
Mar. 2000:	The Commission refuses to authorize the release of the third instalment of aid to Olympic Airways
Jun. 2000:	Deal between the Greek government and British Airways collapses
Dec. 2000:	The Greek government unveils tender for the sale of a majority stake of the entire Olympic Airways group
Feb. 2002:	Privatization process collapses
Feb. 2002:	The Greek government unveils plan for a salami-slicing approach to the privatization of Olympic Airways The flying operations of OA to be sold separately from the group's subsidiaries
Mar. 2002:	The Commission launches investigation on illegal state aid to OA the period 1998–2002

Dec. 2002:	The Commission rules that OA had benefited from €160 million of illegal state aid since 1998. The Greek government announces intention to appeal the decision to the ECJ
Feb. 2003:	Privatization process collapses
Aug. 2003:	The Greek government passes law (3185/03) establishing Olympic Airlines
Jan. 2004:	Olympic Airlines begins its operations
Mar. 2004:	The Commission launches investigation on illegal state aid to Olympic Airways/Airlines by the Greek government for the period since 2002
Jan. 2005:	The Greek government unveils tender for the sale of a majority stake of Olympic Airlines
May 2005:	The ECJ upholds the Commission's decision on illegal state aids to Olympic for the period 1998–2002
Sep. 2005:	The Commission rules that Olympic Airways had benefited from €540 million of illegal state aid by the Greek government since 2002
Sep. 2005:	PM Karamanlis announces that 'Olympic can no longer continue its operations in the present form'
Jan. 2006:	Pantheon (Airlines) is set up as a vehicle for attracting investors on the promise that the owners of the new airline could 'purchase' Olympic's assets (name, logo, slots) if the latter is forced into liquidation
Apr. 2006:	The Commission sends a reasoned opinion to the Greek government over its failure to comply with the 2005 ECJ ruling.

7
Conclusions

What are the lessons to be drawn from this study? The overarching theme of the case studies has been *the limits to Europeanization*: that is, stimuli from the EU for domestic change have produced only modest policy reforms in the selected sectors of Greece.[1] The first task of this chapter is to try to explain *why* by reviewing the three case studies in the context of the theoretical frames discussed in Chapters 2 and 3.

More generally, in referring to the *limits to Europeanization*, the book has sought to address two major dimensions:

- The nature of EU action ('commitment devices') in stimulating economic and social reform at the domestic level
- The *'reform capacity'* of a particular member state – Greece, constituting a 'critical case' – to adapt and enact reform consistent with the EU pressure

The case studies have outlined the nature of the EU stimuli in each of the three sectors. The form of the stimuli has varied both within and across the sectors. It is now the stage to reflect on this 'independent variable' for what it says about the EU's role to coordinate and manage a programme of economic reform. At the same time, the case studies have elaborated the degree of policy change in Greece: the 'dependent variable', raising questions of domestic governance and the scope for reform.

7.1 The original hypotheses: Explaining what happened

Chapters 2 and 3 considered different theoretical frameworks and developed various hypotheses to 'test' in the case studies. The theoretical dimension serves to highlight the key conditions ('intervening variables') explaining the outcomes. They also help to connect the empirical findings here with those from elsewhere, to avoid the isolation of the study.

Chapter 2 placed Greece in the context of the 'external' pressures emanating from the EU. It proposed three hypotheses. How far have they been borne out by the case studies? The first hypothesis focussed on the domestic implications of the form of EU pressure:

H1a. EU-level commitments provide a resource by which domestic actors in Greece can shape their environment, restructuring interests and/or ideas, but the outcome of this EU–domestic interaction will vary according to the type of EU pressure (hierarchical, facilitating) and the configuration of domestic conditions (institutional capacity, timing of EU policies, domestic policy structure).

A further hypothesis suggested that

H1b. The domestic impact of EU stimuli will vary according to the type of 'commitment device' involved. EU institutions will determine the nature of domestic change upto the limits of the 'coercion' available to them.

Domestic change was not seen as an inevitable outcome of EU stimuli; rather, the latter constituted an available resource or tool that needed to be activated at the domestic level by actors with their own distinct ideas and interests and within the given institutional setting with all its particular features. Moreover, the domestic impact was likely to vary according to the type of 'commitment device' developed by EU governance. The case studies amply bore out the contingent nature of EU stimuli, the relevance of their form, and their association with the domestic response in Greece.

Across the three policy areas considered, successive Greek governments have endeavoured to deploy EU commitments as a resource within the domestic policy process:

• *Pensions:* The Simitis Government sought to place reform initiatives in the context of a debate about a new 'social state' in Greece, attempting to broaden the frame within which issues were discussed. The need for reform was linked to the experience of other European states, highlighting shared policy problems. Indeed, successive Greek governments had called in 'outside' experts to help define the agenda and reform options on pensions. The external dimension was relevant, therefore, but there was little specific from the EU to download until 'national strategy reports' led to EU recommendations after 2003. The Greek reform initiatives pre-dated EU action in the context of the Lisbon Programme and the OMC process.

More directly relevant were the burgeoning costs of the national system and the pressures of EMU entry on the basis of the Maastricht criteria that involved a tight fiscal constraint. The fiscal constraint was evident in the report of the Committee for the Study of Long-Term Economic Policy (Spraos Committee) on pensions in 1997, which referred to the cost of no reform. It was explicit: 'there is the nightmare scenario of continuous burdening of production for the purpose of financing social security. In the context of EMU and the single currency this means a shift of production out of Greece and unemployment' (Committee for the Study of Long-Term Economic Policy, 1997). It sought reform 'so that the social security system can play an important role in the attainment of the macro-economic goals, on the basis of which the eligibility of EU member states for participation in EMU will be assessed' (Committee for the Study of Long-Term Economic Policy, 1997). Indeed, Greek entry into the 'euro' system came with private intergovernmental pressure for the Athens government to reform pensions.

So, the 'hard' (EMU) fiscal constraint stimulated action as a link between it and pension costs was established, solutions were partially defined by outside experts, and recommendations were given from the EU Council/Commission as part of the OMC benchmarking process on reform. That said, the specific content of domestic reform had to be set within the peculiarities of the Greek system.

- *Labour Market*: The policy agenda of increasing employment flexibility also reflected a combination of external empowerment and domestic imperatives. Ideationally, the EU leadership in this area was significant. The macroeconomic dimension of EMU, the Delors White Paper of 1993, the Ciampi Advisory Group in 1995, the Amsterdam Treaty of June 1997, and the European Employment Strategy of the following November with its 'National Action Plans', each of these initiatives sustained a debate that was seen in Greece as carrying implications for adaptation. Many of the basic principles of the agenda were consciously downloaded affecting the relevant discourse.

  The Simitis Government's initiatives were indeed shaped by Greece's European vocation. He later made this evident in his 2005 memoirs: Greece's participation in the integration process was 'the strongest lever for our exit from a reality' of economic and social retardation (Simitis, 2005: 125). In the election of 2000, Simitis had made it clear that his new government would focus its attention on structural reform, allowing Greece to compete successfully with other eurozone members (*To Vima*, 5 March 2000).

Yet in the domestic pursuit of labour market reform, the legitimizing power of Europe was only marginally utilized. Here, the pressing and very tangible (unlike pensions) problem of unemployment offered the government a range of domestically inspired arguments to support its agenda. While the EU offered ideas on how to tackle Greece's unemployment problem, it lacked a clear blueprint for action and it most certainly lacked strong sanction mechanisms for non-compliance. Thus, in instrumental terms, the four reform packages of recent years (two under Simitis's government and two under Karamanlis's) displayed little leverage from the EU. Rather, their outcome was the result of the strategic interaction between the government and the social partners. In this context, issues of agenda setting, timing, leadership, and strategy seemed to have determined the fate of the various reform initiatives.

• *Restructuring Olympic Airways:* Rather like pensions, pressure for reform of Olympic started domestically due to a severe fiscal burden. Yet EU initiatives soon defined the domestic agenda and they were of a coercive form to circumscribe the reform options. Three packages of liberalization measures for air transport between 1987 and 1992, the toughening stance of the EU Commission on illegal state aids wielding the executive authority granted to it under 'Competition Policy', the signals emanating from the Commission in favour of privatization as a solution to Europe's ailing state airlines, and the general need to reduce the government deficit and debt to qualify for EMU, each of these constraints shaped the Greek policy agenda and defined the options. Indeed, from 1994 to the present, the EU Commissioner for Competition has been the ultimate arbiter of the domestic 'solutions', ruling on rescues and state aids. Yet, given the domestic pressures, Greek governments have asserted a distinct set of normative preferences: for a 'softer' transition to ease the adaptation process.

Greek governments have felt an EU pressure in each sector and have sought to accommodate themselves to it. Each involved some mix of 'hard' and 'soft' EU constraints. In strategic terms it is somehow ironic that even 'hard' EU contraints (like the case of state aids and Olympic) did not reach to the domestic implementation of preferred solutions. The application of EU rules appeared a highly negotiated process affording plenty of opportunities for the governemnts in Athens for delay and procrastination. As the EU lacked the power to directly coerce a defined outcome, external pressures were a cumbersome stimuli for domestic change. In ideational terms all three cases revealed significant convergence between European and domestic norms. At no point did the Greek government challenge the basic principles of the EU position in the three policy areas: a competitive airline industry, financially sustainable pensions, and greater labour market flexibility. Yet the distance between convergence of norms and policy delivery at the domestic level appreared immense. In the absence of strong EU coercisve leverages, domestic veto points pushed the Greek government towards 'defection' from EU commitments.

The key theme of domestic *reform capacity* in the face of Europeanization pressures was hypothesied in Chapter 2:

> *H2a. The extent of domestic adaptation will depend on (a) the degree of 'policy misfit' with respect to the content of EU stimuli and (b) the availability of a domestic coalition pressing for such reform.*

> *H2b. In the absence of formal veto players and with an electoral system strongly biased in favour of single party governments (with comfortable parliamentary majorities), effective opposition (informal veto points) will be found among those stakeholders with accumulated privileges and it is the strategic interaction between government and the latter, and the relative resources of each, that will determine the outcome of reform.*

> *H3a. Where regulatory compliance is an issue and domestic opponents are entrenched, reform actors will define their interests in terms of manipulating the timing of compliance with EU obligations and postponing effective implementation.*

> *H3b. In the absence of a clear EU obligation to comply (or a strong 'commitment device'), an individual Minister will be left politically isolated to battle reform against domestic opposition and his/her success will depend on the availability of a legitimating public discourse of the risk of Greece's marginalization from 'Europe'.*

As noted in Chapter 2, the notion of 'policy misfit' is problematic given the differences in the type of EU stimuli – 'hard' and 'soft' law – forming varied types of commitment device. In none of the three cases was the Greek policy 'misfit' actually low: the pensions and labour market regime stood in stark contrast to the notions of the Lisbon

Programme; and the position of Olympic Airways, with its illegal state aids, was found to be in breach of the very 'hard' law of EU Competition Policy. Was the misfit, in each case, simply too big for Greece to reconcile itself to? Though tempting to settle for such a crisp explanation, this would be an incomplete answer. The nature of the misfit varied according to the specificity of content and its relevance needs to be related to the strength of the EU legal constraint. In other words, the explanation returns to the kind of EU stimulus that existed in each sector. The stimuli varied within and between each sector. In the cases of pensions and Olympic, the pressure for reform was strengthened by a clear fiscal constraint emanating from the rules for entry into the 'euro'. Though indirect, the constraint was certainly a tough one for Greece and was accepted domestically as such. Yet partly because it was an indirect constraint, domestic adaptation was limited and slow in both sectors. In the case of pensions and the labour market the EU stimuli – the basis of the measure of the 'misfit' – became direct but softer with the onset of the Lisbon Programme and the OMC. In both sectors, the content of the EU stimuli remained defined in rather general terms, precluding a specific reform model. The scope for different types of adaptation was considerable, allowing the measurement of misfit to be somewhat fuzzy, but in reality the degree of domestic reform remained very limited. For Olympic, the Commission's actions on the basis of Competition Policy were direct and became as tough as possible. Yet this 'hard law' still involved negotiations with Athens, and reform of Olympic remained problematic with no stable solution. The domestic strategy sought 'wriggle-room' from the EU constraint. For all of these reasons, the hypothesis based on misfit seems inadequate.

The other part of the hypothesis, however, seems more promising in directing attention to the interests and preferences of key domestic actors. Hypothesis 2b targets the critical area. It extends the perspective of writers such as Boerzel (2000) and Haverland (2003) in identifying the conditions hindering reform. The crucial constraint in all three was the clash of interests between the ministerial agenda and the vested interests of unions and pension funds, with employers' organizations as relevant but somewhat lesser players on labour market reform. The strategic dimension was strong: the 'win-sets' of the key protagonists defined limited scope for agreement. Other constraints were embedded within the wider Greek system – conflicting political interests within the governing party; the problems of a legitimating technical discourse; the limitations of the state administration; non-liberal cultural attitudes and habits; the weaknesses of the domestic market – but it was government's differences with the unions that had the greatest profile:

- *Pensions:* The major unions took fright at the prospect of current privileges being taken away and overall provision being lessened, with little else to compensate. Moreover, with reason, the unions doubted government intentions and commitment within the process of 'social dialogue' from 1997 onwards. Dialogue was replaced by public demonstrations and strike action (1992; 2001 twice; 2005). The confrontation of interests was stark. The confrontation with the unions was extremely costly to the Simitis Government. The Karamanlis Government of 2004 understood this lesson well and postponed any further action to its second term. Intraparty tensions (in both PASOK and ND) have dissipated government commitment to reform – partly in response to union reaction.
- *Labour market:* Unions had held protests and strikes in 1998 (against Papaioannou's Law), in 2000 (against Giannitsis's Law), and in 2005 (against Sioufas's Law on opening hours and Panagiotopoulos's labour market Law). The relevant unions sought to defend the employment conditions of those in the public sector (such privileges are often seen as compensation for relatively low wages), the calculation of the working time, the limits to collective redundancies, and national character of the minimum wage; to prevent the expansion of part-time work in the public sector; to restrict voluntary and compulsory overtime; and to improve the position of those on fixed-term contracts. Each of these provisions was seen, variously, by government and business as imposing rigidities and higher labour costs in the Greek market. Again, government attempts to produce consensus on reform via a social pact (1997) or dialogue largely ran aground as a result of inconsistency and disputed purpose, mistrust, and recrimination on all sides.

Pressure from the EU on domestic reform within Greece was identified in the reactions of the unions and the Greek Left to government (of both PASOK and ND) proposals. In the 2007 election campaign SYRIZA (Coalition of the Radical Left/Συνασπισμός της Ριζοσπαστικής Αριστεράς), the Synaspismos-led coalition of the reformist Left, warned voters, with regard to employment and social policy, that 'ND and PASOK have consistently built on each other's anti-worker measures with the blessings of the European Union' (SYRIZA, 2007). The KKE's fierce opposition to the Lisbon Programme (and the EU more generally) also featured prominently in its pre-election manifesto (KKE, 2007).

- *Olympic:* The reform attempts of successive governments clashed with the myriad of unions operating on behalf of the company's workforce, who sought to defend their rights and positions in the face of threatened job cuts. Moreover, union pressure (and an embedded clientelistic culture in combination with government) undermined the strength and independence of management, which was often made weak and pliant to one or both. The strategy of the Verelis's Law of 2003 was devised to enable the government to 'divide and rule' among the company unions.

Hypothesis 3a was sector specific. It was borne out by the case of Verelis and then Liapis seeking to 'play for time' with the EU Commission in relation to the restructuring process for Olympic Airways/Airlines. It was directly related to the nature of the EU's processes on competition: seeking to influence the 'arbiter', hoping an easier deal could be pressed recognizing that the Commission had some discretion in its action. The tactic was consistent with elements of Greek culture: the small guy seeks help, pushing the boundaries of that discretion. Here, it stemmed from Greek ministers being forced to participate in a 'nested game': placating and manipulating EU pressures, devising a way through the severe domestic constraints. For political reasons, Greek ministers remained committed to a near seamless transition from the existing Olympic company to a new one, reducing the negative impact of job losses and market disruption. This prompted overtures to the Commission to ease the path and be more flexible on the solution.

The nature of the EU constraint – 'commitment device' – inevitably helps to define the strategy and tactics of the relevant domestic Minister. For Olympic, Commission discretion produced Greek lobbying. 'Hard' and 'soft' EU laws involve different degrees of commitment and offer the national Minister contrasting domestic leverage. The EU imperative to act has much less strategic potency if it stems from the Lisbon Programme than from EU directives, executive responsibility on the part of the Commission, or the Maastricht convergence criteria. The case studies displayed the degree of isolation a reform Minister in Athens may face. An individual portfolio responsibility to act exists in a context of intragovernment conflicts over the costs of reform (especially when liberalization measures conflict with established clientelistic and electoral interests) and the support of the Prime Minister may not be firm or consistent, as was apparently the case with Simitis and pension reform (or with Karamanlis and Olympic), for example. Moreover, ministers cannot expect high value policy inputs from his/her ministerial bureaucracy or from domestic think tanks, as the latter are few in number and lack resources. Thus, ministers are left to confront the process of gaining the support or acquiescence of unions and business for reform (and adaptation to the EU) with only public opinion there as a potential ally. Strong public support for Greece avoiding 'exclusion' from the EU or its core policies can legitimize action, as with the acceptance of fiscal measures to gain entry into the 'euro', but it remains general and unspecific in the face of vested interests battling over distributional issues of jobs and pensions.

The problems posed for structural reform by the position and interests of the unions are exemplified by the general hypothesis developed in Chapter 3. This was derived from literatures that are focussed on the domestic system. An amalgam of the 'neo-corporatism' and 'varieties of capitalism' approaches suggested that

> *Market liberalizing reforms (e.g. employment flexibility, privatization) encounter a weak domestic constituency for support as the structure of interest mediation favours the interests of the public sector and the privileged position of the few large private corporations. As a result, the key social partners defend the current privileges and protection, fearing the risks of more open competition and the consequences of low state welfare provision. Similarly, pension reform will be resisted if it threatens current privileges or market stability, with workers anxious as to the lack of wider welfare support and firms as to the threat to current labour conditions. Stop-go incremental policy reform is the most likely outcome.*

The three case studies showed the very substantial relevance of these propositions. The distinctive nature of interest mediation – 'disjointed corporatism', 'parentela' culture, noted in Chapter 3 – structured the voices deployed in the reform process. The reform initiatives on pensions and the labour market incurred the wrath of the major unions, as noted above. Moreover, the strongest union voices – GSEE, ADEDY – were deployed on behalf of the interests of public sector workers, protecting their pension benefits and their employment position. As outlined in Chapter 3, the mode of representation was shown to be skewed to the interests of such workers. The low rate of unionization across the plethora of SMEs in Greece meant there was no corresponding voice from that quarter, one that would have had a greater affinity with the interests of liberalization and flexibility. The voice of the bodies representing SME employers – a natural constituency for liberalization measures – was much weaker in the policy process (reflecting major distortions in the way in which these interests are articulated within their supposedly representative association, GSEVEE). Government strategy has been shaped by this context.

In the case of the two labour market reforms of 2005, the Karamanlis Government succeeded in its limited reform objectives only by crafting a package deal that divided the opposition and delivered some side payments to most players on the negotiating table. The DEKO reform was much more bold, however. Here the government took on and defeated the powerful unions of the state-controlled enterprises, even though that risked alienating some of the party's own trade unionists. The latter case is an exception from the general pattern of reform initiatives (although significant aspects of the DEKO reform are yet to be implemented).

The economic setting has structured actor interests. Given the low provision of the Greek welfare regime – limited unemployment benefits, little support for mobility or retraining – it is in the interests of public sector workers, who are also relatively poorly paid on the whole – to act in a manner that protects their accumulated privileges and employment status. The pensions and labour market case studies bore out such interests – rational to the system – and the agendas of the relevant workers. The attempts by government to broaden the agenda of negotiation – in the context of the social dialogue – were weak and inconsistent, offering limited resources for flanking measures related to welfare or mobility. The 'game' was not restructured and actor interests remained stable. The structure of the economy – numerically dominated by small and microfirms – meant that those often assumed to have a stronger predisposition towards liberalization were too small and diffuse to project an effective alternative agenda. The private sector has too few medium-sized players to offer a sizeable constituency and voice on behalf of liberalization. Ultimately, *the system, rather than personalities or parties, told the essential story of both voice and interest.*

The position of SEV, as the representative body of large firms, is intriguing in this context. Structurally, it has a relatively small coverage, in EU terms, of firms as a proportion of the total, given the plethora of very small enterprises. It is dominated by a few large corporations, including some of those that have recently undergone (partial) privatization. SEV's rhetoric has espoused a conventional agenda of market liberalization, but at the same time it remained committed to consensus-driven reforms. The deal between SEV and GSEE, prior to the Giannitsis labour market reform, suggested the extent to which the organization was determined to protect the stability of a dysfunctioning market regime. This inevitably raised the question of whether large firms in a

198 The Limits of Europeanization

small pool had grown complacent, secure in the knowledge that the status quo offered barriers to new entrants, via high levels of regulation,
and peace.[2] SEV's impact on reform can be gauged from the case studies.
While rhetorically committed to greater labour market flexibility and the
lowering of the cost of pension provision to the economy, SEV has been
unable (whether through a question of will or capability) to take a leading role in shaping reform agendas or outcomes. In the debate over
Olympic's restructuring, its voice was hardly heard at all. Hence, to a
large extent, its overall attitude to the domestic reform game is compatible with the 'varieties of capitalism' assumptions elaborated at the end
of Chapter 3. Lavdas (1997: 248) also noted that the impact of SEV on
the politics of privatization was 'limited because of the emergence of
considerable intra-business interest divisions. . . . SEV's role did not
expand beyond a general advocacy for privatisation'.

The three empirical case studies give a strong signal as to the constraints on structural reform within Greece. The conceptual frames of
'Europeanization' and 'varieties of capitalism', despite their very different starting points, actually converge in highlighting the key area of
blockage: government's relations with the major social partners. This is
an area with a distinctive institutional setting and culture, one that
seemingly structures skewed representation, relations of mistrust, and
conflicts of economic and political interest. It is within this complex set
of relations that the main informal veto points to liberalizing reform
exist.

The case studies were primarily focussed on how policy reform was
pursued and what was achieved. In doing so, coverage was given to
strategies and tactics as well as institutional mechanisms. They gave
scope to identifying how domestic actors responded to EU initiatives
and sought to use them. By contrast, the studies were not centrally concerned with the origination of commitments at the EU level. As such,
the focus of explanation has been on the domestic setting and the features within it that promoted or blocked adaptation. Chapters 2 and 3
sought to borrow from the contrasting conceptual frames perspectives
by which to understand that domestic response. In the event, the
frames converge and complement each other, facilitating a more complete picture. That is, combined they say more about the nature of the
EU stimuli (the independent variable) and its variations, and give a
more complete coverage as to how 'Europe' is seen domestically and the
institutional structures affecting the response to its initiatives.

Moreover, such a combination of conceptual frames is facilitated by
the fact that neither posits deterministic outcomes – as noted at the end

of Chapter 3 – and as such they leave space for other factors to be taken into account. Both are accounts of systemic features affecting continuity and change, convergence and divergence. In this sense, the limits to the coverage of 'Europeanization' are taken up by models of interest mediation and capitalism. At the same time, the latter have difficulty in incorporating how domestic actors may respond to external stimuli – not least from the EU – affecting their ideas and interests. Such stimuli are a resource over and above an actors' location and the resource needs to be interpreted and mediated.

7.2   Reform capacity: Can Greece live with Europe?

Together, the three case studies raise a fundamental question about governance in contemporary Greece: that is, the strength of the system's reform capacity. Lavdas (1997), in his study of the impact of the EU in pre-Simitis Greece, argued that there were limits to the domestic effects. Simitis's rise to power offered grounds for optimism. But, there were reasons for skepticism. In particular, the problems of 'bureaucratic politics' were added to the need for 'systems of interest intermediation capable of reaching intersectoral agreements over policy adjustments' (1997: 253). Indeed, he noted 'a form of defensive nationalism' as a threat to Greece's 'Europeanization', though he identified this as a matter of high defence costs in the context of perceived regional threats. The volume of papers in Allison and Nicolaides (1997) concluded that Greece represented a paradox: its underlying potential was not matched by its economic and political performance. Greek society needed to be 'modernized' to overcome this paradox. Clearly, some reform has occurred and there has been some improvement in performance, but whether it is still best to define the issue as a paradox of this kind is unclear. The key problem remains of reform capacity. If the authors contributing to the volume foreshadowed the start of the Simitis governmental project, then Pagoulatos (2003) was writing in its midst. He finished his study of Greece's post-war economic development on a relatively upbeat note. Greece had made the transition from a weak and incomplete 'development state' (dependent on state-controlled finance) to a fully fledged 'stabilization state', operating in the context of the EMU and financial liberalization (2003: 204).[3] Particularly, for 'a small peripheral country in need of structural adjustments, such as Greece, increased competition under EMU creates a strong external push for advancing liberalisation in the product, services and labour markets, including greater flexibility in wage and employment conditions to offset the loss of control over monetary policy' (2003: 208-9). The external stimuli would also encourage neo-corporatist social pacts at home, 'as the Greek case well into the 1990s demonstrated' (2003: 198). In truth, Pagoulatos's concern was more with the general implications of the new international economy than the specifics of recent Greek policy responses. As such his comments were well founded. Yet the implications for domestic adjustment in Greece have not been realized.

The main problems identified in the case studies here were of a *systemic* nature. The individual personalities of the key actors and the identity of the party in power are of lesser importance in this sense: it is the system that constitutes the problem and all are confined by it. The 'system' here is not used as some bland, 'black-box' not to be penetrated. Rather it denotes that the problem of reform capacity arises from a combination of structural constraints that have already been identified. Tellingly, Simitis himself, out of office, has commented in a similar fashion. 'The "lack of will"', he has written recently, 'is the most common interpretation of the lack of change or of the change that did not go far enough . . . [This interpretation] ignores [the fact] that insecurity, persistence with the status quo, interests and the lack of knowledge have proved stronger than political will' (Simitis, 2007: 32). Greek politics occur in a context that is dominated by political parties and their interests, clientelistic networks and localism (Simitis, 2007: 31). In such a context, policies are dictated by vested interests, cost avoidance, and traditional mentalities in a way that 'does not violate the extant equilibria' (Simitis, 2007: 30). The lack of trust on the part of the citizens, the lack of an informed public and of an active civil society, the limited diffusion of knowledge, and the absence of a public space of deliberation result in the humiliation of all the policy and political actors, the undermining of social dialogue, and eventually to the depreciation of the 'political' (Simitis, 2007: 33–4). These comments are consistent with what is argued here and, as such, they offer important endorsement from the 'inside' of the process.

The question '*Who governs?*' is often based on a liberal conception of the position of government in society. The problems in achieving reform, elaborated in the three case studies, might lead to a simple denunciation of union power in Greece. This would be an inadequate response. The reality is more complex: institutional roles are undermined by structural deficiencies, cultural norms, and conflicts of interest. The problem of reform capacity in Greece rests on a *paradox of governance*. At the top, the government is normally very strong and faces few formal veto points. Yet the government is itself institutionally weak, with a large, low-skilled, and ill-coordinated bureaucracy. An embedded culture of clientelism pervades the state's relationship with wider society, exchanging favours and interests and undermining liberal values of the separation of institutional roles and values. State resources are there to be used by the prevailing interests. This is paralleled by a culture of corruption, often petty, sometimes large. Government's relations with the social partners is marked by strong conflict: disjointed corporatism skews representation and prohibits consensus. The contrasts are stark: unrestrained leadership, but lacking implementational strength; liberal democratic norms and structures with 'rent-seeking' behaviour; social dialogue and distorted interest representation; and a small state facing daunting external challenges with a domestic structure not of consensus but of severe conflict. Against this background, the puzzle may not be seen as explaining stagnation but as accounting for change.

Yet it is also true that Greece's reform capacity has varied between sectors. It has not been a consistent problem. There have been cases of successful policy reform alongside those of a more sluggish nature. The difference is telling with respect to the nature of the respective policy processes. For both the Simitis (1996–2004) and Karamanlis (2004–7) Governments, the record of policy reform has been patchy – displaying areas of much improvement alongside sectors of limited and incremental reform. The management of macroeconomic (and monetary) policy has been relatively successful.[4] Economic growth has been consistently among the highest in Europe, well above the eurozone average. Indeed, growth in 2006 accelerated: up from 3.7% of GDP in 2005 to 4.3%, exceeding all official (Greek and European) forecasts as well as the national average for the previous decade of 4.1% (Bank of Greece Annual Report, 2006). Entry into the 'eurozone' has imposed monetary discipline. The recent recalibration of the government's fiscal indicators (deficit, debt), in collaboration with the EU, and Greece's exit from the 'excessive deficit procedure' of the Stability and Growth Pact show a major improvement in budgetary policy. The requirements of the EMU and the SGP have enveloped fiscal management. A medium-term fiscal framework exists, setting targets for subsequent years.

The problem, therefore, is not so much one of macroeconomic growth nor of the management of monetary policy. The headline indicators on these have mostly been going in the desired direction. Moreover, in these areas, two notable features of the policy process stand out: there is an external *'commitment device'* from the EU levering domestic change; at home, Ministers enjoy *relatively high autonomy* and operate within an *enclosed and elite sphere*. Both features appear crucial to the good performance in macroeconomic management. Relative to other sectors, Ministers have both the will and capability to act. By contrast, the problem for Greece is of how to introduce 'supply-side' reforms to sustain the longer-term economic position and, at the same time, 'modernize' social policies to address iniquities and gaps in coverage. In these sectors, the policy process is more *diffuse* and it is difficult to maintain leadership or control. The EU does not impose a similar set of commitment devices, equivalent to the criteria and timetable of Maastricht. The 'Lisbon Programme' and the OMC hit home softly. As already noted, the domestic policy process in these areas involves powerful sectoral interests. The political interests of government questions its unity of purpose: intragovernment tensions pit electoral cost and clientelistic habits against the benefits of reform.

The three case studies presented here tell a story of relatively *small, incremental reform steps*. The pattern of limited, gradual reform is also evident in other policy sectors in Greece. In other words, the pattern of the three case studies is not unique. Two further examples can be cited, to support this general point.

Environmental policy was a relative vacuum for Greece before it entered the EC in 1981. It subsequently rose up the policy agenda. Rapid urbanization since the 1950s, especially in Athens, has left a legacy of poor planning and low quality infrastructure. The smog (or 'nefos') in Athens has been legendary. Successive governments have sought to address these problems: for example, by controlling the daily circulation of traffic, by building a modern and high quality public transport infrastructure, and by enhancing the appearance of the urban environment. The onset of the 2004 Olympics was a major focus for such improvements. Yet Greece has had a poor record in the transposition of EU legislation – 'hard law' – in environmental policy. Boerzel (2000), for example, noted that Greece was next to Italy in its low rate of transposition and high number of infringement proceedings from the EU Commission (Boerzel, 2000: 144). Beriatos (2004) noted the administrative and organizational weaknesses of the Greek state in implementing environmental and physical planning. Indeed, he notes that 'there is a whole mesh of social interests, which finds expression in the political superstructure and influences the planning procedures at all levels of administration and decision-making' (2004: 442). Koutalakis (2004) highlighted the lack of 'institutional opportunities' for non-state actors in Greece to press for implementation of EU environmental policies, leading to a higher number of complaints to EU bodies.

Successive governments have taken measures to promote (re-)foresta-tion and to prevent forest fires. Yet counteracting political pressures have undermined the political will and capability to act decisively. It is widely suspected that some forest fires have been started deliberately as part of a local 'land-grab' by would-be developers, in a society that has tolerated much illegal building. Moreover, the application of the law by local officials has on occasions been thwarted by political pressures from on high (*Kathimerini*, 24 July 2007). A corrupt and inefficient planning system has been a long-term feature. The weaknesses of the system were highlighted very strongly by the tragic fires of summer 2007, which were the worst in modern Greek history. The combination of a weak and inefficient public administration with a culture of corruption and clientelism has prevented effective management in the sector.

Turning to *education*, the level of public spending (as a percentage of GDP) in Greece is the second lowest in the EU (OECD, 2006: 228). Much of this spending is wasteful. The education system exhibits a number of failures: relatively low numbers finishing secondary (the fifth lowest in the EU) and tertiary education (the eighth lowest) (OECD, 2006: 38). Even more strikingly, there is a derisory participation rate in continuing education (the third lowest in EU) and the lowest levels of educational attainment (as measured by PISA scores) in the EU (OECD, 2006: 81; OECD, 2005b: 81). School pupils are required to digest material, rather than to analyse and explain. The number of students choosing scientific or technology degrees has been low. Spending on research and devel-opment is the third worst in the EU, with a rate of growth below the annual average. Such a performance contrasts with the high social priority attached to education by Greek families, the large numbers attending out-of-school tuition and language classes, and the high numbers of students moving to study in universities abroad. Culturally, Greece prioritizes education. Institutionally, however, the Greek state system too often fails to deliver.

The higher-education sector displays a number of blockages to reform. University management is highly politicized at all levels and this has negative effects on reforms that challenge current privileges. It also prevents the promotion of best performance and practice. For the student body, opposition comes from long-term, largely fictional, 'students' – an entrenched minority with a loud representational voice – and from political interests raising fears of encroaching privatization.

The capability to act of successive governments has been undermined by the political pressures emanating from within the universities. The Karamanlis Government initiated limited reforms of the university system in 2005, with a degree of support from the main opposition party (PASOK). Though the government's strategy can be questioned – it broadened the essential reform issues into a wider agenda of constitutional reform to allow non-state universities, for example – there were clear constraints on the ability to implement the reforms. These came from a combination of supine university management and a distorted student representation that favoured the rights of the 'fictional' students. The public sector succoured failure and privilege. Yet reform and enhancement appeared to many to be desperately needed to meet national priorities.

The record of structural reform in the economic and social areas is not, of course, one without success. In their various ways, both the Simitis and Karamanlis Governments have embraced, as a programmatic discourse, the mix of liberal and social reforms elaborated in the EU's Lisbon Programme. The Karamanlis Government displayed will and guile in its 2005 package of reforms on public sector contracts, using the so-called OTE model developed in the partially privatized telecoms corporation. It has continued privatization and the deregulation of the banking and financial sector. In 2007, the government expected to raise some €1.7 billion in privatization revenues, via further sell-offs of OTE, the telecoms corporation, and TT, the postal savings bank. It is notable that such sell-offs are incremental, involving the sale of portions of the state's stake.

These exceptions attest to the wider rule of the limits to reform. The Bank of Greece's Annual Report in April 2007 diagnosed what remained to be done: 'structural reforms must continue over a wide range of sectors of the economy in order to reduce rigidities in the labour and product markets, upgrade human capital, improve the efficiency of public administration and, eventually, restructure the economy's production base' (Bank of Greece, 2007: 58). The inadequacies stem from successive Greek governments being severely constrained by the systemic features highlighted in the three case studies.

The evidence points to a general problem of governance: one of (partial) system failure to deliver prioritized reforms. Sectional interests are able to defend privileges against a wider societal interest. Governments are weakened by poor institutional support and cultural traits of clientelism and corruption. Divided political interests undermine government's ability to engage in a 'top-down' conflict management with the social partners, a rather stronger manifestation of the lack of consensus associated with the 'MME' model and found by Molina and Rhodes in their study of Spain and Italy (Hancke et al., 2007). Moreover, reform in Greece via consensus within a stable social dialogue is barely an option, given the conflictual nature of an interest mediation based on skewed representation and interests. Attempts at social dialogue are irregular and ill-defined. The problem of governance questions Greece's ability to remain part of the EU's core – its ability to implement reforms that mix market liberalization and social inclusion, as with the Lisbon Programme.

The demands emanating from the EU may be expected to fluctuate over time. The EU's progress on integration and its agenda on economic reform are not time consistent, but rather can be spasmodic. The change of political leadership among the major member states can alter the drive behind particular agendas. One such example occurred in 2007 with the newly elected French President, Nicholas Sarkozy, successfully pressing a Treaty change to seemingly downgrade the EU's commitment to internal competition. Yet even this change was disputed – its legal significance was doubted – with many EU leaders, notably Tony Blair, claiming it was business as usual. Moreover, the EU has proclaimed its Lisbon Programme since 2000 and the single market since 1985. In other words, domestic actors in Greece cannot reasonably assume that the EU will drop its commitments to open and flexible markets and national deregulation. Greece cannot both sit it out and hope to remain at the core.

It is this mix of pressures for reform – not only the domestic but also the European – that has created tensions the like of which Greece has not previously encountered. New cleavages of interest are created, while the incapacities of the system are highlighted. With the pressures and constraints, Greece has become harder to govern. There is little prospect of an apocalypse as there is unlikely to be a key decision point in time. Rather, the risk is of a lethargic system adapting just enough to remain within the EU, but too little to significantly enhance its relative position or to erase repeated dismay and self-doubt as a result of its performance.

7.3 Does Greece want to adapt to 'Europe'?

A more radical adaptation to the EU agenda may well threaten a number of embedded values, norms, and practices associated with the Greek identity. Indeed, behind the reform incapacities exhibited by contemporary Greece may lie not only strategic weakness but also a set of normative objections. Does Greece want to undertake major change? The question refers to a clash of cultures, as noted in Chapter 3.

At one level, this is an agenda of how to continue macroeconomic success and address matters of social solidarity. The deeper reality is that the defence of current interests and privileges can serve to sustain social exclusion and inequities of coverage (as with opposition to labour market and pension reforms) and gross inequalities in employment conditions (as in the case of Olympic employee benefits relative to other groups of workers). Some of this defence may be a rational reaction to the limits of compensating benefits in the context of a poor welfare regime, as with the desire to maintain the conditions of current public sector contracts in the absence of measures to aid mobility such as adequate unemployment benefits.

Moreover, the resistance to liberalization may stem from objections to a change of economic and social model. This can be a matter of generalized images, contrasting cultural stereotypes. Yet Greeks do not refer to their system being based on a 'model'. It is not the result of an ideological choice and it is difficult to define. It exists, but it has few who support it in the round.

That said, there are social norms that a majority of the Greek public probably holds dear and which may be perceived as clashing with EU pressures. Such norms are ones of solidarity and mutual support, particularly within extended families, peer networks, and localities. These can fill gaps created by poor welfare provision, lack of information and expertise. The philanthropic donations to those affected by the forest fires in 2007 were undoubtedly sensitive to the lack of household insurance to compensate the victims, but also to the inadequacies of normal state provision. They showed values of social solidarity. In the job market, nepotism and favours to one's group help to protect individuals from the vicissitudes of limited welfare provision and a long-term problem of unemployment. Using the state to hide unemployment or to avoid redundancies, as apparently countenanced in the case of Olympic, helps to avoid the costs of poor welfare. Such norms clash with liberal notions of competition and meritocracy. Lifestyle matters of time away from work, and leisure based on the family and peers create a means of social integration that might be threatened by employment reforms.

While it is important to recognize that normative issues form part of the political context, the problems of reform capacity identified in

Greece are not primarily the result of defending a crafted 'social model'. The latter barely exists; rather it is an accumulation of a jigsaw of interests, with actors defending corners in the knowledge that the system has many holes and risks many vulnerabilities. The key issue of governance is the relative structural power of government vis-à-vis sectional interests. This is a politics of bare interests, rather than of social choice. It is not a matter of Greek society choosing or not choosing 'Europe'. Those who *can* defend their current privileges and the system stagnates as a result.

7.4 The EU as an actor in the domestic reform process

For its part, the effectiveness of the EU's actions in the three case studies has not been impressive. The extent of policy change has been limited. The tools deployed by the Commission to lever domestic reform – while varied – have been found wanting. At times, individual strategies and tactics have undermined the impact – as with the disputed signals and communications between Brussels and Athens at the time of the Verelis rescue plan for Olympic. As for the Greek state, so for the EU institutions: there is an apparent contrast between the will and capability to act.

In conceptual terms, the three case studies combine a variety of governance features associated with 'Europeanization'. The cases of pensions and labour market reform involved negative constraints (the convergence criteria of EMU) on Greek fiscal policy, while Lisbon and the OMC process offered 'framing' for policy debates (Knill and Lehmkuhl, 1999). The latter lacked implementational strength. The case of Olympic was even more mixed: including, as it did, positive (the creation of an internal EU market), negative (anti-state-aids policy), and framing (the encouragement to privatization) qualities. The Commission sought to marshal a set of policy instruments that are varied in type and strength and that cover its apparent agenda incompletely. 'Will' had seemingly outstretched 'capability'.

Whatever the current governance structure, the EU has delivered on reform inadequately. It has declared an agenda of structural reform to parallel that of the single market and the EMU since Delors's White Paper of 1993 and, more emphatically, with the Lisbon Programme of 2000. The European Council's revision of the Lisbon Programme in 2005 was a clear recognition of the failings of the process to date. Across member states, the pattern of reform to the state's role in the market and of its welfare provision has shown marked variation, sustaining major differences. The three Greek case studies have illustrated the intensity of the problem in one national setting. While showing signs of exceptionalism in this respect, the failure to enact domestic reform is by no means unique.

Faced with the challenges of reform, the EU actually displays both divided will and contrasting capabilities. The variation in domestic performances with respect to reform is shaped by differences of political interpretation of the EU agenda. The instruments available to the EU to stimulate domestic reform are differentiated by the myriad of treaty provisions and accumulated EU legislation. These exemplify a lack of unity of political purpose and a governance structure characterized as much by stealth as by any attempt at holistic design.

The position of the EU is seemingly more institutionally complex than that faced domestically by the Greek government. It also faces a different kind of paradox. Its capability to act may prove relatively easier to strengthen given the repeated institutional reforms of the EU's structures. By contrast, its will to act seems set to be subject to continued fluctuation owing to the turnover of political leadership and shifting pressures and priorities.

The uncertain will to act means a greater degree of tolerance to member states exhibiting lesser reform. The reality is that the EU has had to learn to accommodate states like Greece because of this variation in reform performance. The variation has been exacerbated by the continued enlargement of the EU to incorporate states that have great reform challenges. This is a process that stretches from the 2004 accession of eight states from central and eastern Europe to the entrance of Bulgaria and Romania in 2007 to the expected incorporation of Croatia and possibly to the arrival of Turkey after 2016.

The threat to Greece would come from a strengthening of the EU's unity of purpose and a concomitant step change in the economic integration process. This might occur with a new Franco-German rapprochement, for example, leading a long-heralded push for a deepening of integration among a core set of EU members. In these circumstances, of a bold initiative on structural reform, Greece may well find it difficult to keep pace with the conditions for participation. Thus, Greece should hope that its rhetorical commitment to further integration does not become a reality with this agenda too soon. The likelihood, however, of France and Germany agreeing to a liberal reform agenda appears slim, even after the election of Sarkozy. A significant, but lesser, threat to Greece may come from some variation on this agenda in the macroeconomic field.

7.5 The limits to Europeanization

This book has elaborated a set of processes and outcomes that can be encapsulated as the *'limits to Europeanization'*. The latter comprise

- the *divided will* and *contrasting capability* of the EU to stimulate economic and social reform at the domestic level;
- the *low reform capacity* of a state such as Greece to enact reform in these areas, as evidenced by its record of policy initiatives. More specifically, the *impediments* to an effective EU stimulus formed by the structural power of key domestic actors, with conflicting interests stemming from their political and economic position (including current privileges), buttressed by an embedded culture that seeks resources from the state and undermines liberal role conceptions.

The limits to Europeanization, inevitably, involve a dual set of governance issues: those at the EU and the domestic levels, which are of a distinctive character and subject to different sorts of pressure.

There are contrasting implications for the EU and for states like Greece as they contemplate their futures. To a considerable extent, the most important implications are systemic, concerned with structures of power and capability and these are not overcome easily. The agenda of economic and social reform is central to the political choices faced at both the EU level and within domestic systems. This book has helped to contextualize and explain these dilemmas of governance. The *limits to Europeanization* will be a crucial part of the both the national and European agendas in the coming decades.

Appendix

List of interviewees

1. Alogoskoufis, George (Minister of Economy, MP, ND)
2. Analytis, Nikos (Vice President, SEV)
3. Aranitou, Valia (Researcher, ESEE)
4. Christodoulakis, Nikos (Minister of Economy, MP, PASOK)
5. Christodoulou, Efthimios (Governor, Bank of Greece)
6. Christou, Taxiarchis (President, EISF)
7. Davilas, George (General Manager for Human Resources, OTE)
8. Diamantouros, Nikiforos (European Ombudsman, University of Athens)
9. Doganis, Rigas (CEO, Olympic Airways)
10. Drosopoulos, Giannis (Adviser to the Minister of Finance)
11. Garganas, Nikos (Governor, Bank of Greece)
12. Giannakou, Marietta (Minister for Social Security, MP, ND)
13. Giannakourou, Matina (Researcher, OKE)
14. Giannitsis,Tasos (Minister for Labour, PASOK)
15. Glynos, George (Chef de Cabinet to the EU Commissioner of Social Affairs)
16. Halikias, Tasos (Governor, Bank of Greece)
17. Ioakimides, Takis (University of Athens)
18. Kefalas, Haralambos (Adviser, ESEE)
19. Kintis, Andreas, (President, OKE)
20. Kolias, Konstantinos (ADEDY, OKE)
21. Kollia, Vaso (Reseracher, ND)
22. Kousoulakos, Giannis (Secretary General, Ministry of Finance)
23. Koutsikou-Giannakou, Marietta (Ministry of Welfare and Social Insurance)
24. Kouzis, Nikos (Panteion University, Institute of Labour)
25. Lymberaki, Antigoni (Panteion University, Adviser to the Ministry of Labour)
26. Mandelis, Tasos (Minister of Transport, MP, PASOK)
27. Manolis, Giannis (GSEE, OKE)
28. Manos, Stefanos (Minister of National Economy, MP, ND/PASOK)
29. Matsaganis, Manos (Prime Minister's Office)
30. Mitsos, Achilleas (DG, European Commission)
31. Pagalos, Theodoros (Minister of Transport, MP, PASOK)
32. Paleokrassas, Giannis (Minister of Finance, MP, ND)
33. Papadakis, Giannis (Adviser to the Minister of Finance)
34. Papademos, Loukas (Governor, Bank of Greece)
35. Papadimitriou, Babis (Journalist)
36. Papagiannidis, Antonis (Journalist)
37. Papaioannou, Miltiadis (Minister of Labour, MP, PASOK)
38. Papandoniou, Giannos (Minister of Economy, MP, PASOK)
39. Papanikos, Grigoris (Secretary General, OKE)
40. Patestos, Manolis (President, OSPA)
41. Pochet, Phillippe (Observatoire Social Européen, Brussels)

42. Polizogopoulos, Christos (President, GSEE)
43. Protopapas, Christos (Deputy Minister of Labour)
44. Robolis, Savvas (Panteion University, Scientific Director, Institute of Labour)
45. Sabethai, Isaac (Director of Research, Bank of Greece)
46. Sagos, Evangelos (President, EXPA)
47. Spraos, Giannis (Adviser to the Prime Minister)
48. Spyropoulos, Rovertos (Deputy Minister of Labour, MP, PASOK)
49. Stournaras, Giannis (President of the Council of Economic Advisers)
50. Tinios, Platon (Prime Minister's Office)
51. Tsoumani, Evgenia (SEV)
52. Verelis, Christos (Minister of Transport, MP, PASOK)
53. Vlachos, George (Adviser to the Minister of National Economy)
54. Vlamis, Leonardos (CEO, Olympic Airlines)

Notes

Preface

1. Featherstone Kevin and Dimitris Papadimitriou. 2007. Manipulating Rules, Contesting Solutions: Europeanization and the Politics of Restructuring Olympic Airways. *Government and Opposition* 42 (1): 46–72; Featherstone Kevin. 2005. Introduction: 'Modernisation' and the Structural Constraints of Greek Politics. *West European Politics* 28 (2): 223–41; Papadimitriou Dimitris. 2005. The Limits of Engineering Collective Escape: The 2000 Reform of the Greek Labour Market. *West European Politics* 28 (2): 381–401; Featherstone Kevin. 2003. Greece and EMU: Between External Empowerment and Domestic Vulnerability. *Journal of Common Market Studies* 41 (5): 923–40; Featherstone Kevin, Kazamias George, and Papadimitriou Dimitris. 2001. The Limits of External Empowerment: EMU, Technocracy and Reform of the Greek Pension System. *Political Studies* 49 (3): 462–80; Featherstone Kevin, Kazamias George, and Papadimitriou Dimitris. 2000. Greece and the Negotiation of Economic and Monetary Union: Preferences, Strategies, and Institutions. *Journal of Modern Greek Studies* 18: 393–414; Featherstone Kevin. 1998. The 'Europeanisation' of the Centre–Periphery: The Case of Greece in the 1990s. *South European Society and Politics* 3 (1): 23–39.

1 Introduction

1. In fact the OMC approach can be dated back to 1994 (Schelkle, 2005) and the Broad Economic Policy Guidelines, European Employment Strategy, etc.
2. Dimitrakopoulos (2007) makes a case for a more nuanced interpretation of such EU records. Nevertheless a problem clearly exists.
3. Archbishop Christodoulos died on 28 January 2008. His earlier profile had been diminished by a series of financial and sexual scandals involving senior clerics in Spring 2005.
4. LAOS entered the Greek parliament for the first time in September 2007, having won ten seats on the basis of 3.8% of the vote. See Table 3.3.
5. Arsenis was also associated with the nationalist tradition.
6. Simitis secured 53 votes in the first round, the same as Tsochatzopoulos, with Arsenis just behind at 50 (and Giannis Charalambopoulos, a PASOK veteran, at 11). In the second round, Simitis defeated Tsochatzopoulos by 86 votes to 75.
7. The background here is that George Alogoskoufis, as the new Minister of Economics and Finance in 2004, initiated an audit of the relevant data. This was a highly charged act, challenging the key economic achievement of the Simitis Government. The audit led the Greek authorities in September 2004 to significantly adjust the data that had been reported just before the election. This was taken up by EUROSTAT and reported to the Commission and ECOFIN

(Report by EUROSTAT on the revision of the Greek Government Deficit and Debt Figures, 22 November 2004). Such a revision of the data was exceptional; the most recent deficit was 4.6% of GDP, well above the 3% limit of the Stability and Growth Pact (SGP), rather than a virtuous 1.7%. The figures for 2001 and 2002 had also been revised by more than two percentage points. Following a further investigation by EUROSTAT and the Greek authorities, it was also reported that the deficits and debt levels for the previous three years (1997–9) had also to be revised upwards significantly. Tellingly, Greece had never met the 3% rule on the public deficit in the relevant reference period. In hindsight, Greece's euro entry appeared misjudged, even fraudulent.

The response of PASOK was one of fury, as evident in the parliamentary debate on 21 December. The next day a letter was published from Simitis in the *Financial Times* decrying the fact that Alogoskoufis's audit had not involved any independent agency and that it had 'bent previously accepted rules' (22 December 2004). Simitis's reputation had been based on his 'clean hands'. He argued that the main reason why the figures diverged was because of 'the retroactive application of a new method for estimating defence expenditure', a practice that should be outlawed as it undermined stability. Simitis noted that the effect was to shift expenditure from the future to the past, easing the current government's position prior to the next elections. A few days later, the head of EUROSTAT, Gunther Hanreich, replied in the same newspaper denying that there had been a retroactive application of new rules (28 December 2004). Indeed, the Greek problem was due to 'a clear under-reporting...of military expenditure irrespective of the accounting method used, an over-reporting of revenues from social security and an incorrect treatment of a significant amount of capitalised interest on government bonds'. Despite assurances from Athens that the rules would be applied, they had not done so, and they had not responded to concerns repeatedly expressed by EUROSTAT. As a result of the Greek case, the Commission rapidly brought forward (in December 2004) a set of proposals to strengthen the position of EUROSTAT and to bolster the independence and accountability of statistical institutes. EUROSTAT carried out a special review of the Greek data, and on 23 October 2006 it declared that it was now satisfied with the compilation of the deficit and debt figures.

Greece was now subject to the 'excessive deficit procedure' (EDP), due to its weakened position. The general government deficit in 2004 was set at 7.8% of GDP. An ECOFIN notice of 17 February 2005 signalled the action expected from Greece. The 2006 Greek budget set a target of 2.6% for the deficit, with 2.4% projected for 2007 and a balanced budget by 2012. In the event EURO-STAT, in April 2007, reported that Greece's deficit in 2006 had indeed been 2.6% of GDP, pending further examination, and ECOFIN the following month agreed to lift the EDP from Greece. The public debt levels were also projected to fall beneath 100% of GDP – to 91.3% by 2009, though in 2006 they still stood at 104.6%. Alogoskoufis – an internationally renowned economist – argued that the projections he had offered were realistic on the basis of high growth, rising primary surpluses (containing spending and improved tax efficiency), falling debt, and higher proceeds from privatization. The Greek SGP of 2006 had received a very positive endorsement by ECOFIN on 6 February 2007, as had the government strategy from the IMF on 25 January.

The economic position had been boosted earlier by a remarkable upward revision of GDP data on the part of the National Statistical Service of Greece (NSSG). Its head, Emmanuel Kontopyrakis, had conducted a review in accordance with EU rules requiring periodic reassessment. The previous such revision had been undertaken in 1994. The new review led to an upward revision of Greek GDP by over 20%. The review had taken into account new survey information and the most recent census, enabling a more accurate picture of economic activity in the services sector (especially wholesale and retail trade, transportation, construction, and tourism). The foreign press highlighted the fact that the upgrade was due to new estimates on the black economy, including money laundering and prostitution (*Financial Times*, 29 September 2006). The higher GDP figure was to be reviewed by EUROSTAT; in the meantime, the Greek budget and SGP projections were based on the old GDP levels. If accepted, the new GDP data would mean that the government deficit in 2006 would be 2.1% (not 2.6%) and in 2007 it would be 1.9% (not 2.1%). More strikingly, given the higher GDP level, public debt would be reduced from 107.5% to 85% (*Financial Times*, 29 September 2006) or 83% (IMF Report, 25 January 2007). At a stroke, Greece's relative performance in the euro -zone would be significantly improved. In October 2007, the EU Commission proposed an upward revision of 9.6%, rather than 20% – still a significant upward adjustment of the Greek indicators.

2   The Europeanization Process and the Greek Political System

1. Featherstone notes in the same volume that the term 'Europeanization' has been applied to a range of subjects with little or no connection to EU politics: the export of cultural norms; shifts of ethnic groups; colonialization; transnational cultural diffusion; and habits, identities, and citizenship (2003: 5–12).
2. The discussion here follows that of Featherstone and Kazamias (2001: 7–9).
3. Note that Ioakimides's use of the term 'intended' is distinct from that of Bache and Jordan (2006).
4. We are grateful for the comments given here by Eleni Xiarchogiannopoulou.

3   The Domestic Constraints on Reform

We are grateful for the comments given on earlier drafts of this chapter by David Soskice, George Pagoulatos and Dimitris Sotiropoulos. Any errors that remain are ours alone.

1. For a general background, see the excellent work by Koliopoulos and Veremis (2002). Also, Diamandouros (2002).
2. The number of governments is the total number where a government has had the same prime minister and lasted through the period from one parliamentary election to another.
3. We are indebted to the review offered in Hall and Soskice (2001).
4. Hancke et al. (2007) note that French policymakers used EU competition regulations to justify domestic reforms desired for non-EU reasons, but long-established state-business networks shaped how the policy was enacted

at home. They see this as consistent with the path dependency of the varieties of capitalism model. The comment neglects, though, the leverage that stems from EU commitments to produce change that may not have been realizable otherwise and it fails to highlight the role of actors seeking to restructure power relations in a particular sector. The comment neatly summarizes the limitations of both 'varieties of capitalism' and 'Europeanization'.

5. Two institutions are complementary when the existence of one increases the efficiency of the other (see Amable, 2003: 6).
6. Matsaganis et al. argue that it should be seen in the context of other flanking measures (2003).
7. They contest, however, the notion that in general the systems of all four states are more generous than those found elsewhere in the EU.
8. In July 2007, the Greek daily *Kathimerini* reported local outrage when the Finance Ministry, apparently bowing to pressure from illegal builders, transferred the head of the state land service in Aitolacarnania, in western Greece, who had sought to apply the law against land grabbers in Mesolongi (*Kathimerini*, 24 July 2007).
9. We are grateful to David Soskice here for his help. Any errors remain ours.
10. It might also be added that the media reflects the stress on personalistic politics, failing to compensate for the lack of a wider policy input from the civil society, and its major corporations are themselves engaged in an incestuous relationship with one or other of the parties – in the expectation of material self-gain should the party enter office.
11. Greek firms have, however, accepted much greater risk in their entry into foreign, largely Balkan, markets in recent years.

4 Whose Benefits? The Elusive Reform of the Greek Pension System

1. Comment made by senior member of Greek government in personal interview, January 2003.
2. See Council decision 2000/436/EC, 29 June 2000.
3. More specifically, the eleven agreed objectives were adequacy (prevent social exclusion in old age, allow people to maintain their living standards, promote solidarity between and within generations), financial sustainability (raise employment levels, extend working lives, ensure sustainable pensions in a context of sound public finances, adjust benefits and contributions so as to share the financial consequences of ageing in a balanced way between the generations, ensure that private pension provision is adequate and financially sound), responding to changing needs (adapt to more flexible employment and career patterns, meet the aspirations for greater equality of women and men, make pension systems more transparent and demonstrate their ability to meet the challenges).
4. This section is based on Featherstone et al. (2001).
5. This was the second-highest percentage (behind Italy) in the OECD. A decade earlier pension payments accounted for 8.2% of the GDP. See Bank of Greece (1990: 145 and 162).

6. Employees' contributions for primary pension were increased by 1%, from 4.75% to 5.75%. Employers' contributions for primary pension were raised by 2%, from 9.50% to 11.50%. Contribution for auxiliary pensions remained unchanged at 3% for employees and 3% for employers. Contributions for health care also remained unchanged at 2.25% for employees and 4.50% for employers.

7. For the full text of GSEE's alternative report, see GSEE (1999: 61–81).

8. For the preparation of the IMF report, the government had also invited British officials with expertise on the preparation of actuarial studies for pension systems. An extensive summary of the IMF report was published in *To Vima*, 19 July 1992.

9. Dimitris Sioufas was appointed Minister for Health, Welfare and Social Security on 7 August 1991 replacing Marietta Giannakou-Koutsikou who had been in this post since the formation of Mitsotakis's first government in April 1990. Keesing's Record of World Events, 38403.

10. This section is based on Featherstone et al. (2001).

11. For the Committee's other reports on inflation and income policy, use of public revenues, public administration, agriculture, public expenditure, and industry, see *Avgi*, 17 January 1998.

12. See, for example, the wave of detailed reporting on the content of the report that appeared in many daily newspapers two weeks before its official publication (*Ta Nea*, 30 September 1997; *Eleftheros*, 1 October 1997; *Kathimerini*, 1 October 1997).

13. In the course of the presentation of the report, Spraos said that unless the tendency is somehow reversed, in a few years the ratio between workers and pensioners would be nearly 1:1; 'in this case we do not need pension funds: we can give to the pensioner the worker's address and he can go live with him' (since the worker will be supporting the pensioner anyway...). See *Eleftherotypia*, 14 October 1999.

14. An early draft of the report was much more substantial and included more number crunching than the finished product. A minority within the committee supported maintaining the technical side of the report, but eventually the decision was taken to produce a report, easily digestible by the public. It is interesting that the much more technical report of the OECD of 1997 was substantially more critical of the problem; yet due to its 'technical' nature, the OECD report received very little attention.

15. See, for example, the views expressed by the PM's chief economic adviser, Gikas Chardouvellis (*To Vima*, 20 January 2001). These seemed to be rather different from the views of the PM's political office where the influential Platon Tinios was based (*in.gr*, 3 July 2001) and with the Ministry of Labour which remained in close working relationship with the British officials in charge of the preparation of the actuarial study on the Greek pension system (*To Vima*, 26 November 2000 and *Ta Nea*, 27 December 2000).

16. This would be achieved through (a) the incorporation of the pension funds of the banking sector and state-owned companies into IKA (the largest existing fund covering private sector employees); (b) the incorporation of the so-called noble pension funds of doctors, lawyers, and engineers into OAEE (the existing fund covering the self-employed); (c) the creation of a new pension fund for those employed in the state administration (whose

pensions are currently paid directly by the budget); and (d) the continuation in its present form of OGA, the pension fund covering farmers. (See *Ta Nea*, 27 December 2001)

17. It was estimated that more than 70% of Greek employees could chose retirement before the age of 65. See *Ta Nea*, 17 April 2001.

18. Those who entered after 1993 were already subjected to the provisions of the 1992 law.

19. A notable exception of this rule was former Prime Minister Constantinos Mitsotakis who was reportedly supportive of the government's plans (*Eleftherotipia*, 18 April 2001).

20. For Pagalos's interview in which he criticized the government over its handling of the labour market reform, see *To Ethnos*, 19 November 2000.

21. For example, the new package made no attempt to reform the system of disability pensions which was the subject of widespread abuse. Also the pension rights of those employed in 'arduous and unhealthy' occupations remained unchanged (in some cases they became even more generous). The regime of early retirements was too subjected to very little change (in some cases it became more generous).

22. Some groups of employees could also qualify for a minimum pension after 3500 days of service.

23. However, some of these loses were counterbalanced by the introduction of a more generous model of calculating the overall level of pension entitlement.

24. The pension fund of DEI, the state-controlled electricity company, was exempted for this provision.

25. Vasilis Magginas remained in his post after ND election victory in September 2007.

5 The Puzzle of Jobless Growth: The Challenge of Reforming the Greek Labour Market

1. These include personal income taxes plus employees' and employers' social security contributions as well as payroll taxes.

2. For example, despite its de facto use for many decades, part-time employment was legally recognized only in 1990 (Law 1892/90). Similarly, legislation on the regulation of atypical forms of employment (mainly contract work) was introduced as late as 1998 (Law 2639/98). Even more astonishingly, until 1998, the law prohibited the operation of private employment agencies (even after the adoption of the 2639/98 Law the operation of these agencies is heavily regulated).

3. For industrial workers the severance pay stipulated by the Greek legislation is more convergent with the EU average.

4. Prior to the introduction of the Law 2874/2000 the monthly limits on collective redundancies were as follows: (a) up to five employees for businesses employing between 20 and 49 staff, (b) between one and four employees for businesses employing between 50 and 250 staff, and (c) up to 2% of the total workforce for businesses employing over 250 staff. Under Law 2874/2000 these limits were altered as follows: (a) up to four employees for businesses

employing between 29 and 250 staff and (b) up to 2% of the total workforce for businesses employing over 250 staff.

5. The legal framework on working time provided further restrictions on flexible employment. Until 1990 working time (the statutory 40 hours – a week) was strictly calculated on a weekly basis. By the end of the 1990s, the reference period for the calculation of working time was extended to six months (under Laws 1892/90 and 2639/98), but such an extension had been subjected to a number of restrictions and required full union consent. Throughout the 1990s not a single company was able to make use of this provision.

6. The measure 'temporary suspension' (διαθεσιμότητα) originates from the mid-1950s (Law 3198/55). During the period of their temporary suspension, employees are remunerated at 50% of their average wage during the last two months prior to their suspension.

7. 'Normal overtime' referred to employment over 48 hours a week, which was remunerated, depending on the length of overtime, with up to 75% over and above normal pay.

8. In July 2001 the government invited a second wave of legalization applications. Some 280,000 foreign workers responded to this invitation but as of summer 2003 it was not clear how many of them received their green cards.

9. Further confusion has been caused by the fluidity surrounding the institutional position and competences of labour watchdogs such as the Labour Inspectorate (responsible for upholding standards on working conditions).

10. The 19 subject areas were maintaining increases in real income under conditions of low inflation, public investment, private investment, investment in human resources, banking, 'lame duck' companies, industrial policy, effectiveness of the public sector, collective bargaining, pay and wages, working time, part-time work, social protection for those working in new forms of employment, territorial employment pacts, conditions for working pensioners, rights and obligations under the law 2434/96 on employment and vocational training, and employment policy in the EU.

11. The idea of pursuing a far-reaching reform of the Greek pension system had been shelved following the opposition to the Spaos committee's recommendations in 1996. For more detail, see Featherstone et al. (2001).

12. These were Christos Protopapas, deputy Minister of Labour; Apostolos Fotiadis, deputy Minister of Economics; and Tasos Giannitsis, chief economic adviser to the Prime Minister.

13. Each delegate represented GSEE's three largest party-political fractions participating in the process: PASKE on behalf of PASOK, DAKE on behalf of ND, and Αυτόνομη Παρέμβαση on behalf of Synaspismos. The KKE-controlled faction of GSEE (PAME), the third-largest force within GSEE, from the outset refused to join the process. Representatives of the public sector union, ADEDY, also participated in the Political Secretariat when the agenda included issues relating to public sector employees.

14. 'Compulsory overtime' has been a peculiarity of the Greek labour market since 1975. It related to the management's derogative of forcing employees to work overtime for eight hours a week (over and above the normal 40-hour

week) with a pay increase of 25%. Any employment over a 48-hour week was considered 'normal' overtime. Pay for such overtime ranged from 25%–75% (depending on the total number of overtime hours worked) over and above the normal pay.

15. On 23 October 1997, GSEE went on a one-day strike accusing the government for inflexibility in the social dialogue and demanding above-inflation pay rises for 1998–9.
16. Protopapas had been President of GSEE during 1993 to 1996.
17. Professor Aggelos Aggelopoulos has been one of the most influential Greek economists of the twentieth century with close associations to the Greek left. During the German occupation of Greece he has been one of the key figures in the partisan-controlled provisional government and he later served briefly in the first post-war unity government under George Papandreou. He also held professorial positions at the University of Athens and the Panteion University and in 1974 he was appointed a member of the Greek Academy.
18. These were (1) EU Community Support Framework; (2) Qualitative improvement of support mechanisms for employment policies; (3) Fiscal, income, and anti-inflationary policy; (4) Structural policies for competitiveness; (5) Policies for the development of entrepreneurship; (6) Institutional framework for human resources policies; (7) Initiatives for high-unemployment areas; (8) Active employment policies; (9) Safety net against exclusion, inequality, and poverty.
19. On 10 October 2000, GSEE organized a one-day strike against the government's plans on labour market reform. See also *To Vima*, 1 October 2000 and 15 October 2000.
20. See, for instance, the stormy discussions during PASOK's National Conference on Unemployment (3–4 November 2000) and the joint meeting of PASOK's Parliamentary Group on Employment with the party's trade unionists (23 November). During these discussions, PASOK's Secretary General, Costas Scandalidis, and Deputy Minister of Labour, Christos Protopapas, played an instrumental role in winning over party doubters. On this, see *Eleftherotypia*, 3 November 2000; 5 November 2000; and 20 November 2000).
21. For businesses that operated six-days-a-week compulsory overtime would extend to eight hours per week (41–8).
22. The membership of this committee would consist of two union representatives, two representatives from employers associations, and one member of the Labour Inspectorate.
23. The move caused a fierce attack by GSEE and prompted the opposition to accuse the government of a parliamentary coup (*in.gr*, 22 July 2005).
24. Extended to 21:00 in the summer months.
25. In tourist areas, longer opening hours applied. Also there were no legal restrictions on the opening hours of certain categories of shops such as tobacconists (περίπτερα), florists, 'corner shops', and liquor shops.
26. This tension is also reflected in the growing importance of the Greek Federation of Retail Enterprises (SELPE/ΣΕΛΠΕ: Συνδέσμου Επιχειρήσεων Λιανικής Πώλησης Ελλάδος), representing some of the largest retail chains in the country, which was a key proponent of the government's proposals and pushed for even longer opening hours, including Sundays.

6   Destination Nowhere: Restructuring Olympic Airways/Airlines

1. For more statistics, see http://ec.europa.eu/transport/air_portal/internal_market/index_en.htm.
2. The right of an air carrier to undertake the air transport of passengers, cargo, or mail between two States other than the State in which it is registered.
3. The right of an air carrier licensed in one State to put down, in the territory of another State, passengers, cargo or mail taken up in the State in which it is registered.
4. The right of an air carrier licensed in one State to take on, in the territory of another State, passengers, cargo, or mail for off-loading in the State in which it is registered.
5. These provisions were extended to freight in December 1990.
6. For further background information, see http://www.europa.eu.int/comm/transport/air/rules/competition_en.htm.
7. Loyola De Palacio was a leading member of the centre-right Partido Popular in Spain, having previously served as Minister of Agriculture and as a member of the European Parliament (briefly). She was appointed as Vice President of the Commission, responsible for relations with the European Parliament, alongside the Transport and Energy portfolios, under President Romano Prodi. Previously, Neil Kinnock, formerly leader of the British Labour Party, held the Transport portfolio in the Commission of Jacques Santer, 1995–9.
8. Between 1990 and 2000 the government awarded over 14 consultancy contracts that covered the whole range of the activities performed by the OA group.
9. Twenty-one of those aircrafts belonged to the OA's subsidiary Olympic Aviation.
10. In the 1994 restructuring plan, the Greek government had predicted profits of ECU62.8 million for 1997.
11. Greece entered ERM II on 14 March 1998.
12. In 1999 OA employed 7000 permanent and 3000 seasonal staff. See *To Vima*, 14 April 2002.
13. Sixty more pilots agreed to be redeployed in the Civil Aviation Authority.
14. This issue has been the subject of a separate case pursued by the lawyers of the Greek Ministry of Transport under instructions from Christos Verelis.
15. The lease of aircraft and crew changed at an hourly rate.
16. Jacques Barrot took over the post of Commissioner of Energy and Transport from Loloya De Palacio in November 2004.
17. In the Commission's reasoned opinion in April 2006 the state aid repayable to the Greek state amounted to €161 million.
18. The divestment strategy was consistent with an array of potential solutions: placing OA under a major foreign strategic partner, seeking a foreign purchaser, and creating a new company as part of a radical restructuring plan. Each was intended to bring to an end the continuing drain on the state posed by OA's position; in that sense, they were indeed compatible with an end to state aids and the shift of OA to a fully commercial criteria of operation.

7 Conclusions

1. Greece has not been in a position to 'upload' its preferences and policies in these areas to any significant extent.
2. A notable exception of this pattern is the banking sector, which throughout the 1990s saw considerable domestic restructuring and major entrepreneurial initiatives to break into neighbouring markets in Southeast Europe.
3. Pagoulatos argues that the transition had been brought about by a mix of Greece's own inherent development, EU membership, and international changes (structural and ideological).
4. Inflation remains above the eurozone average, though it narrowed in 2006 to 1.1 percentage points (from 1.3 in 2005).

Bibliography

Allison Graham T. and Nicolaides Kalypso (eds). 1997. *The Greek Paradox, Promise vs. Performance*. Cambridge, MA: MIT Press.

Alvarez Michael R., Garrett Geoffrey, and Lange Peter. 1991. Government Partisanship, Labor Organisation, and Macroeconomic Performance. *American Political Science Review* 85 (2): 539–56.

Amable Bruno. 2000. Institutional Complementarity and Diversity of Social Systems of Innovation and Production. *Review of International Political Economy* 7 (4): 645–87.

———. 2003. *The Diversity of Modern Capitalism*. Oxford: Oxford University Press.

Amable Bruno, Barré Rémi, and Boyer Robert. 1997. *Les Systèmes d'innovation à l'ère de la Globalisation*. Paris: Economica.

Apogevmatini (various dates).

Athens News Agency (various dates).

Athinaiki (various dates).

Avgi (various dates).

Avriani (various dates).

Bache Ian and Jordan Andrew. 2006. Europeanization of British Politics? In *The Europeanization of British Politics*, edited by Ian Bache and Andrew Jordan. Basingstoke: Palgrave Macmillan.

Bank of Greece. 1990. Report of the Governor for the Year 1989. Athens: Bank of Greece.

———. 1991. Report of the Governor for the Year 1990. Athens: Bank of Greece.

———. 2006. Annual Report 2005. Athens: Bank of Greece.

———. 2007. Annual Report 2007. Athens: Bank of Greece.

Berger Suzanne. 1981. Regime and Interest Representation. In *Organizing Interests in Western Europe*, edited by Berger Suzanne. Cambridge: Cambridge University Press.

Boersch-Supan Axel and Meinhard Miegel. 2001. *Pension Reform in Six Countries*. Heidelberg, New York, Tokyo: Springer.

Boerzel Tanja A. 2000. Why There Is No 'Southern Problem'. On Environmental Leaders and Laggards in the EU. *Journal of European Public Policy* 7 (1): 141–62.

Bonoli Guiliano. 2000. *The Politics of Pension Reform: Institutions and Policy Change in Western Europe*. Cambridge: Cambridge University Press.

Boyer Robert. 2005. Coherence, Diversity and Evolution of Capitalisms: The Institutional Complementarity Hypothesis. In *CEPREMAP*. Unpublished mimeo.

Brady Henry E. and Collier David (eds). 2004. *Rethinking Social Enquiry: Diverse Tools, Shared Standards*. Lanham, MD: Rowman & Littlefield.

Bulmer Simon. 2007. Theorizing Europeanization. In *Europeanization: New Research Agendas*, edited by Graziano Paolo and Vink Maarten P. Basingstoke: Palgrave, Macmillan.

Bulmer Simon and Radaelli Claudio M. 2005. The Europeanisation of Public Policy? In *The Member States of the European Union*, edited by Lesquene Christian and Bulmer Simon. Oxford: Oxford University Press.

Bulmer Simon and Lesquene Christian. 2005. Introduction. In *The Member States of the European Union*, edited by Lesquene Christian and Bulmer Simon. Oxford: Oxford University Press.

Bulmer Simon and Burch Martin. 1998. Organising for Europe – Whitehall, the British State and the European Union. *Public Administration* 76 (4): 601–28.

Bulmer Simon and Burch Martin. 2000b. The Europeanisation of British Central Government. In *Transforming British Government*, edited by Rhodes Roderick Arthur W. London: Macmillan, 46–62.

———. 2000. The Europeanisation of British Central Government. In *Transforming British Government*, edited by Rhodes Roderick Arthur W. London: Macmillan.

Button Kenneth. 2001. Deregulation and Liberalization of European Air transport Markets. *Innovation: The European Journal of the Social Sciences* 14 (3): 255–75.

Carli Guido. 1993. *Fifty Years of Italian Life (Cinquant' Anni di Vita Italiana)*. Rome: Laterza.

Cawson Alan. 1986. *Corporatism and Political Theory*. Oxford: Basil Blackwell.

Checkel Jeffrey T. 1999. Social Construction and Integration. *Journal of European Public Policy*, special issue 6 (4): 545–60.

Cini Michelle and McGowan Lee. 1998. *Competition Policy in the European Union*. London: Macmillan.

Commission of the European Communities. 1986. Third Annual Report to the European Parliament on Commission Monitoring of the Application of Community Law. *COM(86) 204 Final, Official Journal of the European Communities, C 220 1/9/1986* 29.

———. 1992. Ninth Annual Report on Commission Monitoring of the Application of Community Law. *COM(92) 136 Final*.

Committee for the Study of Long-Term Economic Policy. 1997. Pensions and the Greek Economy: A Contribution to the Public Debate. Athens: Prime Minister's Office.

Confidence Pact between the Government and the Social Partners towards the Year 2000 [Σύμφωνο Εμπιστοσύνης Κυβέρνησης και Κοινωνικών Εταίρων στην Πορεία προς το 2000]. Concluding document of the social dialogue. Athens, 10.11.1997.

Court of Justice of the European Communities. 2005. Judgement of the Court of 12 May 2005 in Case C-415/03. *Official Journal of the European Union 182/10, 23.07.2005*.

———. 2007. Judgment of the Court of First Instance of 12 September 2007 in Case T-68/03. *Official Journal of the European Union C 247/22, 20.10. 2007*.

Crouch Colin. 2005. Complementarity and Fit in the Study of Capitalisms. In *Hanging Capitalisms? Internationalization, Institutional Change, and Systems of Economic Organization*, edited by Morgan Glenn, Whitley Richard, and Moen Eli. Oxford: Oxford University Press.

de la Porte Caroline and Pochet Philippe. 2002. Public Pension Reform: European Actors, Discourses and Outcomes. In *Building Social Europe through the Open Method of Co-ordination*, edited by de la Porte Caroline and Pochet Philippe. Brussels: P.I.E.–Peter Lang.

Dell'Anno Roberto and Schneider Friedrich. 2003. *The Shadow Economy of Italy and Other OECD Countries: What Do We Know?* [last cited 30.10.2007]. Available from http://ideas.repec.org/p/zbw/ifwedp/5523.html.

Demertzis Nikos. 1994. *The Greek Political Culture Today* [Η Ελληνική Κουλτούρα Εήμερα]. Athens: Odysseas.

de Palacio Loyola. 2002. Energy Market Liberalisation: Pitfalls and Benefits. Speech given at the World Economic Forum. New York, 3.02.2002.

————. 2004. Future Challenges in the Air Cargo Transport. Speech given at the Air Cargo Forum. Bilbao, 15.09.2004.

Diamandouros Nikiforos. 1994. Cultural Dualism and Political Change in Post-Authoritarian Greece. *Working paper No. 50*. Madrid: Instituto Juan March.

————. 2000. Cultural Dualism and Political Change in Post-Dictatorship Greece [Πολιτισμικός Δυϊσμός και Πολιτική Αλλαγή στην Ελλάδα της Μεταπολίτευσης]. Athens: Alexandria.

————. 2002. *The Origination of the Constitution of the Modern State in Greece, 1821–1828*. Athens: National Bank of Greece Cultural Foundation.

Dimitrakopoulos Dionyssis. 2007. Institutions and the Implementation of EU Public Policy in Greece: The Case of Public Procurement. *Hellenic Observatory Papers on Greece and Southeast Europe* (2).

Doganis Rigas. 2001. *The Airline Industry in the 21st Century*. London: Routledge.

Dyson Kenneth and Featherstone Kevin. 1999. *The Road to Maastricht: Negotiating Economic and Monetary Union*. Oxford: Oxford University Press.

Dyson Kenneth and Klaus H. Goetz. 2003. Living with Europe: Power, Constraint and Contestation. In *Living with Europe: Germany, Europe and the Politics of Constraint*, edited by Dyson Kenneth and Goetz Klaus H. Oxford: Published for the British Academy by Oxford University Press.

Eckstein Harry. 1975. Case Study and Theory in Political Science. In *Handbook of Political Science*, edited by Greenstein Fred and Polsby Nelson. Reading, MA: Addison-Wesley.

Economic and Social Committee of Greece (OKE). 1998. *Opinion on Draft Bill 'Regulation of Labour Relations and Other Provisions'* [Γνώμη της Ο.Κ.Ε. 'Ρύθμιση Εργασιακών Σχέσεων και άλλες Διατάξεις', Σχέδιο Νόμου]. Athens: OKE.

————. 2001. *Opinion on Draft Bill 'Promotion of Employment and Other Provisions* [Γνώμη της Ο.Κ.Ε 'Προώθηση Απασχόλησης και άλλες Διατάξεις, Σχέδιο Νόμου]. Athens: OKE.

————. 2003. *Social Dialogue in Greece: Assessment, Trends and Prospects* [Γνώμη της Ο.Κ.Ε 'Ο Κοινωνικός Διάλογος στην Ελλάδα – Αποτίμηση – Τάσεις-Προοπτικές']. Athens: OKE.

Economic Policy Committee (EPC). 2000. Progress Report to the Ecofin Council on the Impact of Ageing Population on Public Pension Systems. *EPC/ECFIN/ 581/00-EN FINAL. Brussels, 6.11.2000.*

Efimerida tis Kyverniseos. 1996. Vol. B, 18 October 1996.

EIRO online. 1998. Law Changes Terms and Conditions at Olympic Airways [last cited 05.11.2007]. Available from http://www.eurofound.europa.eu/eiro/1998/ 04/feature/gr9804166f.htm.

————. 2000. Government Proposes Changes to Industrial Relations [last cited 05.11.2007]. Available from http://www.eurofound.europa.eu/eiro/2000/07/ feature/gr0007178f.htm.

————. 2002. Industrial Relations in the EU Member States and Candidate Countries [last cited 14.10.2007]. Available from http://www.eurofound. europa.eu/eiro/2002/07/feature/tn0207104f.htm.

————. 2004. Trade Union Membership 1993–2003 [last cited 8.10.2007]. Available from http://www.eurofound.europa.eu/eiro/2004/03/update/tn0403105u.htm.

Eleftheriadis Pavlos. 2005. The Reform Agenda: The Citizen and the State Constitutional Reform and the Rule of Law in Greece. In *Politics and Policy in Greece: The Challenge of Modernisation,* edited by Featherstone Kevin. Oxon, New York: Routledge.

Eleftheros (various dates).

Eleftheros Typos (various dates).

Eleftherotypia (various dates).

Elias Beriatos. 2004. Environmental Policy and Spatial Planning in Greece: Institutional aspects. *Water Air and Soil Pollution: Focus* 4 (4–5): 433–44.

Employment Taskforce. 2003. *Jobs, Jobs, Jobs: Creating More Employment in Europe* (the 'Kok' report). Brussels, November.

Esping-Andersen, Gosta. 1990. *The Three Worlds of Welfare Capitalism.* Cambridge: Polity Press.

European Commission. 1985a. Eurobarometer: Public Opinion in the European Community. (24).

————. 1985b. Eurobarometer: Public Opinion in the European Community. (23).

————. 1990. Eurobarometer: Public Opinion in the European Community. (34).

————. 1994. Decision on Aid Granted by Greece to Olympic Airways. *Official Journal of the European Communities L 273, 25.10.1994, Brussels, 7.10.1994.*

————. 1996. State Aid C 14/94 – Greece. *Official Journal of the European Communities C 176, 19.6.1996, Brussels, 19.6.1996.*

————. 1995. Eurobarometer: Public Opinion in the European Commission. (43).

————. 1997. Single Market Scoreboard. (1).

————. 1998. Decision on Aid Granted by Greece to Olympic Airways. *Official Journal of the European Communities L 128/1, 21.5.1999, Brussels, 14.08.1998.*

————. 1999a. XVIth Report on Monitoring the Application of Community Law. *COM(1999)301 Final, 9.7.1999.*

————. 1999b. A Concerted Strategy for Modernising Social Protection. *COM(99)347 Final, Brussels.*

————. 2000a. Single Market Scoreboard. (6).

————. 2000b. The Future Evolution of Social Protection from a Long-Term Point of View: Safe and Sustainable Pensions. *COM(2000)622 Final, Brussels, 11.10.2000.*

————. 2001. Eurobarometer: Public Opinion in the European Union. (54).

————. 2002a. *Employment in Europe, 2002: Recent Trends and Prospects.* Brussels: Directorate General for Employment and Social Affairs.

————. 2002b. Taking Stock of Five Years of the European Employment Strategy. *COM(2002)416 Final, Brussels, 17.07.2002.*

————. 2002c. Decision on Aid Granted by Greece to Olympic Airways. *Official Journal of the European Communities L 132/1, 28.5.2003, Brussels, 11.12.2002.*

————. 2003a. Internal Market Scoreboard. (12).

————. 2003b. *Indicators for Monitoring the 2003 Employment Guidelines* [latest update 15.12.2003]. Brussels: Directorate General for Employment and Social Affairs.

————. 2004a. Report from the Commission to the Spring European Council: Delivering Lisbon, Reforms for the Enlarged Union. *COM (2004) 29 Final/2, Brussels, 20.2.2004.*

————. 2004b. Eurobarometer Spring 2004: Public Opinion in the European Union. (61).

————. 2004c. Eurobarometre: Public Opinion in the European Community. (60).

————. 2004d. Report on the Accountability Issue Related to the Revision of Greek Budgetary Data. *COM(2004) 784 Final, Brussels, 1.12.2004.*

————. 2005a. 22eme Rapport Annuel Sur le Controle De'l application Du Droit Communitaire (2004). Document de Travail des Services de la Commission Annexes Statistiques Annexe au COM (2005)570. *SEC(2005) 1447, Brussels 23.12.2005.*

————. 2005b. Working Together for Growth and Jobs: A New Start for the Lisbon Strategy. *COM(2005)24, Brussels, 02.02.2005.*

————. 2005c. Commission Finds that Greece Has Granted Illegal State Aid to Olympic Airways and Olympic Airlines. *Press Release IP/05/1139, Brussels, 14.09.2005.*

————. 2006a. Recommendation for a Council Recommendation on the 2007 Up-date of the Broad Guidelines for the Economic Policies of the Member States and the Community and on the Implementation of Member States' Employment Policies. *COM(2006) 816 Final Part III, Brussels, 12.12.2006.*

————. 2006b. Document de Travail des Services de la Commission. Annex au 23eme Rapport Annuel de la Commission Sur le Controle De'l Application Du Droit Communitaire (2005). *COM(2006) 416 Final, SEC(2006) 1005, Brussels 27.7.2006.*

————. 2006c. Internal Market Scoreboard. (15).

————. 2006d. Eurobarometer: Public Opinion in the European Union. (64).

————. 2006e. Greece Must Comply with Court Judgment on Illegal Subsidies Granted before 2002 to Olympic. *Press Release IP/06/425, Brussels 04.04.2006.*

————. 2006f. European Commission Takes Greece to Court for Aid to Olympic. *Press Release IP/06/531, Brussels 26.04.2006.*

————. 2007. *Fourth Report of Economic and Social Cohesion: Growing Regions, Growing Europe.* European Union: Regional Policy.

European Commission/Council. 2003. Adequate and Sustainable Pensions: Joint Report by the Commission and the Council. *CS 7165/03, Brussels, 18.03.2003.*

————. 2006. Adequate and Sustainable Pensions: Synthesis Report. *SEC(2006)304, Brussels, 27.2.2006.*

————. 2001. Council Recommendation on the Implementation of Member States' Employment Policies. *Official Journal of the European Communities L 22, Brussels, 24.1.2001.*

European Council. 1999. Presidency Conclusions. *Cologne European Council, 3 and 4.06.2000.*

————. 2000a. Presidency Conclusions. *Lisbon European Council, 23 and 24.3.2000* DOC/00/8.

————. 2000b. Presidency Conclusions, *Feira European Council, 19 and 20.06.2000*

————. 2000c. Decision 436 of 29 June 2000: Setting up a Social Protection Committee. *Official Journal of the European Communities L 172, 12.07.2000.*

————. 2005. Presidency Conclusions. *Brussels European Council, 22 and 23.3.2005* DOC/05/1.

European Parliament. 1999. *Debates of the European Parliament.* 16.11.1999.

Eurostat. 2003. *Quarterly Accounts: First Quarter 2003 – Expenditure and Output Approach to GDP – First EUROSTAT Estimates* [last cited 15.07.2003]. Available from europa.eu.int.

―――. 2004. Key Economic Indicators in the EU [last cited 07.02.2005]. Available from: http://europa.eu.int/comm/eurostat/newcronos.

―――. 2006. Economy and Finance [last cited 30.10.2007]. Available from http://epp.eurostat.ec.europa.eu/portal/page?_pageid=0,1136173,0_45570704&_dad=portal&_schema=PORTAL.

―――. 2007. Euro Indicators [cited 30.10.2007]. Available from http://epp.eurostat.ec.europa.eu/portal/page?_pageid=1194,47855358,1194_47869485&_dad=portal&_schema=PORTAL#NA.

Falkner Gerda, Treib Oliver, Hartlapp Miriam, and Leiber Simone. 2005. *Complying with Europe: EU Harmonisation and Soft Law in the Member States.* Cambridge: Cambridge University Press.

Featherstone Kevin. 1988. *Socialist Parties and European Integration: A Comparative History.* Manchester: Manchester University Press.

―――. 1990. The 'Party-State' in Greece and the Fall of Papandreou. *West European Politics* 13 (1): 101–15.

―――. 1998. The Europeanisation of the Centre Periphery: The Case of Greece in the 1990s. *South European Society and Politics* 3 (1): 23–39.

―――. 2003. Greece and EMU: Between External Empowerment and Domestic Vulnerability. *Journal of Common Market Studies* 41 (5): 923–40.

―――. 2004. The Political Dynamics of External Empowerment: The Emergence of EMU and the Challenge to the European Social Model. In *Euros and Europeans: Monetary Integration and the European Model of Society,* edited by Martin Andrew and Ross George. Cambridge: Cambridge University Press.

―――. 2005. Introduction: 'Modernisation' and the Structural Constraints of Greek Politics. *West European Politics* 28 (2): 223–41 (also in the book *Politics and Policy in Greece: The Challenge of 'Modernisation',* edited by Featherstone Kevin. London: Routledge).

Featherstone Kevin and Katsoudas Dimitrios (eds). 1987. *Political Change in Greece: Before and after the Colonels.* London: Croom Helm.

Featherstone Kevin and Kazamias George. 1997. In the Absence of Charisma: The Greek Elections of September 1996. *West European Politics* 20 (2): 157–64.

Featherstone Kevin and Papadimitriou Dimitris. 2003. When Do Prisoners Escape? The Limits of Social Dialogue and Labour Market Reform in Greece. Paper read at 8th EUSA conference, 27–9 March, at Nashville.

Featherstone Kevin, Kazamias George, and Papadimitriou Dimitris. 2000. Greece and the Negotiation of Economic and Monetary Union: Preferences, Strategies, and Institutions. *Journal of Modern Greek Studies* 18: 393–414.

―――. 2001. The Limits of External Empowerment: EMU, Technocracy and Reform of the Greek Pension System. *Political Studies* 49 (3): 462–80.

Featherstone Kevin and Radaelli Claudio M. (eds). 2003. *The Politics of Europeanization.* Oxford: Oxford University Press.

Featherstone Kevin and Tinios Platon. 2006. Facing up the Gordian Knot: The Political Economy of Pension Reform. In *Social Policy Developments in Greece,* edited by Maria Petmesidou and Elias Mossialos. London: Ashgate.

Featherstone Kevin and Dimitris Papadimitriou. 2007. Manipulating Rules, Contesting Solutions: Europeanization and the Politics of Restructuring Olympic Airways. *Government and Opposition* 42 (1): 46–72.

Ferrera Maurizio. 1996. The Southern Model of Welfare in Social Europe. *Journal of European Social Policy* 6 (1): 17–37.

Financial Times (various dates).

Flyvbjerg Brent. 2006. Five Misunderstandings about Case-Study Research. *Qualitative Inquiry* 12 (2): 219–45.

Giner Salvador. 1982. Political Economy, Legitimation and the State in Southern Europe. *The British Journal of Sociology* 33 (2): 172–99.

Goetz Klaus H. 2000. European Integration and National Executives: A Cause in Search of an Effect? *West European Politics* 23 (4): 211–31.

———. 2001. European Integration and National Executives: A Cause in Search of an Effect? In *Europeanised Politics? European Integration and National Political Systems*, edited by Goetz Klaus H. and Hix Simon. Portland, OR: Frank Cass.

———. 2006. *Territory, Temporality and Clustered Europeanization*. Vienna: Institute for Advanced Studies.

Goldthorpe John. 1984. The End of Convergence: Corporatist and Dualist Tendencies in Modern Western Societies. In *Order and Conflict in Contemporary Capitalism*, edited by Goldthorpe John. Oxford: Clarendon Press.

Grabbe Heather. 2003. Europeanization Goes East: Power and Uncertainty in the EU Accession Process. In *The Politics of Europeanization*, edited by Featherstone Kevin and Radaelli Claudio M. Oxford: Oxford University Press.

GSEE. 1999. *The System of Social Security in Greece. GSEE's Alternative Solution* [Το Σύστημα Κοινωνικής Ασφάλισης στην Ελλάδα. Η Ενναλακτική Πρόταση της Γ.Σ.Ε.Ε.]. January. Athens: GSEE.

Gunther Richard, Diamandouros Nikiforos, and Puhle Hans-Jurgen (eds). 1995. *The Politics of Democratic Consolidation: Southern Europe in Comparative Perspective*. Baltimore: Johns Hopkins University Press.

Hall Peter. 2007. The Evolution of Varieties of Capitalism in Europe. In *Beyond Varieties of Capitalism: Conflict, Contradiction, and Complementarities in the European Economy*, edited by Hancke Bob, Rhodes Martin, and Thatcher Mark. Oxford: Oxford University Press.

Hall Peter and Soskice David (eds). 2001. *Varieties of Capitalism: The Institutional Foundations of Comparative Advantage*. Oxford: Oxford University Press.

Hall Peter and Taylor Rosemary C. R. 1996. A Political Science and the Three New Institutionalisms. *Political Studies* 44: 936–57.

Hancke Bob and Goyer Michael. 2005. Degrees of Freedom: Rethinking the Institutional Analysis of Economic Change. In *Changing Capitalisms? Internationalization, Institutional Change, and Systems of Economic Organization*, edited by Morgan Glenn, Whitley Richard, and Moen Eli. Oxford: Oxford University Press.

Hancke Bob and Rhodes Martin. 2005. EMU and Labour Market Institutions in Europe. *Work and Occupations* 32 (2): 196–228.

Hancke Bob, Rhodes Martin, and Thatcher Mark (eds). 2007. *Beyond Varieties of Capitalism Conflict, Contradiction, and Complementarities in the European Economy*. Oxford: Oxford University Press.

Haverland Marcus. 2000. National Adaptation to European Integration: The Importance of Institutional Veto Points. *Journal of Public Policy* 20 (1): 83–103.
———. 2003. The Impact of the European Union on Environmental Policies. In *The Politics of Europeanization*, edited by Featherstone Kevin and Radaelli Claudio. Oxford: Oxford University Press.
Hay Colin and Wincott Daniel. 1998. Structure, Agency Political Studies and Historical Institutionalism. *Political Studies* 46 (5): 951–7.
Hellenic Parliament 1998. *Minutes of Parliamentary Sessions* [Πρακτικά Συνεδριάσεων], 5–7.08.1998
———. 2000. *Minutes of Parliamentary Sessions* [Πρακτικά Συνεδριάσεων], 4–7.12.2000.
Hennis Marjoleine. 2001. Europeanization and Globalization: The Missing Link. *Journal of Common Market Studies* 39 (5): 829–50.
Heritier Adrienne and Knill Christoph. 2001. Differential Responses to European Policies: A Comparison. In *Differential Europe: The European Union Impact on National Policymaking*, edited by Heritier Adrienne, Kerwer Dieter, Knill Christoph, Lehmkuhl Dirk, and Teutsch Michael. A-C Douillet: Rowman & Littlefield Publishers.
http://www.in.gr (various dates).
I Niki (various dates).
Imerisia (various dates).
Immergut Ellen. 1992. *Health Politics and Institutions in Western Europe*. New York: Cambridge University Press.
Ioakimides Panagiotis. 1998. *European Union and the Greek State* [Η Ευρωπαϊκή 'Ενωση και το Ελληνικό Κράτος]. Athens: Themelio.
———. 2001. The Europeanization of Greece: An Overall Assessment. In *Europeanization and the Southern Periphery*, edited by Featherstone Kevin and Kazamias George. London: Frank Cass.
Ioannou Christos A. 2000. Social Pacts in Hellenic Industrial Relations: Odysseys or Sisyphus. In *Social Pacts in Europe—New Dynamics*, edited by Fajertag Giuseppe and Pochet Philippe. Brussels: ETUI.
Iversen Torben and Soskice David. 2006. Electoral Institutions and the Politics of Coalitions: Why Some Democracies Distribute More Than Others. *American Political Science Review* 100 (2): 165–81.
John Peter. 1998. *Analysing Public Policy*. London: Casell.
Kathimerini (various dates).
Katrougalos George and Lazaridis Gabriella. 2003. *Southern European Welfare States: Problems, Challenges and Prospects*. Basingstoke: Palgrave Macmillan.
Katz Ritchard and Mair Peter. 1995. Changing Models of Party Organisation and Party Democracy: The Emergence of the Cartel Party. *Party Politics* 1 (1): 5–28.
Kaufmann Daniel, Kraay Aart, and Mastruzzi Massimo. 2007. Governance Matters VI: Aggregate and Individual Governance Indicators. In *World Bank Policy Research Working Paper No 4280*: World Bank.
Keesing's Record of World Events. *37721*. London: Keesing's.
———. *38403*. London: Keesing's.
Kitschelt Herbert. 1986. Political Opportunity Structures and Political Protest: Anti-Nuclear Movements in Four Democracies. *British Journal of Political Science* 16 (1): 57–85.

————. 2000. Citizens, Politicians, and Party Cartellization: Political Representation and the State Failure in Post-Industrial Democracies. *European Journal of Political Research* 37 (2): 149–79.

KKE. 2007. Elections 2007 [last cited 9.10.2007]. Available from http://www.kke.gr/filladia/exeispolylogo.php.

Knill Christoph. 1998. European Policies: The Impact of National Administrative Traditions. *Journal of Public Policy* 18 (1): 1–28.

Knill Christoph and Lehmkuhl Dirk. 1999. How Europe Matters. Different Mechanisms of Europeanisation. *European Integration Online Papers (EIoP) 3 (7)* [last cited 30.10.2007]. Available at http://eiop.or.at/eiop/texte/1999-007a.htm.

————. 2002. The National Impact of European Union Regulatory Policy: Three Europeanization Mechanisms. *European Journal of Political Research* 41 (2): 255–80.

Knill Christoph and Lenschow Andrea. 1998. Coping with Europe: The Impact of British and German Administrations on the Implementation of EU Environmental Policy. *Journal of European Public Policy* 5 (4): 595–614.

Koliopoulos John and Veremis Thanos. 2002. *Greece: The Modern Sequel*. London: Hurst & Co.

Koutalakis Charalambos. 2004. Environmental Compliance in Italy and Greece: The Role of Non-state Actors. *Environmental Politics* 13 (4): 755–75.

Kouzis Giannis. 2000. Labour Relations and Social Dialogue. In *Issues of Social Dialogue* [Ζητήματα Κοινωνικού Διαλόγου], edited by Kouzis Giannis and Robolis Savvas. Athens: Gutenberg.

————. 2001. *Labour Relations and European Integration* [Εργασιακές Σχέσεις και Ευρωπαϊκή Ολοκλήρωση]. Athens: INE/GSEE.

Ladrech Robert. 1994. Europeanization of Domestic Politics and Institutions: The Case of France. *Journal of Common Market Studies* 32 (1): 69–88.

Lavdas Kostas. 1997. *The Europeanisation of Greece: Interest Politics and the Crises of Integration*. London: Macmillan.

Leon George. 1976. *The Greek Socialist Movement and the First World War: The Road to Unity*. New York: Boulder, Col.

Lijphart Arend. 1975. *The Politics of Accommodation: Pluralism and Democracy in the Netherlands*. 2nd edn, revised edn. Berkeley; London: University of California Press.

Lopez-Claros Augusto, Porter Michael E., Sala-i-Martin Xavier, and Schwab Klaus (eds). 2006. *Global Competitiveness Report 2006–2007: Creating an Improved Business Environment*. Edited by World Economic Forum. Houndmills, Basingstoke; Hampshire, New York: Palgrave Macmillan.

Loulis John. 1981. New Democracy: The New Face of Conservatism. In *Greece at the Polls: The National Elections of 1974 and 1977*, edited by Penimman Howard. Washington: American Enterprise for Public Policy Research.

Lyberaki Antigoni and Paraskevopoulos Christos. 2002. Social Capital Measurement in Greece. Paper read at International Conference of the Organisation for Economic Co-operation and Development (OECD), 25–7 September, at London.

Lyrintzis Christos. 1984. Political Parties in Post-Junta Greece: A Case of Bureaucratic Clientelism? *West European Politics* 7 (2): 99–118.

————. 2005. The Changing Party System: Stable Democracy, Contested 'Modernisation'. In *Politics and Policy in Greece the Challenge of 'Modernisation'*, edited by Featherstone Kevin. Oxon, New York: Routledge.

March James G. and Johan P. Olsen. 1984. The New Institutionalism: Organizational Factors in Political Life. *American Political Science Review* 78 (3): 734–49.

———. 1989. *Rediscovering Institutions: The Organizational Basis of Politics*. New York: Free Press.

Martin Andrew and Ross George. 1999. European Unions Face the Millennium. In *The Brave New World of European Labour: European Trade Unions at the Millennium*, edited by Martin Andrew and Ross George. Oxford: Berghahn Books.

Matsaganis Manos. 2002. Yet Another Piece of Pension Reform in Greece. *South European Society and Politics* 7 (3): 109–22.

Matsaganis Manos, Ferrera Maurizio, Capucha Luís, and Moreno Luis. 2003. Mending Nets in the South: Anti-Poverty Policies in Greece, Italy, Portugal and Spain. *Social Policy & Administration* 37 (6): 639–55.

Mavrogordatos George Th. 1988. *Between Pityokamptis and Procroustis: Professional Associations in Today's Greece* [Μεταξύ Πιτυοκάμπη και Προκρούστη. Οι Επαγγελματικές Οργανώσεις στη Σημερινή Ελλάδα]. Athens: Odysseas.

McMenamin Iain. 2004. Varieties of Capitalist Democracy: What Difference Does East-Central Europe Make? *Journal of Public Policy* 24 (3): 259–74.

Menz Georg. 2005. *Varieties of Capitalism and Europeanization: National Response Strategies to the Single European Market*. Oxford New York: Oxford University Press.

Ministry of Development. 2005. Annual Competitiveness Report. Athens.

Ministry of Interior. 2004. Results of the National Elections 2004 [Αποτελέσματα Εθνικών Εκλογών 2004] 2004 [last cited 14.10.2007]. Available from http://www.ypes.gr/ekloges/content/gr/elec_data/2004NE_epi_res.asp.

———. 2007. National Elections 2007 [last cited 14.10.2007]. Available from http://www.ekloges.ypes.gr/pages/index.html.

Ministry of Labour. 1997. *Framework for the Social Dialogue on Development, Competitiveness and Employment* [Πλαίσιο Κοινωνικού Διαλόγου για την Ανάπτυξη, την Ανταγωνιστικότητα και την Απασχόληση]. Athens. 14.04.1997.

———. 2000. *Policies of Employment and Combating Unemployment* [Πολιτικές για την Απασχόληση και την Καταπολέμηση της Ανεργίας]. Athens. September.

Molina Oscar and Rhodes Martin. 2005. Varieties of Capitalism and Mixed Market Economies. *APSA-EPS Newsletter*.

Morgan Eleanor J. and McGuire Steven. 2004. Transatlantic Divergence: GE-Honeywell and the EU's Merger Policy. *Journal of European Public Policy*, 11 (1): 39–56.

Morgan Glenn, Whitley Richard, and Moen Eli (eds). 2005. *Changing Capitalisms? Internationalization, Institutional Change, and Systems of Economic Organization*. Oxford: Oxford University Press.

Mörth Ulrika. 2003. Europeanization as Interpretation, Translation, and Editing of Public Policies. In *The Politics of Europeanization*, edited by Featherstone Kevin and Radaelli Claudio M. Oxford: Oxford University Press, 159–78.

Mouriki Aliki. 2002. Labour Relations and Social Dialogue in Greece [Εργασιακές Σχέσεις και Κοινωνικός Διάλογος]. In *Social Portrait of Greece 2001* [Το Κοινωνικό Πορτραίτο της Ελλάδας, 2001], edited by Maratou-Alpranti Laura, Bagkavos Crhistos, Papadakis Michalis, and Papliakou Vassiliki. Athens: EKKE.

Mouzelis Nikos. 1978. *Modern Greek Society: Facets of Underdevelopment*. Athens: Exantas.

————. 1993. The State in Late Development. *Greek Political Science Review* 1: 53–89.

————. 1996. The Concept of Modernization: Its Relevance for Greece. *Journal of Modern Greek Studies* 14 (2): 215–27.

Mouzelis Nikos and Pagoulatos George. 2005. Civil Society and Citizenship in Postwar Greece. In *Citizenship and the Nation State in Greece and Turkey*, edited by Birtek Faruk and Dragona Thalia. Abington and New York: Routledge.

Mylonas Paul and De la Maisonneuve Christine. 1999. The Problems and Prospects Faced by Pay-As-You-Go Pension Systems: A Case Study of Greece. *OECD Working Paper No. 215*. Paris: OECD Economics Department.

Natali David and Rhodes Martin. 2004. The 'New Politics' of the Bismarckian Welfare State: Pension Reforms in Continental Europe. *EUI SPS Working Papers No 10*.

New Democracy. 2004. *Election Manifesto*. Athens: New Democracy.

Nikolakopoulos Ilias. 2005. Elections and Voters, 1974–2004: Old Cleavages and New Issues. In *Politics and Policy in Greece the Challenge of 'Modernisation'*, edited by Featherstone Kevin. Oxon, New York: Routledge.

O'Donnell Owen and Tinios Platon. 2003. The Politics of Pension Reform: Lessons from Public Attitudes in Greece. *Political Studies* 51 (2): 262–81.

Olsen Johan P. 2002. The Many Faces of Europeanization. *Journal of Common Market Studies* 40 (5): 921–52.

Organisation of Economic Cooperation and Development (OECD). 1997. *Economic Survey of Greece*. Paris: OECD.

————. 2004. Social Expenditure Database [last cited 12.10.2007]. Available from http://www.oecd.org/document/9/0,3343,en_2649_34637_38141385_1_1_1_1,00. html.

————. 2005a. Product Market Regulation in OECD Countries: 1998 to 2003.

————. 2005b. Education at a Glance: OECD.

————. 2006. Education at a Glance: OECD.

————. 2007a. OECD Economic Outlook Sources and Methods 2007 [cited 8.10.2007]. Available from http://www.oecd.org/eco/sources-and-methods.

————. 2007b. OECD Economic Outlook 81: Statistical Annex Tables 2007 [cited 8.10.2007]. Available from http://www.oecd.org/document/61/0,2340, en_2825_32066506_2483901_1_1_1_1,00.html.

————. 2007c. Employment Outlook: OECD.

————. 2007d. Economic Surveys: Greece. In *OECD Economic Surveys No 5*: OECD.

Pagoulatos George. 2003. *Greece's New Political Economy: State, Finance and Growth from Postwar to EMU*. Edited by Oxford, *St. Antony's Series*. Basingstoke and New York: Palgrave Macmillan.

————. 2004. Believing in National Exceptionalism: Ideas and Economic Divergence in Southern Europe. *West European Politics* 27 (1): 45–70.

————. 2005. The Politics of Privatisation: Rewarding the Public–Private Boundary. In *Politics and Policy in Greece: The Challenge of 'Modernisation'*, edited by Featherstone Kevin. Oxon, New York: Routledge.

Papadimitriou Dimitris. 2005. The Limits of Engineering Collective Escape: The 2000 Reform of the Greek Labour Market. *West European Politics* 28 (2): 381–401 (also in the book *Politics and Policy in Greece: The Challenge of 'Modernisation'*, edited by Featherstone Kevin. London: Routledge).

Pappas Takis. 1999. *Making Party Democracy in Greece*. Basingstoke: Macmillan.

————. 2003. The Transformation of the Greek Party System Since 1951. *West European Politics* 26 (2): 90–114.

Pelkmans Jacques. 2001. Making EU Network Markets Competitive. *Oxford Review of Economic Policy* 17 (3): 432–56.

Petronoti Marina and Triandafyllidou Anna. 2003. Recent Immigration Flows to Greece [Σύγχρονα Μεταναστευτικά Ρεύματα στην Ελλάδα] [last cited 30.10.2007]. Available from http://www.migrantsingreece.org/resources.asp.

Pierson Paul. 1998. Irresistible Forces, Immovable Objects. *Journal of European Public Policy* 5 (4): 539–60.

————(ed.). 2001. *The New Politics of the Welfare State*. Oxford: Oxford University Press.

Pitelis Christos and Clarke Thomas. 1993. Introduction: The Political Economy of Privatization. In *The Political Economy of Privatization*, edited by Clarke Thomas and Pitelis Christos. London: Routledge.

Pochet Philippe. 1999. *Economic and Monetary Union and Collective Bargaining in Europe*. Brussels: P.I.E.–Peter Lang.

Politis Takis. 2007. Entrepreneurship in Greece: Main Trends and Characteristics. Paper read at the Hellenic Observatory Research Seminars, 13 March, at London.

Pollis Adamandia. 1987. The State, the Law and Human Rights in Greece. *Human Rights Quarterly* 9 (4): 587–614.

Provopoulos George and Tinios Platon. 1993. Pensions and the Fiscal Crisis of the Greek State. In *Greece, the New Europe and the Changing International Order* edited by Psomiades Harry and Thomadakis Stavros B. New York: Pella.

Putnam Robert D. 1993. *Making Democracy Work. Civic Traditions in Modern Italy*. Princeton, NJ: Princeton University Press.

Radaelli Claudio. 2003. The Europeanization of Public Policy. In *The Politics of Europeanization*, edited by Featherstone Kevin and Radaelli Claudio M. Oxford: Oxford University Press.

Sabethai Isaac D. 2000. The Greek Labour Market: Features, Problem and Policies [Η Ελληνική Αγορά Εργασίας: Χαρακτηριστικά, Προβλήματα και Πολιτικές]. In *Economic Bulletin No. 16, 16.12.2000*, edited by the Bank of Greece.

Sargent Jane. 1985. Corporatism and the European Community. In *The Political Economy of Corporatism*, edited by Wyn Grant. London: Macmillan.

Scharpf Fritz W. 1987. A Game-Theoretical Interpretation of Inflation and Unemployment in Western Europe. *Journal of Public Policy* 7 (1): 227–57.

————. 1991. *Crisis and Choice in European Social Democracy*. Ithaca, NY: Cornell University Press.

————. 1997. *Games Real Actors Play. Actor-Centered Institutionalism in Policy Research*. Boulder: Westview.

Schelkle Waltraud. 2005. Understanding New Forms of European Integration: A Study in Competing Political Economy Explanations. In *The Political Economy of European Integration: Theory and Analysis*, edited by Jones Eric and Verdun Amy. London: Routledge.

Schimmelfennig Frank and Ulrich Sedelmeier. 2004. Governance by Conditionality: EU Rule Transfer to the Candidate Countries of Central and Eastern Europe. *Journal of European Public Policy* 11 (4): 661–79.

Schmidt Vivien A. 2002. *The Futures of the European Capitalism*. Oxford: Oxford University Press.

Schmidt Vivien A. and Radaelli Claudio M. 2004. Policy Change and Discourse in Europe: Conceptual and Methodological Issues. *West European Politics* 27 (2): 183–210.

Schmidt Vivien A. (ed.). 2006. *Democracy in Europe: The EU and National Polities.* Oxford: Oxford University Press.

Schmitter Philippe C. 1977. Models of Interest Intermediation and Models of Societal Change in Western Europe. *Comparative Political Studies* 1 (1): 2–38.

Schmitter Philippe C. and Lehmbruch Gerard. 1979. *Trends toward Corporatist Intermediation.* London, Beverly Hills: Sage Publications.

Schneider Martin and Mihai Panuescu. 2004 Wettbewerbsfahigkeit und Dynamik institutioneller Standortbedingungen: ein Empirischer Test des 'Varieties of Capitalism' – Ansatzes. *Schmollers Jahrbuch: Zeitshrift fur Wirtschafts und Sozialwissenschaften / Journal of Applied Social Science Studies* 124 (1): 31–59.

Sebastiani Mario. 2002. Il Settore Aereo Fra Liberalizzazione e Concentrazione' [Liberalisation and Consolidation in Air Transport Market']. *Industria*, XXIII (1):107–26.

Sedelmeier Ulrich and Schimmelfennig Frank. Governance by Conditionality: EU Rule Transfer to the Candidate Countries of Central and Eastern Europe. *Journal of European Public Policy* 11 (4): 661–79.

Simitis Constantinos. 2005. *Policy for a Creative Greece 1996–2004* [Πολιτική για Μια Δημιουργική Ελλάδα 1996–2004]. Athens: Polis.

———. 2007. *Goals, Strategy and Perspectives* [Στόχοι, Στρατηγική και Προοπτικές]. Athens: Polis.

Sotiropoulos Dimitris A. 1993. A Colossus with Feet of Clay: The State in Post-Authoritarian Greece. In *Greece, the New Europe and Changing International Order*, edited by Psomiades Harry and Thomadakis Stavros. New York: Pella.

——— (ed.). 2004. *The Unknown Civil Society: Social Mobilisations, Volunteerism and the Statein Contemporary Greece* [Η Άγνωστη Κοινωνία Πολιτών: Κοινωνικές Κινητοποιήσεις, Εθελοντισμός και Κράτος στη Σύγχρονη Ελλάδα]. Athens: Potamos.

Streeck Wolfgangand and Thelen Kathleen. 2005. *Beyond Continuity: Institutional Change in Advanced Political Economies.* Oxford; New York: Oxford University Press.

SYRIZA. 2007. Social State and Social Rights 2007 [last cited 9 October 2007]. Available from http://www.syriza.gr/theseis/ergasia-asfalisi/koinoniko-kratos-kai-koinonika-dikaimata.

Ta Nea (various dates).

Tallagreg Jonas. (2002). Paths to Compliance: Enforcement, Management and the European Union. *International Organisation* 56 (3): 609–43.

Thatcher Mark. 2004. Varieties of Capitalism in an Internationalized World: Domestic Institutional Change in European Telecommunications. *Comparative Political Studies* 37 (7): 1–30.

———. 2007. Reforming National Regulatory Institutions: The EU and Cross-National Variety in European Network Industries. In *Beyond Varieties of Capitalism Conflict, Contradiction, and Complementarities in the European Economy*, edited by Hanke Bob, Rhodes Martin, and Thatcher Mark. Oxford: Oxford University Press.

The Independent (various dates).

The Observer (various dates).

The Times (various dates).
To Ethnos (various dates).
To Vima (various dates).
Transparency International. 2005. Global Corruption Report 2005.
Tsebelis George. 1995. Decision Making in Political Systems: Veto Players in Presidentialism, Parliamentarism, Multicameralism, and Multipartism. *British Journal of Political Science* 25: 289–325.
————. 2002. *Veto Players: How Political Institutions Work*. New York: Russell Sage Foundation; Princeton, NJ: Princeton University Press.
Tsoukalas Constantinos. 1991. Enlightened Concepts in the Dark: Power and Freedom, Politics and Society. *Journal of Modern Greek Studies* 9: 1–23.
————. 1993. Greek National Identity in an Integrated Europe and a Changing World Order. In *Greece, the New Europe and The Changing International Order*, edited by Psomiades Harry and Thomadakis Stavros. New York: Pella.
Tsoukalis Loukas. 1997. Beyond the Greek Paradox. In *The Greek Paradox: Promise vs. Performance*, edited by Allison Graham T. and Nicolaidis Kalypso. Cambridge, Massachusetts and London: The MIT Press.
Venieris Dimitrios N. 1996. Dimensions of Social Policy in Greece. *South European Society and Politics* 1 (3): 260–9.
Voulgaris Giannis. 2006. State and Civil Society in Greece: A Relationship to Be Revisited [Κράτος και Κοινωνιά Πολιτών στην Ελλάδα: Μια Σχέση προς Επανεξέταση]. *Greek Review of Political Science* 28: 5–33.
World Bank, International Finance Corporation. 2007. Doing Business 2007: How to Reform. Comparing Regulation in 175 Countries, edited by World Bank. Washington D.C.
World Economic Forum. 2002. The Lisbon Review 2002–2003: An Assessment of Policy and Reforms in Europe. Geneva: World Economic Forum.
————. 2006. Global Competitiveness Report 2005–2006.
Zahariadis Nikolaos. 2003. *Ambiguity and Choice in Public Policy: Political Decision Making in Modern Democracies*. Washington DC: Georgetown University Press.
Zambarloukou Stella. 2006. Collective Bargaining and Social Pacts: Greece in Comparative Perspective. *European Journal of Industrial Relations* 12 (2): 211–29.

Index